Writing for Scholars

SAGE was founded in 1965 by Sara Miller McCune to support the dissemination of usable knowledge by publishing innovative and high-quality research and teaching content. Today, we publish more than 750 journals, including those of more than 300 learned societies, more than 800 new books per year, and a growing range of library products including archives, data, case studies, reports, conference highlights, and video. SAGE remains majority-owned by our founder, and after Sara's lifetime will become owned by a charitable trust that secures our continued independence.

Los Angeles | London | Washington DC | New Delhi | Singapore

Writing for Scholars

A Practical Guide to Making Sense & Being Heard

Lynn P. Nygaard

2nd Edition

$SAGE

Los Angeles | London | New Delhi
Singapore | Washington DC | Boston

Los Angeles | London | New Delhi
Singapore | Washington DC

SAGE Publications Ltd
1 Oliver's Yard
55 City Road
London EC1Y 1SP

SAGE Publications Inc.
2455 Teller Road
Thousand Oaks, California 91320

SAGE Publications India Pvt Ltd
B 1/I 1 Mohan Cooperative Industrial Area
Mathura Road
New Delhi 110 044

SAGE Publications Asia-Pacific Pte Ltd
3 Church Street
#10-04 Samsung Hub
Singapore 049483

Editor: Jai Seaman
Assistant editor: Lily Mehrbod
Production editor: Victoria Nicholas
Proofreader: Andy Baxter
Marketing manager: Catherine Slinn
Cover design: Shaun Mercier
Typeset by: C&M Digitals (P) Ltd, Chennai, India
Printed and bound by CPI Group (UK) Ltd,
Croydon, CR0 4YY

1st edition: © Universitetsforlaget/Scandinavian University
Press, in cooperation with LIBER and Copenhagen Business
School Press, 2008

UNIVERSITETSFORLAGET

2nd edition: © Lynn P. Nygaard, 2015

Library of Congress Control Number: 2014948573

British Library Cataloguing in Publication data

A catalogue record for this book is available from
the British Library

ISBN 978-1-4462-8253-3
ISBN 978-1-4462-8254-0 (pbk)
ISBN 978-8-2150-2555-1 (Norway)

At SAGE we take sustainability seriously. Most of our products are printed in the UK using FSC papers and boards.
When we print overseas we ensure sustainable papers are used as measured by the Egmont grading system.
We undertake an annual audit to monitor our sustainability.

Contents

List of figures

About the author

For almost two decades, Lynn P. Nygaard has provided editorial support and coaching for researchers in a wide variety of disciplines. A native English speaker, Nygaard started as a freelance copy-editor and translator for Norwegian academics looking to publish their work in international journals. In 2000, she became an editorial advisor at the Center for International Climate and Environmental Research – Oslo. This position allowed her to view researchers and the writing process from close quarters. She found that language was seldom the main explanation for what was going wrong, and developed a workshop for academics that focused on developing awareness of audience, formulating the core argument and structuring the story. As a workshop facilitator, she has helped researchers both in Norway and abroad hone their arguments and tailor their work for publication. In 2008, she became a special advisor at the Peace Research Institute Oslo, and continues to develop her expertise in how to support scholars through the writing process. With an undergraduate degree in women's studies from the University of California at Berkeley and a graduate degree in political science from the University of Oslo, she is currently pursuing a doctorate from the Institute of Education, University College London, that focuses on research productivity, academic writing and gender gaps in academia.

Preface

Tap, tap. I'm knocking lightly on the door of one of my researcher colleagues. In my hand is a copy of an article he has co-authored. I've been trying to edit it all morning but I'm just not getting anywhere because, frankly, I can't figure out what the authors are saying.

'Do you have a minute?' I ask. 'I'm working on your article and I was just wondering if you could tell me, in your own words, what exactly you guys are trying to say.'

'Umm, OK', comes the polite but befuddled response. He thinks for a minute, stares at a spot on the wall above my left shoulder and then starts talking. He starts off slow, hesitant. But after a few minutes he warms to his theme. He gets up, draws a series of squiggles on the whiteboard and waves his arms around – his voice clear and confident. I understand *exactly* what he is saying.

'Why didn't you just write that?' I ask, amazed yet again at how the written scholarly article can so utterly and completely fail to communicate the knowledge and passion of the scientist.

'I thought we did', comes the inevitable answer.

And thus was conceived the idea of a writing workshop for scholars.

I had been an editor working at a research institute for several years, so I was prepared for how much scholars needed to work on their writing; I wasn't prepared for how much they *wanted* to. Not only did the workshops become far more popular than I had ever imagined, but to each and every one of them, participants brought such enthusiasm, conscientiousness and genuine love for scholarship that sometimes I was left reeling. I don't know who taught who the most. Over the next few years, I brought what I learned from editing to my workshops, and I brought what I learned from my workshops to my editing. These experiences coalesced into this book, *Writing for Scholars: A Practical Guide to Making Sense & Being Heard*.

The main title is intentionally ambiguous. 'Writing for Scholars' can mean either the writing process as experienced by scholars, or the craft of scholar-to-scholar communication. This book covers both.

First, scholars have a love–hate relationship with writing. Writing is how we communicate our ideas with the rest of the world. For some of us, it's pretty much all we do; if we aren't writing, then we're reading in preparation for more writing. And yet we don't usually think of ourselves as writers. As a result, the writing process is often fraught with unnecessary levels of distress. One of the aims of this book is to help you turn the writing process into something that works *for* you, not against you. And the revised edition of this book provides an illustration of how the writing process is never really finished. When I finished writing the first edition of *Writing for Scholars*, I thought I had said everything I wanted to say about writing for publication in academia. I think that feeling lasted about two months – just long enough to get over the 'I never want to see my own writing again as long as I live' phase. Then I started thinking of things I could add or just tweak. Although my ideas evolved, the book stayed the same way it was when it went to press (including the few inevitable typos that taunted me with their permanence each time I picked up the book). The conversation is never over, and this revised edition allows me to extend, develop or modify some of the points I made in the first edition.

The title *Writing for Scholars* also acknowledges that writing for other scholars is not like writing for the general public. Scholars and scientists are a critical bunch and aren't easily impressed. Scholarly and scientific writing has to be content-rich in a way that most other kinds of writing do not. A short scientific article can represent years, even decades, of meticulous research. A scholarly essay of only a few thousand words can be the culmination of extraordinarily complex thought processes. Both have to withstand the external pressure of criticism and contradictory findings. Thus another main aim of this book is to show you what it takes to reach other scholars and convince them that you have something to say. The first edition of this book had no references to the work of others. I did this somewhat intentionally to ease reading, and also because I wrote from my personal experience as a copy-editor, not as a publishing scholar, nor as someone who has studied scholarly writing as an academic subject. Although the focus of this edition is still on things I have learned as a practitioner, I have made an effort to connect what I say to what others (both other practitioners and scholars of academic writing) have said on the same matters – an important part of writing for a scholarly audience. Another difference in this edition is that it focuses more specifically on scholars from the social sciences. Although the main messages are the same, the examples are more tailored to social science disciplines. It nevertheless still aims to speak to both qualitative and quantitative researchers, as well as those who work non-empirically. Most importantly, the primary focus is still on the challenges of communicating our ideas with other academics through writing.

Without scientific and scholarly writing, our cumulative knowledge would stagnate. I can think of few activities more important or meaningful than pushing the frontiers of knowledge forward. Remember this when you are banging your head against your desk in frustration. Dare to make sense, speak up and be heard. Your work – and your fellow scholars – deserve no less.

Acknowledgements

After many years of helping authors through the writing process, I thought I knew what I was getting myself into when I embarked on a project of my own. Naturally, I didn't have a clue. I suppose it's like thinking you can do open heart surgery just because you've been handing scalpels to the doctor for a few years. And when it came time to work on this second edition of *Writing for Scholars*, I realized that this naivety had actually worked in my favour the first time around, and that knowing more can actually make the writing process harder. I suddenly understood the scholars whom I had been editing in a whole new way.

Fortunately, I had help. First and foremost, I would like to thank my colleagues at the Peace Research Institute Oslo (PRIO) for allowing me to experiment on them mercilessly – trying out new ideas for writing workshops, giving feedback, and perhaps most importantly, by allowing me to grow not just as a practitioner, but also as a scholar. PRIO has generously supported my doctoral studies at the Institute of Education, University College London, where I have been fortunate enough to have two fantastic supervisors, Dr Lesley Gourlay and Professor Richard Andrews. All the participants in my workshops on scholarly writing and writing retreats also deserve acknowledgement; by sharing their work and frustrations, they taught me as much about writing as I taught them.

For this SAGE edition, I would also like to extend my gratitude to my editor Jai Seaman, who has an amazing talent for spotting all those weaknesses in the text that you know are there but hope no one will notice.

Finally, I thank my husband Harald Nygaard, and my children Johan and Marlena, who have no idea what I write about, but who are nevertheless proud to say they have a mom who is a writer. This book is dedicated to them.

Companion website

This book is supported by a brand new companion website (https://study.sagepub.com/nygaard). The website offers a wide range of free learning resources, including:

- **Author Videos** introducing the book and providing top tips for getting started, finding your voice, presenting your work and getting feedback.
- **Library of recommended resources** including links to relevant websites and journal articles.
- **Essential Checklist** for scholarly writing.
- **Glossary** of key terms.

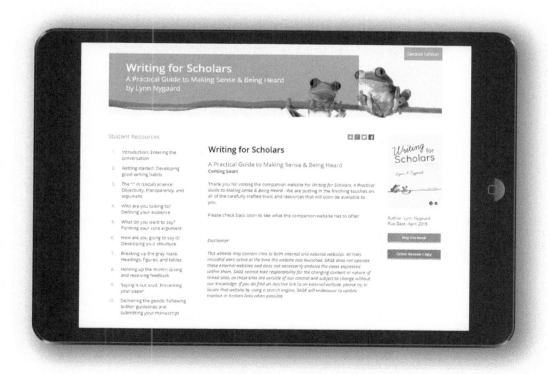

ONE

Introduction
Entering the conversation

Sometimes the only discernible difference between a genius and a lunatic is the ability to communicate. If you run up to a random crowd of people waving your arms around and shouting 'My frogs are blue!' you're more likely to end up in a padded cell next to a guy who picks up alien transmissions through his fillings than on the cover of *Science*.

But if you manage to track down the right group of people (say, other frog researchers), capture their attention ('Hey, do you remember Weinburger's theory that pigmentation at the chromosomal level is fixed at birth in amphibians?'), be specific about exactly what you did and found ('I exposed 50 frogs to ultraviolet light for 547 hours, after which their skin took on a distinctly bluish hue'), and explain what it means ('This shows that Weinburger was wrong!'), you just might find yourself holding a Nobel Prize rather than a bottle of Haldol. It's not enough simply to know something. You must be able to communicate your knowledge to others. To accomplish this, you need to know who you are talking to, what you want to say, and how you are going to say it. This is true for any discipline, for any methodological approach.

As scholars, we communicate with three main audiences: the public, user groups (such as businesses, practitioners, community organizations and government agencies) and other scholars (including aspiring scholars in the form of students)

Think of academic writing as a kind of conversation where a lot of people are talking at once. You need to have a point that the others will be interested in hearing, and to make an opening in a conversation so you can be heard.

When we communicate with the public, we usually do so through the mass media: newspapers, magazines, television programmes and radio. But while the mass media is important for getting a (simple) message across to a large number of people, most scholars find it a frustrating means of communication. Journalism is a language of black and white, and scholars are most fluent in grey. This is because most scholarship is incremental: the *if*s, *and*s and *but*s matter. It's not just the devil that lives in the details, researchers are mighty comfortable there, too.

When we communicate with user groups, we often do so through reports (or sometimes books) written specifically for them. Perhaps a government agency wants to better understand why some young people become criminals, so they can design better crime prevention policies. Or perhaps a business wants to know if blue frogs have commercial applications. Unfortunately, reports are often largely ignored by other researchers for two main reasons. First, they seldom go through the rigorous quality control that academic books and journal articles are subjected to (see the text box 'Explaining the peer review process') and, second, they often make for excruciatingly dull reading. Writing reports gives us a false sense of freedom. Without the word limits imposed by publishers or the structural conventions of journal articles, we think we can write as much as we want and that it will get read – not least because someone cared enough about the subject matter to commission the report in the first place. Because there is a general perception in some circles that quality can be measured in bulk ('You wrote a five-kilo report? It must be good'), and we generally want to give clients their money's worth, entire forests have given their lives for reports that never have their bindings cracked.

Explaining the peer review process

Both journals and book publishers, particularly university presses, rely on peer review to ensure that your manuscript meets the standards for scholarly publishing, but their practices differ.

In *book publishing*, a two-part review process is common – that is, your work is reviewed both by the editor and by outside experts. First, the acquisitions or commissioning editor screens your proposal and a few sample chapters to evaluate whether it might be worthy of publication. Editors need relatively little time to review a proposal, but it may take them a while to get to it if they have a mountain of other ones on their desk. If an editor thinks your proposal seems promising, it may be sent out to peer reviewers - perhaps as many as ten different academics who will give their opinion on how promising the book seems. If the reviews are positive, you may be offered a contract at this point. When the editor receives the complete manuscript, he or she will take a first pass at editing and make suggestions for revision. These suggestions can be related either to the writing or to the substance, and it may take several rounds before the editor is satisfied and ready to send it to outside experts (usually two or more, but sometimes only one) for formal review. The external review process can take from two to six months, depending on whether the manuscript is sent to the referees simultaneously or consecutively. It may take even longer if you are asked to make revisions after each review. What's important to note here is that the decision to publish primarily rests in the hands of the editor and the editorial board of the press; the role of the outside referees is advisory, and their comments are usually general.

For *journals*, peer review plays a much more decisive role. Unlike book submissions – where proposals can be sent to several presses at once, although this is increasingly frowned upon – journal articles can only be submitted to one journal at a time. Journals also expect you to send a full manuscript, not a proposal or query. Once the manuscript is received, it may be sent directly to review, but will probably go through some sort of vetting process first. Because of the high volume of submissions, the editor (or editorial board) weeds out not only articles that are clearly substandard, but also articles that may be scientifically sound but merely unsuitable for the particular journal. The percentage that gets rejected even before review varies widely, depending on the reputation of the journal and the number of submissions; some smaller (or newer) journals may reject almost none offhand, while other very highly ranked journals (particularly in the natural sciences) may reject up to 90 per cent. If the article passes the initial screening, it is usually sent to three reviewers, although there may be as many as five and sometimes (but rarely) only one or two. 'Reviewer fatigue' is a real and increasing problem, so finding suitable reviewers who agree to take on the job may take time – and this is what usually determines how long the review process will take. Three to six months is common. The reviewers make specific comments on both the content and the writing, as well as stating whether they think the article should be accepted, accepted with minor revisions, revised by the author and resubmitted, or rejected. The journal editor almost always follows the advice of the peer reviewers, but may exercise his or her own judgement in cases where the reviewers disagree with one another.

Even if we communicate regularly with the public and user groups, most of us find communicating with other scholars more important and more satisfying. It means that we are participating in the scholarly dialogue,[1] the ongoing conversation among researchers or scholars that constitutes our collective knowledge on a particular subject. Building on work from other scholars and sharing our findings to stimulate further thinking is what research and scholarship are about. But the

---

[1]In this book, I use 'scholarly dialogue' and 'academic discourse' (as well as their variations) interchangeably.

scholarly dialogue is big and noisy, with thousands of voices chiming in. How do you make your voice heard over the din?

For most scholars, the best way to reach other scholars – and thus actively participate in the scholarly conversation – is through academic publishing, and all of the other activities associated with publishing (such as conferences or presentations). What sets academic publishing apart from other types of publishing is that it relies on peer review to ensure quality (see the text box 'What makes scholarly writing *scholarly*?'). This means that other experts in the field have assessed the work – both as a piece of writing and as a piece of scholarship – before it was published. For some disciplines, particularly in the humanities, much scholarly publishing takes place in books (including monographs and anthologies). But for most other disciplines, the pinnacle of scholarly publishing is the journal article.

What makes scholarly writing *scholarly*?

Scholars do a lot of writing, but not all of it is scholarly. To be considered an academic publication, and thus part of the scholarly dialogue, your article, book chapter or book must satisfy these four criteria:

- **It must present new insight**
  'New' doesn't necessarily mean 'revolutionary' or 'only minutes old', but you must have something to add to the conversation that has not been said already – at least to the group of scholars you are talking to. In many contexts, textbooks – no matter how much expertise is needed to write them – do not count as scholarly works because they are not meant to bring new insight, but rather synthesize what is already known by most experts in the field.

- **It must both build on existing insight and be usable for future research in some way**
  Like any conversation, academic discourse flows best when people listen to each other. Showing how your work builds on the work of other scholars, and presenting it in a way (for example, in the form of a claim that can be tested or at least challenged) that will allow others to build on it further (for example, by testing it), ensures that you are keeping the dialogue moving. Popular scientific works – no matter how difficult they are to write and irrespective of whether they offer new ideas – normally do not count as academic output because, being aimed at the general public, they are not intended to keep the *scholarly* dialogue moving forward.

- **It must be accessible to other scholars**
  Muttering to yourself in the back of the room does not constitute participation in the discourse. This means that it doesn't help to write something brilliant only to have it lie around in your bottom desk drawer – or even to circulate it at your workplace. In practical terms, this criterion means you need to publish in a journal or book or on a website that is recognized as an appropriate academic channel. What is considered an 'appropriate channel' might vary from place to place:

some institutes insist that the journal be ranked on the ISI Web of Knowledge, or have a high impact factor. And others might specifically name the target journals they want their staff to aim for. Some might emphasize the importance of open access. Check with your institute to see what kinds of publishers or publishing venues are acceptable, and what kinds are considered especially prestigious.

- **It must be subject to peer review**
  What sets the scholarly dialogue apart from other conversations is the quality control offered by standardized procedures for peer review. Peer review assures the people listening to you that you have something worthwhile to say. This holds for every individual work you publish. Depending on the type of merit system used, your work might not count as scholarly – even if outside experts have offered their opinions – unless the particular journal or press is *recognized* as a scholarly publisher. And even if a journal or press is recognized as scholarly, if your specific work bypassed the peer review process, then it doesn't count: a non-reviewed letter to the editor or book review published in the *Journal of Groundbreaking Research* is not an academic publication.

Do you know what is *not* on this list? Nowhere is it written that academic output has to be boring. Careful and meticulous, yes. Devoid of any life and movement, no.

This list also contains no requirement that the work has to be in English. Although English is unquestionably the lingua franca of the academic world, academic publishing is alive and kicking in many other languages. There are good arguments for publishing in English: your voice becomes part of an international discourse, and you can bring scholarship from your country that would otherwise go unrecognized to a wider audience. However, publishing *only* in English risks eroding the academic discourse, or even popular discourse, in other languages. The choice of language inevitably informs the nature of the discourse, and keeping the discourse going in more than one language can invite more voices and increase the vibrancy of the conversation.

And whether we like it or not, our publications list is the rod by which our academic prowess is measured. Quantity matters, and so does the caliber of the journals that publish our work. More than ever, New Public Management norms in academia require us to prove our worth through publications that we can point to. And for those of us who are dependent on external sources of funding to continue doing research, our publication credentials not only help us move forward in our own careers, but they also keep our funders happy: if we can't show them that we put their money to good use, they won't give us more money to continue our work.

But to publish, we have to learn to write effectively – both for our own sakes and for the sake of our readers. The myth of the tweed-clad scholar suggests that you can lock yourself in your ivory tower, puff contentedly on your pipe and take an infinite amount of time to produce your great work; if it makes sense to you, that's all that matters. Then your readers, awed by your genius, will devote whatever time and energy is required to comprehend your every word. Reality, of course, is somewhat different. You don't have infinite amounts of time, and neither do your readers: they are unlikely to devote even half a minute to anything they do not find compelling in some way. The world of today's academic has fewer leisurely conversations in overstuffed chairs, and more meetings, conferences, students, children and all kinds of other things to distract both you and your potential readers.

So, if you want to be heard in the scholarly dialogue – if you want your work to be read by people who share your area of interest – you need to do more than type up your results or pontificate without restraint. You need to build an argument on paper that will convince your reader from the first paragraph that what you have to say is relevant, important and valid.

The aim of this book is to help you do exactly that. By taking a closer look at what goes into writing good scholarly prose, particularly journal articles, it will show you how to make a strong, convincing, coherent and lucid argument that will reach your intended audience. This book is written mainly for researchers who are new to publishing academically, but it should also be useful for those who have been engaged in scholarly discourse for many years and are now advising young scholars, or would simply like to further hone their own skills. Even the best academic writers have works that were rejected or never satisfactorily finished, and this book can help you identify what went wrong and how to get back on track. Much of what is written here you may already know – you just may not know that you know it. It looks at the basic questions you face as a writer (such as 'Who are you talking to?' and 'What do you really want to say?'), questions so basic that often their answers are never given, merely assumed. Uprooting these assumptions will allow you to transform your tacit knowledge into knowledge that is more explicit, knowledge you can use more consciously as you write.

WHAT CONSTITUTES GOOD SCHOLARLY PROSE?

One of the first assumptions that must be uprooted before going any further is that the ability to write well is bestowed by the gods. Many believe that you either have it or you don't. If you have it, you must bow to the whims of your muse; if you don't have it, you will never learn. It's true that some people are more talented than others, much to the annoyance of those who struggle to put a simple sentence together. But even the best writers put their sentences together one word at a time. While some art is involved, mostly it's about craft. As with any craft, practice makes a huge difference. You cannot skip the practice and go right to perfect. There is a misconception among researchers that academics in the humanities have an easier time writing than others – after all, the humanities is where the words live. But a love of words and language does not guarantee an ability to write, any more than, say, a love of art enables you to paint anything grander than your garage door.

Tip

Build up a library of good writing. Collect articles and books that you think are well written. Ask yourself why you like them. How simple is the language? How complex? How concrete? Did the author use metaphors? Underline passages that strike you as particularly powerful. Re-reading some of these before you start writing can help you find a voice that is less like the articles you want to throw down, and more like the articles that you want to pick up.

And just to make this more complicated, ideals of good academic writing are not the same all over the world (see the text box 'Different cultures of academic writing'). The Anglo-Saxon style of writing – which this book represents – puts the burden of clarity on the author: if your prose is not clear, then it is your job to go back and fix it. The more Francophone or Continental style of academic writing allows for more complexity and more digressions and puts a greater burden on the reader to interpret. The Anglo-Saxons might complain that this style is pompous, off-putting and unnecessarily convoluted, while the counter-argument is that the Anglo-Saxon style is overly simplistic, with little nuance, and does not invite the reader to actively engage. A third tradition, common, for example in Asian countries, is that the author must remain extremely respectful of his or her academic predecessors, and the best way to do this is to use their words as faithfully as possible. While the Anglo-Saxons cry 'plagiarism' and wring their hands over the inability of the author to assert their own voice, the authors from this tradition are shocked at our arrogance and pretentiousness. I make no claim that the Anglo-Saxon style is the 'best' way to write: I do, however, have to acknowledge that this style dominates in academic publishing in English, and that this book is written in accordance with this style.

Different cultures of academic writing

The norms and conventions for what constitutes good academic writing vary not only across disciplines, but also across geographical regions. What might be considered exemplary use of figurative language, description and voice in one region might be considered amateurish in another. Three of the biggest sources of variation are: formality (to what extent you are allowed to use, for example, colloquial language, the first person or contractions); the extent of *hedging* (that is, how many qualifiers the author uses to soften the claim); and *stance* (the author's positioning relative to both the existing literature and the reader). In some cultures, you are expected to make strong claims with minimal hedging and play up your contribution to the field. In others, this would seem both ignorant and arrogant. Which of the following styles sound familiar to you?

(Continued)

(Continued)

'*A is B*. I'm the only one to have ever said this, and now that I have demonstrated this beyond any doubt, the world will shift on its axis.'

'*A* might perhaps under some circumstances resemble *B*, except of course when it does not, which happens at times.'

A is B. Why do I have to keep explaining this?'

'Be patient while I elaborate in detail all my thoughts about *A*, and then all my thoughts about *B*. If you are born wealthy and have plenty of time on your hands, you can devote your life to guessing what I think the relationship between *A* and *B* might be.'

'*A*, being a most prestigious and well-known entity, is indubitably like *B*, another respected phenomenon, because this is obvious to the observant eye.'

Norms of academic writing vary throughout the world

'My professor says that *A is B*, which must make it true. I'm not famous enough yet to use my own words, so you have to read between the lines of the way I put together other people's words to guess what I really think.'

Although there are many variations of the Anglo-Saxon style of writing, there are key important elements they all share. Good scholarly writing in the Anglo-Saxon tradition aims to communicate an idea clearly by breaking it down into logical components and presenting these components in a way that makes sense to the reader. As scholarly writers, our biggest challenge is to explain an idea to people who have not been with us every step of the way through our research. By the time we sit down to write, most of us have been so immersed in our work for so long that we have no idea what in our work is new or difficult to grasp – everything seems obvious. Either we explain too much or we explain too little. Few of us are born knowing how to step outside ourselves and tell the story but, fortunately, most of us can learn.

And learning to write good scholarly prose starts not with mastering the parts of speech or subject–verb agreement but with understanding the nature of academic discourse. The scholarly dialogue is simply the process by which we develop a body of knowledge. For a body of knowledge to keep growing, it requires both theory and empirical evidence (both qualitative and quantitative). Theory provides the ideas that link the data together and give them meaning; and the empirical evidence gives the theory weight. Theory alone is just an idea. Empirical data alone is just isolated experience or piles of numbers. Even disciplines that are almost completely theoretical in nature (philosophy, for example) are not just about coming up with new ideas, but also about tying these ideas to real-world phenomena (even if these phenomena are highly abstract).

Thus, knowing where your work fits into this discourse – what your contribution is and who will be interested in hearing about it – is the key. It is just like any other conversation: the participants all have their own particular interests. Those who are primarily interested in applied research will be more interested in the data; those who are primarily interested in pure research will be more interested in theory.

This applies not only to readers, but also to journal editors and book publishers. Publishers and editors are crucial: you must get published before you can reach your readers. So what do journal editors and book publishers look for when they evaluate an article or book? Let's say you are an editor of a scholarly journal. You want people to read and cite the articles published in your journal. The more your journal's articles are read and cited, the more your journal's prestige grows; the more prestigious the journal, the more scholars will read it and submit their best articles to it. People will read an article if the topic is interesting; they will cite an article if it adds something new to the discourse; and they will quote an article if it is written with precision and grace. So, first off, you will look for articles that will capture a reader's interest and that add something new. If they are well written, so much the better. Likewise, if you are a book publisher, you know that you will never be able to sell a book unless the reader finds it compelling enough to pick up in the first place. Further sales are generated if it is rich enough in content for scholars to refer to in their own scholarly inquiry. Thus relevance and quality are likely to head your list of criteria as you read the hundreds of manuscripts that land on your desk. It is also the first thing any reviewer, for either journal articles or books, will be looking for. So, as a scholarly writer, whether you are writing an article for a journal or a book for a publisher, *relevance* and *quality* are at the top of the essential checklist for scholarly writing (see the text box 'The essential checklist').

The essential checklist

- **Relevance of the topic**
  To the academic discourse:
  Does it push the scholarship forward?
  Does it represent something new or unique?
  To the journal:
  Is it consistent with the journal's preferences for theme and approach?

(Continued)

(Continued)

- **Academic quality**
  Is the method academically sound?
  Is the analytical framework or approach fruitful?
  Are the data valid?
  Is the theoretical anchoring solid?

- **Focus of the core argument**
  Is your research question sufficiently precise and fruitful?
  Does your thesis statement (main conclusion) answer the question, the whole question, and nothing but the question?

- *Organization and coherence*
  Is your structure complete?
  Does your abstract contain your aims and findings?
  Do you adequately set the stage in your introduction?
  Have you explained your method or approach?
  Does your conclusion conclude and not just stop?
  Do the sections and paragraphs have a smooth and logical flow?

- **Sentence flow**
  Do you take the audience into account in your choice of words?
  Are there noticeable problems with grammar or usage?

- **Headings, tables and figures**
  Is your title engaging and suitable?
  Do your headings correspond with the content?
  Do your tables and figures add substance to your argument?
  Are your tables and figures readable?

- **Format and house style**
  Did you follow instructions to the best of your ability?
  Are your references correct and complete?

Relevance

Does your topic add something to the academic discourse? Does it push the scholarship forward or expand the field? If it doesn't, then there is no reason for anyone to publish it. This does not mean that every article you write has to be revolutionary. The very idea of what makes something 'new' or 'innovative' varies drastically from field to field. The scholarship that makes up the body of knowledge for a given discipline or issue area is largely incremental. Sometimes being 'new' means that you look at a familiar problem with updated data to see if anything has changed.

Sometimes a step forward may require taking a step back and providing an overview if such an overview does not already exist. Sometimes 'innovation' means looking at an established discourse through a different theoretical lens, or introducing it to a different audience. In this sense, 'new' or 'innovative' can be very subjective, and not simply a function of fresh data on an unexplored topic resulting in a bold game-changing hypothesis. The only thing that matters is that the reader should not want to roll her eyes and say, 'Oh, please. I have read this a thousand times before.'

Only the experts in the field can determine whether a topic is relevant, which is why peer review is so important. This is particularly true for journal articles, which are supposed to represent the cutting edge of research and scholarship. But even your expert reviewers need to be persuaded a bit, so it is up to you to make a case for the relevance of your topic. But demonstrating relevance is not always straight-forward. Sometimes something can be so new that it generates scepticism, so you have to convince your reader that you are still doing rigorous scholarship. And sometimes a topic can be so familiar that you might have to work hard to show that you have something to say that hasn't been said a hundred times before. Moreover, you need to show that the topic is relevant not only for the academic discourse, but also for the particular journal you have submitted it to. Each journal has a particular focus. One economics journal, for example, may tend toward the theoretical, another toward the empirical; one literary journal may emphasize tex-tual analysis while another focuses on historical context. A paper may contribute to the academic discourse in general, but not be relevant for a particular journal.

Academic quality

No journal wants to publish an article that is not built on solid research or reason-ing. This means that the data must be valid and the method or analysis must be sound. This is discussed further in Chapter 3. To quantitative researchers, who are used to cataloguing their data and describing their method in enough detail so that it could be reproduced by another researcher, this seems obvious, but qualitative researchers (or those who work primarily with theory) often think it does not apply to them. I assure you that it does. When it comes to documenting method and data, the main difference between qualitative and quantitative research is that qualita-tive researchers have a harder time explaining how they went about carrying out their research. Instead of being able simply to describe an established method ('We used a 7-point Likert scale') and concrete data ('12% of men and 40% of women'), qualitative researchers, as well as scholars in the humanities, must meticulously lay out and justify their logic, in addition to linking their study to the work of others. If they don't, their work will come across as weak, overly speculative and not founded on anything substantial. Even if the topic is fascinating or exceptionally timely, journals do not want to publish an article that lacks sound reasoning.

On the other hand, the increasing pressure for journals to increase their impact factors and the opportunities for rapid publication afforded by open access and web-based solutions mean that journals sometimes confuse 'cutting edge' with 'complete balderdash' – especially because it is not always easy to tell the difference. (You might recall the Sokal hoax in 1996, when Alan Sokal submitted an intentionally bogus article to a journal of postmodern cultural studies and it still got published – and later even defended – by the journal.) That said, it is in the best interest of neither you nor the journal to intentionally print 'soap bubbles' or 'Rorschach tests' (see the text box 'Signs of bad academic writing' on p.15).

For most journals, and most peer reviewers, relevance and academic quality are so important that if your work lacks them, the best writing and editing in the world will not make it publishable. Since counting on judgementally impaired editors and peer reviewers is a risky prospect, you are better off aiming for the real deal. And if your topic is relevant and your scholarship is sound, then no matter how badly written or poorly structured your manuscript, it is probably still salvageable. This means that you can work with it as a piece of writing to make it more attractive to a journal or publisher.

Here are some other criteria essential to good scholarly writing, the ones you can do something about even after your research is finished, starting with the most important.

Focus of core argument

It's not enough to have a great topic; you need to know exactly what you want to say about it and make that clear to the reader. The core of your argument is made up of a starting point (your research question) and a destination (your thesis statement). This is explained further in Chapter 5. The research question defines the specific focus of your inquiry, and the thesis statement sums up what you want to say about it. When it comes to making an argument your reader can follow, definitiveness or correctness probably takes a back seat to actually responding to the question that was asked. Consider these two research questions: 'Can online learning achieve the same kind of learning outcomes as classroom learning?' and 'How can learning developers ensure that online courses result in desired learning outcomes?' The answer to the first might be something like 'No, not according to my new data', while the second might be 'Online learning requires learning developers to conceptualize and implement innovative approaches to measuring learning outcomes, including uses of peer feedback.' In both cases the topic is the same – online courses – but each has a different focus. The first is a 'yes or no' question, and the second is a 'how' question. What is important here is that the question and answer are related to one another. In your paper, the answer to 'Can online learning achieve the same kind of learning outcomes as classroom learning?' could just as well be 'The evidence is unclear.' The answer, however, should not be 'Online learning requires learning developers to conceptualize and implement innovative approaches to measuring learning outcomes, including uses of peer feedback.' This is the answer to a slightly different question, and your readers will be confused. What your reviewers will be looking for is a well-formulated question that actually gets addressed in some way or another – even if the answer is 'The evidence is unclear.'

What questions are you asking? What answers are you providing? A good core argument has a relevant question that you answer with evidence that supports your claim.

Organization and coherence

Once you have a starting point and an end point, you still have many choices to make about how you move from one to the other. In other words, there are a lot of different ways you can choose to organize your paper. An effective structure will help you tell the story you want to tell (this is explained in more detail in Chapter 6). The introduction presents and demonstrates the relevance of your research question, and prepares the reader for what will follow. The way you present your method or approach will convince your readers that your findings are valid and your analysis logical – and that it's worth their while to keep reading. The results or analysis you present will provide solid evidence for your argument, and your discussion (or conclusion) allows you to lay out the logic of your thesis statement in full, as well as to discuss any implications this might have (which also increases the relevance of your inquiry). Each paragraph should flow logically to the next. Poor organization and lack of coherence will almost certainly be noted by reviewers and hurt your chances of publication.

Sentence flow

Authors who are not writing in their native language often feel they are at an unfair disadvantage when they submit manuscripts for publication. Although their papers will often (but by no means always) require more copy-editing than manuscripts written by native speakers, grammatical errors, awkward usage and sentence flow are fairly easy to fix – which is why this criterion is not at the very top of the list (and since many other books cover writing at the sentence level, it will not be discussed further in this book). If the core argument is clear and the structure is sound, any halfway decent editor can clean up the language without breaking a sweat. Moreover, scholars are often willing to put up with some seriously challenging prose if the payoff is solid scholarship. Scholarly writing is one place where it is perhaps better to have a good argument expressed badly than a bad argument expressed well.

Headings, tables and figures

Your manuscript is likely to contain more than body text (see Chapter 7 for a more detailed discussion). At the very least, you will have a title. You will probably also have separate headings for each section. The reviewers will be looking for a title that accurately reflects the content of the entire paper and headings that reflect the content of the section that follows. Tables and figures allow you to tell your story through more than just words. Sometimes, this is simply a supplement to text, giving readers an opportunity to understand your point through more than one medium. But for quantitative researchers, the presentation of your data in the form of a table or figure might be even more important than the text you write to describe these data. For this reason, comprehensibility is the main concern: do your tables and figures help clarify your argument, or do they seem tangential or confusing?

Format and house style

Each journal or publishing house has its own set of standards for formatting and conventions with respect to spelling, punctuation, capitalization and typography. (See Chapter 10 for more on this.) These standards and conventions are often referred to collectively as the 'house style'. The goal of a house style is to achieve a certain consistency across issues of a journal or books published by a press. References are a good example: different disciplines have different conventions, and some journals want authors' names spelled out in full, others want a first initial and so on. Because formatting and style errors are by far the easiest problem for an editor to fix, they are at the bottom of the list. This does not mean that format and style do not matter, only that getting it wrong will seldom stand in the way of your getting published.

The 'Essential checklist' shows that a good core argument is more important than sentence flow, which is more important than formatting. But this is no excuse to write sloppily or put no effort into your reference list. Excellence in meeting the criteria at the bottom of the list may help make up for shortcomings closer to the top. Say your core argument is strong but your structure is wobbly. The editor could go either way: accept or reject. If your sentences are engaging and your reference list impeccable, the editor might give you the opportunity to revise your paper. If your sentences are incomprehensible and your references a mess, you probably won't get the benefit of the doubt.

Signs of bad academic writing: A typology

If good academic writing remembers that it is part of a conversation, bad academic writing forgets this in one way or another. Unfortunately, just because something has been published does not mean it is exemplary prose. Here is a typology of typical types of bad writing you might have seen in the wild, and their warning signs so you can try to avoid making the same mistake.

The Soap Bubble

The prose looks pretty but can withstand no external pressure – such as an intelligent reader. Identifiable by an overabundance of colourful figures but an almost total lack of substance. Warning sign: spending more time on layout than on content.

The Coconut

The opposite of the soap bubble, this structure seems determined to keep the reader out. Impenetrable sentences, convoluted logic and a complete lack of overview will discourage everyone but the most determined. The payoff is often worth it, but few will be hardy enough to find out. Warning sign: sentences that are a paragraph long.

The Tourist

With no clear direction, the writer wanders from one supposed point of interest to another – 'Hey, this looks interesting … have you seen this over here? … Ooh, this reminds me of something we saw last year.' Warning sign: writing the entire draft in one sitting, no revising.

Shock and Awe

Taking a cue from the military, the writer attempts to blind readers with facts. Designed to intimidate and confuse, this technique requires the writer to detonate bombs of empirical evidence so rapidly that the hapless reader has neither the time nor the opportunity to make sense of the data. Warning sign: more numbers or quotes than your own words.

The Emperor's New Clothes

Similar to the logic of shock and awe, but with verbosity rather than empirical evidence in the arsenal. Fearing that if the reader actually understands the words on the page she will discover the utter lack of content, the author's strategy is to assault the reader with verbiage until he cries uncle. Warning sign: multisyllabic, quasi-synonyms for otherwise comprehensible words.

The Attic

The article where nothing is thrown away and perfectly good ideas go to die a dusty and forgotten death because readers can't see them beneath all the other junk lying around. Also known as the *burrito* style of research publication (as opposed to the

(Continued)

(Continued)

salami slicing style), because the author puts in everything he can think of with only the thinnest of excuses holding it all together. Warning sign: no deletions in your revision.

The Channel Surfer
This results from felony cut-and-paste abuse. The writer gleefully moves random sentences and paragraphs around without taking time to rewrite the transitions between the pieces. The result is no connection or flow between ideas. Warning sign: a 'second' with no 'first'.

The Inkblot
Sometimes writing is a process of discovery, and sometimes it's just a process. Here, even the writer isn't sure what the message is, so he circles around it from a variety of angles hoping one of them might make sense to someone. Like the famous Rorschach test, this strategy takes advantage of lack of clarity: There is something in it for everyone. Warning sign: a single citation from such a work can be offered as support for diametrically opposed arguments.

A NOTE ON CO-AUTHORSHIP

This book is written as if you were the sole author of every paper you write. For many of us, however, sole authorship is the exception rather than the rule. For quantitative researchers in particular, not only is co-authorship the norm, but works by single authors are viewed with scepticism.

But in the context of this book, is writing as a co-author substantially different from writing as a single author? Answering this question requires a closer look at the concept of authorship. In theory, this is obvious: the author is the person who did the research and wrote the paper. In practice, however, modern merit systems (which tend to reward quantity of publication) have led to some unfortunate developments: researchers can be listed as co-authors for such less-than-significant contributions as providing a single photograph, filling in one or two points of data or chatting with the lead author over drinks. In some fields, it is common for a doctoral supervisor to be listed as co-author (or even lead author) of manuscripts written by their students, even if they have had no direct involvement in either the research or the writing. In some areas, the extreme competition to inflate publication lists forces researchers to make deals: 'I'll add you to my list if you add me to yours.' The incentive structure is such that simply sharing an elevator with someone seems to merit a co-authorship credit; the traditional system of listing lesser contributors in an acknowledgements section is no longer seen as sufficient. Recent highly publicized incidents of data falsification, where co-authors protested that they had no knowledge of what the lead author was up to, illustrate how dangerous this development is. This is why the Vancouver rules were established (and updated in December 2013). The rules, formally known as 'The Uniform Requirements for

Manuscripts Submitted to Biomedical Journals: Writing and Editing for Biomedical Publication', are a set of ethical guidelines for conducting and reporting research. (For a complete description of the rules, see: www.icmje.org.) The requirements for authorship are as follows:

- Authorship credit should be based on: (1) substantial contributions to conception or design of the work, or the acquisition, analysis or interpretation of data for the work; AND (2) drafting the work or revising it critically for important intellectual content; AND (3) final approval of the version to be published; AND (4) agreement to be accountable for all aspects of the work in ensuring that questions related to the accuracy or integrity of any part of the work are appropriately investigated and resolved.
- All those designated as authors should meet all four criteria for authorship, and all who meet the four criteria should be identified as authors.

While the rules were designed for biomedical research, their relevance for other fields is clear. What these rules say, essentially, is that just because your name is at the bottom of the list of ten authors is no excuse for letting the others do all the work and bear all the responsibility. Moreover, simply acting as supervisor, acquiring funding or collecting some data is not enough to be listed as a co-author. Nor is commenting on and editing the manuscript. This is what the acknowledgements section is for.

While some researchers find that working with co-authors makes them work more effectively – partly because they tend to give co-authored work higher priority, and partly because they have someone to bounce ideas off of – the truth is that working with other authors can be even more challenging than doing it all yourself: you have to iron out disagreements, reach compromises and accommodate one another's writing styles and working habits. The more you work on content-driven research rather than data-driven research, the more difficult working with co-authors can be, and the harder it is for you to maintain your own voice and sense of ownership of the material. This is particularly relevant for joint authorship that involves more than one discipline. In return, the end result can be better than anything you might have managed by yourself: you have colleagues to brainstorm with and additional expertise to draw from; the risk of veering dangerously off course is mini-

Co-authoring in the social sciences often means extra work - making sure everyone agrees on a common framework - but the payoff can be both a higher quality product and the satisfaction of working as a team.

Source: Photo by Ilan Kelman

mized. The point is that multi-authored papers do not write themselves. Putting everyone's contribution in a Petri dish and turning on a heat lamp does not grow a publishable manuscript.

Thus your responsibility in a multi-author work is the same as it is when you are on your own: you participate in the research itself, you participate in the writing and you participate in the preparation of the manuscript for submission. Whether you are the sole author, the lead author or the fifteenth co-author, this book is designed to guide you through the process of shaping your ideas and research into a valuable contribution to the scientific dialogue.

ORGANIZATION OF THIS BOOK

Many books on scholarly publishing focus on what you can do when you *finish* writing – how to fiddle with your sentences, straighten out your margins, get your manuscript ready for submission and so on. Taking its point of departure from the 'Essential checklist', this book is designed to be useful much earlier, when you are struggling with such questions as: 'How do I get my thoughts together?' 'How do I get what's in my head onto the paper?' and 'How do I make it comprehensible to other people?'

Chapter 2, *Getting started: Developing good writing habits*, talks about how you can get the most out of the writing process by approaching writing as a way to discover and develop your ideas. You don't have to have your article totally worked out in your head before you set pen to paper.

Chapter 3, *The 'I' in (social) science: Objectivity, transparency and argument*, introduces a central idea of the book: that academic writing is argumentative and not merely descriptive. This idea is developed more fully in Chapters 4–6.

Chapter 4, *Who are you talking to? Defining your audience*, helps you develop a sensitivity to who you are writing for and what they need from you. Chapter 5, *What do you want to say? Forming your core argument*, explains what a research question and thesis statement are, the relationship between them and their importance to your paper. Chapter 6, *How are you going to say it? Developing your structure*, describes the central elements of structure and how you can use them to build a convincing argument.

Chapter 7, *Breaking up the grey mass: Headings, figures and tables*, points out that your article consists of more than just body text and discusses how you can use headings (including your title), tables and figures to make your argument more clear, and also underscore your structure.

Chapters 8 and 9 address an often overlooked point: that actively participating in the scholarly dialogue requires more than simply publishing journal articles and books. Chapter 8, *Holding up the mirror: Giving and receiving feedback*, looks at how you can get the most out of the review process, both as a reviewer of others' work and as the one whose work is being reviewed. Chapter 9, *Saying it out loud: Presenting your paper*, discusses how you can make your presentations more effective, and how you can use them to develop your ideas and help you in the writing process.

Chapter 10, *Delivering the goods: Following author guidelines and submitting your manuscript*, gives you advice on the kinds of details you should really focus on before submitting (or resubmitting) your work.

This book is rooted in my years of experience as an academic editor and workshop facilitator. Throughout, I present practical exercises that can be used either in a classroom setting or for self-study. The chapters can be read in sequence from beginning to end, but you can also read them in any order depending on your interests and needs. This second edition also draws from some of my own research on writing and research productivity.

Remember

Social science is an ongoing conversation that takes place mainly through peer-reviewed books and journals.

Understanding how the scholarly dialogue works will help you make sense to, and be heard by, those you want to reach.

FURTHER READING

- Becker, Howard S. (2008) *Writing for Social Scientists: How to Start and Finish Your Thesis, Book, or Article*, 2nd revd edn, Chicago, IL: University of Chicago Press. Chapter 2, 'Persona and authority', addresses many of the myths of the academic voice and persona, and essentially what academic writing is supposed to be about. Chapter 3 attacks the notion of the 'one right way'.
- Germano, William (2008) *Getting it Published: A Guide for Scholars and Anyone Else Serious about Serious Books*, 2nd edn, Chicago, IL: University of Chicago Press. A more straightforward how-to book, it covers the entire process of book publishing, from proposal, to dealing with feedback and publication.
- McKay, Sandra Lee (2003) 'Reflections on being a gatekeeper', in Christine Pearson Casanave and Stephanie Vandrick (eds), *Writing for Scholarly Publication: Behind the Scenes in Language Education*, London: Lawrence Erlbaum Associates, pp. 109–23. This chapter gives a good discussion about the peer review process.
- Murray, Rowena (2013) *Writing for Academic Journals*, 3rd edn, Maidenhead: Open University Press. Murray provides a good all-round introduction to writing journal articles, including a good discussion about why to do it in the first place and what might be stopping you.
- Sword, Helen (2012) *Stylish Academic Writing*, Cambridge, MA: Harvard University Press. With a focus on developing voice and telling the story, this book has a refreshing take on the norms of academic writing. Sword builds on her own research and analyzes style conventions from several different disciplines. She also includes exercises to help liven up your prose.

TWO

Getting started
Developing good writing habits

It's not without reason that the writing process is often compared to being pregnant. Both start off with such promise, but before long, we start wondering what we have gotten ourselves into. We suffer through frustration, boredom, bouts of nausea and hours that feel like weeks. Looming up ahead is a deadline that feels both too distant and too soon. When the result is finally delivered, it's a miracle – and we cannot possibly imagine doing it again any time soon.

But we do. As scholars and researchers, we communicate our ideas primarily through writing, so most of us are working on several writing projects at once. When one is completed, there's no time or spare energy to hand around the cigars because another one is calling. Yet to most of us the writing process still feels foreign, mysterious and maybe a little scary. As students, we procrastinated till just before a paper was due, then brought on the caffeine and pulled a couple of all-nighters. As researchers, we don't seem to do much better: we get funding for, say, a year-long project. We spend eleven months researching, three weeks writing and one week revising and then, only then, do we finally discover what we want to say. By the time we've rewritten the entire paper and finished all the revisions, we are six months behind; not only have we spent all the money budgeted for that project, but we're also rapidly running out of the money budgeted for the next. We feel like failures; we swear that *next time* it will be different. But it won't – not unless we make some changes in the way we tackle this essential part of a researcher's work.

This chapter aims to help you do just that. It demystifies the writing process and shows how to make writing an ongoing part of your research, instead of a dreaded trial that comes at the end of it. (See the text box 'What the research says about research productivity' for a discussion of the academic discourse on what makes some researchers produce more than others.)

What the research says about research productivity

Research productivity, that is, the amount and kind of writing that is published as a result of your research, is a field of study heavily dominated by quantitative research into the individual and environmental factors that are associated with higher or lower degrees of productivity. A common observation in this field is that productivity is highly skewed: in virtually all research-producing settings, about 15 to 20 per cent of the staff produces more than half of the published research. So, what do these super-producers have in common? Most of the research has looked at age, rank, gender and discipline as explanatory individual factors. The consensus, if one can say that there is any consensus at all, is that age has an inverted U function: productivity increases up until the age of about 50–60 and then starts decreasing – unless you are one of those super-producers. Professors outpublish scholars of lower ranks by an order of magnitude. And men seem to outpublish women – although this effect disappears almost entirely when controlled for age, rank and discipline. Discipline is a difficult category, because even more so than the rest of these categories, it all depends on what you measure and how you measure it. But what is most clear when you look at discipline is that different fields have different patterns of publishing. Researchers in the hard sciences seldom publish anything other than journal articles. Book publishing is most common in the humanities. Social scientists are somewhere in between: they publish more books than researchers in the hard sciences, but not as many as those in the humanities. Co-authoring follows a similar pattern: co-authoring occurs most in the hard sciences, least in the humanities and the social sciences are somewhere in-between. Important environmental factors include funding for research and an institute that places a value on producing research. Oddly enough, although it is assumed that native language should matter (in the sense that the assumption is that researchers publishing in a non-native language are at a strong disadvantage), it has not been investigated to any large degree, and most cross-national studies don't show an obvious advantage for those institutes located in English-speaking countries.

Since most of us cannot choose to be native-English-speaking male professors around the age of 50, we are better off looking at what the research says that productive researchers do: first off, they are motivated to do research – they do not see it as a necessary evil. More important, they are motivated to do the writing. They may not always love it (and may often hate it), but they make a point of writing regularly (sometimes as little as 30 minutes a day, but regularly). They are also aware of what they are good at, and of when they need help. They might form writing groups, or just know when they need a second opinion. They may be ambitious, but they don't let themselves get paralyzed by unrealistically high expectations for each and every sentence they construct. They attend international conferences, where they present their work and get inspiration from others in their field, which often leads to future collaboration. They know how to handle setbacks and how to organize their time; they know what it takes for *them* to stay on track. In my own experience as a writing coach, it seems that the more you publish, the more you publish. It takes time to learn the genre, to learn about yourself as a writer and to build a foundation of knowledge that you can build on. But once you start publishing and get the hang of it, it builds its own momentum. Writing and publishing become part of your lifestyle. The point of this chapter is to focus on those very things you need to learn to get to know yourself as a writer.

For more reading on productivity, see:

- Boice, Robert (1985) 'The neglected third factor in writing: Productivity', *College Composition and Communication*, 36 (4): 472-80.
- Costas, Rodrigo, van Leeuwen, Thed N. and Bordons, Maria (2010) *A Bibliometric Classificatory Approach for the Study and Assessment of Research Performance at the Individual Level: The Effects of Age on Productivity and Impact*, Leiden: Centre for Science and Technology Studies (CWTS).
- Creamer, Elizabeth G. (1998) *Assessing Faculty Publication Productivity: Issues of Equity*, Washington, DC: Graduate School of Education and Human Development, George Washington University.
- Kyvik, Svein (1991) *Productivity in Academia: Scientific Publishing at Norwegian Universities*, Oslo: Universitetsforlaget.
- Mayrath, Michael C. (2008) 'Attributions of productive authors in educational psychology journals', *Educational Psychology Review*, 20: 41-56.
- Teodorescu, Daniel (2000) 'Correlates of faculty publication productivity: A cross-national analysis', *Higher Education*, 39: 201-22.
- White, Charles, James, Karen, Burke, Lisa A. and Allen, Richard S. (2012) 'What makes a "research star"? Factors influencing the research productivity of business faculty', *International Journal of Productivity and Performance Management*, 61 (6): 584-602.

WRITING AS A PROCESS OF DISCOVERY

Most of us are not like Mozart, who could compose a symphony in his head and simply write it down in its full perfection afterwards. Most of us need a few tries to get it right. It's tempting to think of all those early drafts as a waste of time and paper, but they aren't. Sometimes the only thing that separates a mediocre piece of writing from a truly great piece of writing is the number of drafts the author was willing to put effort into. Putting words on paper helps us think things through. Suddenly gaps in logic become visible. Things we thought we knew thwart our every attempt to describe them. At the same time, innovative, previously

Sometimes you do not know what you know – or what you do not know – until you try to write it down

unimaginable solutions can leap out at us once we start writing. This is why so many 'Aha!' moments happen while we think we are polishing up our final draft. But no matter how often it happens, it still takes us by surprise.

The surprise comes in part because we don't appreciate the difference between what we think we know, and what we know well enough to explain to someone else. Ideas float around in our heads without explicit connections between them. We may sense a connection, but until we try to describe it on paper it remains ephemeral. In our own minds, we can get away with a lot. Paper is less forgiving. In scholarly writing you can't get away with 'It's kinda like, you know, totally …' accompanied by sweeping hand gestures and eloquent facial expressions.

To get the most out of the writing process, we have to start writing *before* we think we are ready, *before* we have 'thought it all through' – and *long* before funding runs out. We also need to realize that proficient writing is rarely produced in a single sustained session. Some ideas simply need time to mature. Whenever we pick up work that has been lying dormant for a few months, we almost always have something to add, something that didn't occur to us before. College all-nighters may have earned us some pretty good grades, but if we want to write *well*, if we want to develop an idea fully and communicate it in the best way possible, we need to think of writing as a process of discovery. Writing is more than typing up the results of our research: writing is *part* of our research. But before we can make writing work for us as a process of discovery, we need to understand the difference between the creative and critical phases of writing.

Try this: Form a writing group with peers

Writing groups can have many different forms and functions: to provide feedback; to provide inspiration and motivation; and to provide a space to write. If you want a group to provide feedback, see the suggestions in Chapter 8. If you need motivation and space to write, there are a variety of formats that could work for you. You can meet weekly to share writing goals – progress made on the previous goals and the goals for the following week. Here, it is important to keep track of everyone's progress by writing down the goals – and the progress. You might also choose to talk about not just goal-setting, but also other aspects of writing: motivation, time management, the ups and downs. At the very least, this can help you get a better idea of what is 'normal' for writers to struggle with. Some groups meet to create a space for actual writing: after a brief discussion about what the writing goals for the next hour or two will be, they sit down and write.

This works when it is difficult to carve out writing time in a busy schedule: it is harder to re-allocate writing time to something else when you have a group expecting you to be there. No matter what format you choose, what makes a writing group successful is that you all agree on what you want out of the group, and you all commit.

SEPARATING THE CREATIVE AND THE CRITICAL

Whether we are aware of it or not, writing is a two-part process: the creative part, where we put our ideas into words so they make sense to us; and the critical part, where we try to make those words make sense to someone else (see Figure 2.1). In the creative part, we let the ideas flow, make new connections, see implications and draw conclusions. You don't need to write full sentences. You don't have to start from the beginning and write to the end; you can start in the middle, skip around, and write whichever sections you feel inspired to write. You don't need to be grammatically correct either. You don't even need to write in the language you are planning to publish in.

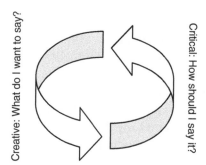

Figure 2.1 The creativity cycle

Trying to refine rough text can lead to renewed bursts of creativity

In the critical part of the process, we emerge from our own little universe and shift our perspective to that of a reader. This is where we fill in the blanks, connect the dots, and generally put into words everything the reader needs to draw the same conclusion we draw, or to see the same connection we see.

The important thing to remember here is that we cannot do both at the same time. Creativity does not thrive when we get hung up on punctuation, spelling and subject–verb agreement. Perfectionism makes you your own worst enemy. In the creative phase, what's important is to capture our threads of thought and pin them down on paper. Likewise, in the critical phase, we cannot focus properly on giving our readers what they need from us if we are constantly spinning off in our own universe and rethinking our entire thesis. Think of the creative and the critical as muscles that pull in opposite directions: if you contract only your bicep, your arm bends; if you contract only your triceps, your arm straightens; if you contract one at a time, you can create fluid movement, but if you try to do both at once, your arm just gets stiff.

Concentrating on one phase at a time does not necessarily mean that we do all the creative work first, and only then move on to the critical. Most of us flip back and forth between the two many times during a single writing project, sometimes in the space of a few minutes. Indeed, the two phases build on one another. While struggling to explain our ideas to another person, we come up with new ideas, or perceive new facets in old ones. This new burst of creative thought requires us to follow through by refining yet again to make sure other people understand what we mean. We develop and refine our ideas by moving from creative to critical to creative, over and over again. What's important is that we don't expect ourselves to do both at once.

I should mention here that those of us who are more quantitatively oriented often experience the creative process a little differently than qualitative or theoretically oriented researchers: the more quantitative the research design, the more creative energy goes into designing the method and analyzing the data numerically. Putting together the tables and figures then feels like being finished. The writing feels anti-climactic – or worse, depressing and frustrating because it doesn't come out as straightforwardly as expected. While those of us who are more qualitative and theoretically oriented may be more used to how things change during the writing, and how putting an argument into words shapes the direction it takes, quantitative researchers can sometimes feel that the struggle to express themselves in words just means they are bad writers. The truth is that academic writers of every flavour can expect to go back and forth between thinking about what they really want to say, and how they want to say it.

Because writing critically is so different from writing creatively, these phases each require a very different focus. If you think of the creative phase as digging deeper toward the 'truth', the crux of your research and what you really want to say, you can think of the critical phase as climbing back out of your hole to join the rest of the world and help them appreciate your discovery. The critical phase thus requires you to step outside yourself: your focus is on understanding your audience, making your argument coherent and concise, and presenting your material as comprehensibly as possible. Since the remaining chapters of this book concentrate on developing these skills, the rest of this chapter will focus on developing skills to stimulate creativity – that is, learning how to (temporarily) shut out the critical voice.

STIMULATING CREATIVITY

Stimulating creativity is not about forcing yourself to be creative, but rather about creating an environment where creativity can thrive. For most of us, this does not happen of its own accord. Most of us work in environments that outright squelch the creative process. We are pulled in conflicting directions by administrative demands, family obligations, funding concerns, classwork and other circumstances over which we have little control. In my own research I've seen that it is not just the actual interruptions that can derail a train of thought, but the mere possibility of interruptions that can make it difficult to slip into the deep concentration you need to write. This means that we must take active steps to counteract these influences. Here are some steps that anyone can take.

Set aside time and space

Waiting for inspiration to strike is a lot like waiting for Godot. We think that when inspiration finally arrives, we will sit down and write. Inspiration's arrival, however, is not guaranteed, and deadlines can't be deferred till inspiration shows up. So we have to find a way to be productive while we're waiting. This requires some self-discipline, because when we ask ourselves, 'Do I feel like writing right now?' our answer will probably be a resounding 'No' or 'Not yet, I just have to [fill in the blank] first.' Once a writing momentum is established, finding time becomes easier. The question is how to get momentum in the absence of inspiration.

A great way to establish momentum is to try immersing yourself in writing for a period of a few days – a kind of writing retreat. If you can remove yourself to another location entirely, like a cabin in the woods, all the better. But you can achieve the same thing by moving to a different office, moving to a different place in your own office, or merely disconnecting yourself from the phone and Internet for a while. The point is that for the next period of time, your main focus will be on one particular writing project. Three days is an ideal length of time: day 1 is usually spent being incredibly ineffective and struggling to figure out where to start. On day 2, you finally manage to get some words on paper, and by day 3, you've gotten a sufficient amount to work with that you can re-enter the real world again and still maintain some sort of flow even though you may not have an opportunity to write full time.

Try this: Structured writing time with a partner

If you are having trouble getting started and need a friendly push, try structured writing time with a partner. Spend 15 minutes or so asking each other basic trigger questions (see Chapter 8), such as: 'What are your biggest challenges with this manuscript?' 'What do you most want your audience to understand?' and so on. Then spend a couple of minutes explaining exactly what you want to achieve in the following writing session, which can be between 30 and 90 minutes long – just make sure that you agree with your partner on how long it should be. When you have both stated your writing goals, set the timer and *write* for the allotted period of time. When the time is up, *stop*. Take a deep breath, walk around,

(Continued)

(Continued)

stretch. Make sure your break is at least 15 minutes long. Meet with your partner at the beginning or end of the break and spend a few minutes talking about what you will do for the next writing session. When the break is over, set the clock again, and start writing. Try spending about two to three hours doing this, broken up in chunks of time as you see fit. For example, start with a 20-minute discussion and an hour of writing, followed by a half-hour break. Then 45 minutes of writing, followed by a 15-minute break. Then you can finish up with a sprint of 30 minutes of writing, followed by a discussion about what you will do the next time you sit down and write. This technique not only gets you started putting words on paper, but also makes it clear when you can stop – and not feel guilty about stopping.

The key to maintaining momentum once you have established it is to schedule specific chunks of time that will be devoted to writing, preferably in a pattern characterized by a certain degree of regularity. And even more important than regularity is to make these time periods *non-optional*. That is, you cannot ask yourself, 'Do I feel like writing?' Because you know what the answer will be. Consider serious athletes. Competitive swimmers, for example, do not ask themselves whether they feel like swimming today; swim practice is from 5 p.m. to 7 p.m., and they show up regardless of what mood they're in. It's the same with writing. Professional writers don't ask themselves if they *feel* like writing. They write whether they feel like it or not. Sometimes they are inspired, and require no self-discipline. Other times they are not inspired, but what makes them professional is that they write anyway. They know that even when they are struggling to compose coherent sentences, the writing itself will often lead to inspiration. They learn to set aside a block of time that generally works well for them. Some write better for a few hours each morning. Others prefer evenings. Some like marathon sessions with a lot of time off in between.

If you think about it, you can probably discern a pattern in your own writing. When are you most productive? Once you discern a pattern, develop a schedule around it. For example, if you are a morning writer, then you can decide that 8 a.m. to 10 a.m. is your writing time every morning (except weekends). This means that you do not get to your desk and say, 'Bleh. Today I don't feel like writing. Maybe I'll just make a few phone calls instead.' If the morning is your writing time, then morning is when you *write*.

It is important, however, to develop a realistic schedule. If you set aside, say, seven hours a day every day, you will do nothing but disappoint yourself. Most people can be truly productive and creative for only a few hours a day. If you set aside two hours a day, you can get a lot done and still have the rest of the day for all your other business. Even one hour a day – or for that matter, 30 minutes – will result in getting far more words on paper than if you do not set aside any time at all. If you prefer marathon sessions, you can set aside two or three days a week, leaving the rest of the week flexible. Whatever you do, you want to avoid a situation where you say to yourself, 'I can get this done if I just work on it eight hours a day all next week.' When Monday rolls around, you will feel overwhelmed by the work ahead. You may tell yourself that since you will be spending the whole week working on your project, you should probably get all of the small tasks off your desk first. Suddenly, the day will be over. So Tuesday you tell yourself, 'This will work if I write ten hours a day for the rest of the week.' By Friday you will have to put in 40 hours in a single day in order to meet your deadline.

For some people, developing a predictable schedule of any kind is unrealistic because the work they do is inherently erratic. Emergency medical personnel, for example, will have a hard time developing a fixed schedule for anything, let alone writing. Others face a battery of administrative duties, financial responsibilities, demands from students, field work that requires varying degrees of attention and so on. An unpredictable and demanding schedule does not relieve you of the obligation to set aside time, but it may make it harder. Instead of finding and institutionalizing your own personal writing rhythm, you will have to set aside irregular chunks of time – in essence, make appointments with yourself.

The less control you exercise over the content of your days, the greater responsibility you must take for sitting down with your calendar and making these appointments. When your schedule is packed with demands beyond your control, it is tempting to view the white spaces on your calendar as 'unscheduled time that may be used for writing if nothing else turns up'. This pretty much guarantees that other things *will* turn up and writing will always come last. But if you fill in those blank spaces *in ink* with 'writing time', it will be easier for you to acknowledge that you need time to write, and that writing time may have to come at the expense of something else. If 'writing time' doesn't sound important enough to you, write something like 'implementation of project 44022'. The actual wording doesn't matter, as long as you indicate to yourself that you have a valid reason to say no to other things that may turn up at that time. But be careful not to overschedule yourself. If on 1 January you make a New Year's resolution to improve your writing habits and block off every single white space in your calendar for the entire year with 'writing time', sooner or later you will be forced to miss one of those appointments. Probably it will be before you finish sweeping up the confetti and polishing off the rest of the champagne. Once you break one appointment, it will be progressively easier to break more appointments, and soon you'll be treating the 'writing time' blocked off in your calendar as just another kind of white space. It is far better to make only a few writing appointments that you know you will keep, than to make many that never have a chance.

Making irregular writing appointments may make it difficult to maintain a writing rhythm, but it will still provide you with chunks of time when you *know* you will be writing, when you will not let yourself do anything else. And getting through the first couple of sessions may give you enough momentum that you will want to write even when it is not on the schedule. (Yes, that is encouraged. No, it does not excuse you from writing during the hours you have scheduled for writing.)

Once you have set aside time to write, you can then sit down and focus on writing without having a nagging feeling that you should be doing something else. But you not only have to make a commitment to yourself; you also have to let everyone else know that you are unavailable. Otherwise you are sure to be interrupted. This is *your* writing time, and you have to take it seriously. If you don't, no one else will. Take your phone off the hook. Turn off your email. Put a sign on your door that says 'Do not disturb. Genius at work'. If that fails, find an alternative work space that will physically remove you from interruption. If you make it clear that certain times are off limits, people will learn to respect it – as long as you do. Once you start to make exceptions – say you let a desperate student come in to talk to you about her thesis that is going nowhere – you're signalling that your writing time isn't all that important after all. There really is no good excuse. You either make time, or you don't. If you make time, you can write. If you don't make time, you can't write. And, ironically, this is just as important if you seem to have all the time in the world. PhD students and others can face a different kind of scheduling pressure: vast, yawning caverns of time, which can be even more intimidating than a full schedule. Because the writing project is so huge, and you have so much time to do it in, it is tempting to do all kinds of other things first as a way of 'clearing your desk'. You may have to physically remove yourself from your usual setting as a signal to yourself that you are going to focus on your writing. You can also use peer pressure to your advantage: the company of others on your writing retreat – as long as they share your goal – will make it harder for you to 'cheat' and do other things.

Cutting yourself off from the outside world by going away or simply making yourself unavailable to others may be very difficult. Most of us want to feel that we are available – to colleagues, to students, to whoever may wish to talk to us. And it is this desire to be available that can make writing so difficult: it's not just the actual interruptions that can prove distracting, but also the threat of interruption. Shutting out the world may feel not only unnatural, but outright rude. But it is possible, and you can avoid the wrath of your colleagues and students by making clear the times when you *are* available – and then being just as conscientious about making yourself available at those times as you are about making yourself unavailable during your sacred writing time.

Develop productive writing rituals

Even if we have set aside predictable writing times, we might not be ready to throw ourselves headlong into writing as soon as we walk through the door. Most of us need at least a few minutes to prepare mentally. This is why we develop rituals. Most of us already have rituals, even though we might not recognize them as such: we make a cup of tea, we read our email, or we straighten out our desk just so.

If you want to create a productive writing environment, you need to take a close look at your rituals, be honest about how well they work for you, and take whatever steps are necessary to change the ones that need changing. Rituals are recognizable by three qualities in particular: they occur at regular and predictable occasions; their content has a regular and predictable pattern; and much of the content serves no other purpose than to put the performer in a specific frame of mind or prepare him for another, more meaningful task. Both religious rituals (the taking of communion, for example) and secular rituals (such as a baseball player putting on his uniform in a specific way) follow this pattern.

Rituals associated with writing ideally help ease the transition to a productive writing state. Buying a double cappuccino with extra foam every morning and sipping it as you walk the few blocks to your office may allow you to feel momentarily occupied while you are mentally getting ready. Because the content of whatever ritual you use requires little active thought (you go to the same Starbucks, order the same latte and walk the same route every time), your thoughts can turn toward writing without having to actually put pen to paper. The lack of pressure to make decisions makes the transition to more focused work easier. But your thoughts will not turn to the work ahead if you have to think about what kind of coffee you want, where to get it and which direction to take afterward. For this reason, we are unlikely to change our rituals during periods of intense creativity and concentration.

Problems occur when your rituals do not prepare you for the task ahead so much as they simply eat up your available time. For example, some people have to tidy up their desk area before they feel ready to write. This is innocuous enough if 'tidy' means that we can find the desk, the chair, the keyboard and the computer screen. If you are more fastidious and you think things like, 'I'll start writing just as soon as I've polished the underside of my Venetian blinds, alphabetized my CDs and organized my rubber bands by size', steps must be taken: you need to either downgrade your idea of 'tidy' or make sure your work area is pristine when you leave it (and remains untouched while you are gone) so when you return you do not need to spend an inordinate amount of time cleaning. This also means that you might have to avoid working at home. If you simply cannot leave a pile of laundry unfolded, then you have to remove yourself to a place where there is no laundry.

Email is another classic offender. How many times have you sat down at your desk intending to write, but you check your mail first? You get distracted reading and answering these mostly unimportant messages, and when you finally finish, your whole morning has disappeared – and, more alarmingly, taken all your writing energy with it. If you cannot start writing until you've read – and answered – the 150 emails waiting for you in your inbox, then it is time to change your email habits. The world will survive if you wait a few hours to open your inbox. If it is truly, truly important, you can probably be reached by phone.

Learn the difference between 'getting things done' and 'looking like you are working'. A walk around your building, a chat with a colleague in the hallway – a good writing ritual may not involve sitting at your desk, but it gets you ready to write

What's important to remember is that any counterproductive rituals you have developed came from a legitimate need to feel prepared. This means that if you purge those negative rituals and replace them with nothing, you will still feel that need to prepare yourself. And if you do not fill the void with a more productive ritual, you will simply fall into old habits. What constitutes a productive ritual? Try taking a printout of your work at the end of the day, and then in the evening spending a short time reading through it and marking it with pencil: you can start the next day by simply addressing the comments you made the night before. The terror of the blank screen can be paralyzing, so a ritual that allows you to have something – anything – to start with can be an effective way of tricking yourself into working effectively. You can also leave notes in your draft of where to start the next day. Anything that leaves you feeling ready to go (and doesn't cut into your writing time) is a productive ritual. Light a candle. Take a bath. It doesn't matter what it is – as long as it works for you.

Warm up

A lot of fruitful writing rituals allow the writer to warm up before writing in earnest. The importance of warming up cannot be stressed enough. Athletes warm up before they compete. And before musicians get down to serious playing, they perform scales over and over again to get their fingers limbered up. We know this, but we don't apply it to writing. When we finally park ourselves in front of the computer after a prolonged absence, we expect perfect sentences to immediately come flowing from our fingertips. Instead, we can't write a word.

Tip

Develop and maintain a regular exercise routine, especially during intense writing periods. In addition to stimulating your creative brain, regular exercise both reduces stress, which in itself helps ideas flow, and helps prevent repetitive stress injuries, which are the bane of writers everywhere and a very real occupational hazard for anyone who writes or works with data. It's easy to convince yourself that you don't have time to exercise or that it isn't important for your work. Many scholars seem to think they exist only from the neck up. But for the brain to function optimally, it has to cooperate with the rest of the body it is attached to.

Warming up is as important for writers as it is for athletes and musicians. For a writer, warming up means writing for the sake of writing. When you're warming up, your writing can be sloppy or repetitive. It doesn't have to relate to the subject of your paper. It doesn't even have to make sense.

All too often, writers get caught in a vicious cycle. We worry so much about producing perfect sentences and finding exactly the right word that the writing dries up – but verbal elegance comes only when we're warmed up, so the more we worry about how bad our writing is, the worse it becomes because we don't write anything and never get warmed up. Giving yourself permission to write badly for a while will help break this cycle. This is particularly important if you have to schedule your writing over irregular intervals: the more time that elapses between writing sessions, the longer it takes to get warmed up, and the more time you must set aside to do just that. Once you are warmed up, your writing will improve. The important thing is to get yourself to that point.

A simple way to warm up is to read through what you've already written, just to find your voice again and remember where you were. Another way to warm up is to write about your research in a non-academic way, perhaps as an opinion piece for a newspaper or a series of recommendations for a user group: sometimes releasing yourself from the pressure of having to 'sound academic' will let the words flow, and you can carry that flow over to your academic writing.

One warm-up technique often used by professional writers in all genres is *free-writing* (also called timed writing). The idea is to write for a certain time – say 10, 15 or 20 minutes – without stopping, without correcting. Your only goal is to warm up the connections between your brain and your fingers, to get your words flowing. The goal is *not* to produce something that you will save. In fact, when you are finished, throw it away. If you keep what you write during these sessions, you will start thinking that you should write something useful – and you will start putting pressure on yourself to do just that. That's not what free-writing is about.

Free-writing comes in at least two variations: freestyle and focused. The freestyle approach means that you write about nothing in particular. Just keep your pen (or your fingers) moving and your thoughts flowing. You do not have to make sense. You do not even have to complete your thoughts. Here is an example:

> Here I am at my desk. This chair is actually too low for me, I realize. My desk is crowded, maybe I should clean it up. On the other hand, I know where things are. What should I make for dinner? I wonder if I have time to go to the conference next week? I have to get – never mind. What happened to the tree that used to be across the street?

The freestyle approach not only helps get your fingers moving, it also helps clear your mind of clutter. Putting these intrusive thoughts on paper gets them out of your head and allows you to focus on more important things. It is similar to the practice of meditation, where you clear your mind by acknowledging the presence of these intruders and then escorting them through the back door of your mind like a skilled party host: 'Hi, Bob! Nice to see you, I've got someone over here I'd like you to meet. Talk to you later.'

Freestyle free-writing is also useful if you are writing in your non-native tongue. It can help you get into the flow of thinking and writing in a different language without the pressure of having to be a genius at the same time.

Freestyle free-writing is harder than it sounds. At least at first, most of us find it difficult to keep writing without reading through what we have written and without feeling as though there has to be a connection between thoughts. Experiment with writing in longhand versus writing on the computer. Many people feel that they can be more creative when they write by hand, while others like the speed offered by touch-typing.

Tip

To keep yourself from looking at what you've written and force your critical mind to take a rest, try turning off your monitor while you write.

When you have mastered the freestyle approach to free-writing – that is, you no longer find it difficult to write about nothing in particular – you can try the focused approach. The focused approach uses free association to help you work through a particular problem that you are having with your paper, such as an unsatisfying conclusion:

> I just can't seem to get my conclusion to work. I stop but it feels like there should be more to say. I look at everything I wrote and I just think, 'so what?' What is the meaning of all this? Why did I even start it in the first place? Oh, yes, now I remember. It was when ...

Try beginning almost every sentence with a fixed phrase that directs your attention to the problem:

> What I really want to say is ...

> What I really want the reader to understand is ...

> What's really new about my work is ...

After you pick a question that focuses your attention where you want it to be focused, just keep answering it over and over again. This frees you from the pressure of having to have the 'right' answer. What is likely to happen is that the first time you answer the question it will come out stiff and sounding like a formal thesis statement. But the more times you answer it, the more your language will relax and become more conversational. After such a session, you can look at all the 'answers' you wrote down and see whether any seem right to you. You can then revise that answer and work it into your paper. At the very least, it may help you focus your thoughts.

In a focused free-writing exercise, if you suddenly veer in another direction midway and lose your focus, that's fine – because the danger with focused free-writing is that you'll start taking the ideas too seriously, thinking too much and caring too much about what you put on the paper. As with freestyle free-writing, the main goal is to warm up, and if you start worrying about what comes out, the purpose will be defeated. If you tend to be a perfectionist, you might want to avoid this variation.

Free-writing (especially the freestyle variant) can be used to start your writing day, perhaps as part of your pre-writing ritual. Or you can use it in the middle of a session, to push past temporary writer's block. No matter how you decide to use free-writing, the time you spend on it is just as important to the final product as the time spent combing through your work looking for mistakes. Writing fluidly about nothing in particular is directly related to your ability to express yourself more seriously afterward. It is far better to write intentional gobbledygook for ten minutes than to spend four hours paralyzed by writer's block because you didn't warm up.

Be ready when ideas come

When we are sufficiently warmed up, we also become more open to epiphany – that sudden moment of clarity where everything comes together and makes sense. Epiphanies are a gift from the writing gods that are bestowed upon us all, but only a few can make proper use of them. Why? Because they have an average lifetime of a photon, and if we don't write them down immediately, they will disappear. We have an idea just before we fall asleep, and because it is such a good one, we are sure that we will remember when we wake up. But we don't.

Experienced writers know that to ignore such a gift is to spite the writing gods, the consequences of which are too dire to contemplate. So they write down these epiphanies, snippets of thought or perfect words. Experienced writers are always ready. Pen and paper are essential ingredients of their briefcase, bag or coat pocket. Post-it notes by the bedside are a given. And like any other divine gift, epiphanies don't come when we want them to, but only of their own accord. The trick is to create an environment that encourages their appearance.

Ideas, epiphanies, sudden Aha!s, or whatever you like to call them, are a product of your right brain, your creative half. But many of us are dominated by our more structured and critical left brain. One way to create an idea-friendly environment is to somehow keep your left brain preoccupied so your right brain has a chance to work unfettered. The key here is repetitious, perhaps monotonous, sound or activity.

Some people find they work well with certain kinds of background noise. Sitting on a train or an airplane or in a busy café often provides this kind of almost hypnotic white noise. Listening to certain kinds of music – classical, for example – can also work. As can standing in the shower.

Other people find that they get some of their best ideas while they are exercising – perhaps jogging, swimming or walking. Note that it has to be somewhat repetitive exercise for this to work. Games like basketball, where you have to pay attention to the ball and the other players, seldom have this effect. You need to find something that demands just enough concentration to keep your left brain preoccupied but not so much that your mind can't wander.

Pay attention to when you get your ideas. This will help you to both recreate the setting if you need to and, more importantly, be prepared to write down the idea when it comes. Obviously, you can't keep a pen and paper with you in every situation; in the shower and swimming pool they aren't exactly practical. But usually it is possible to keep writing materials within reach. And it often doesn't matter if you do not (or cannot) read the notes afterwards: sometimes, the mere act of writing an idea down is enough to sear it into your memory. You don't need to restrict yourself to pen and paper either. Some people record their ideas on tape recorders, dictation machines or even their own cell phones. Others even call their own answering machines and leave a message. It doesn't matter how you do it: just find a way to preserve the idea before it flutters away.

Tip

If you *can't* write down your great idea when it shows up, and it does get away from you, you may be able to get it back by revisiting the scene: try rereading the last couple of pages you wrote or were reading; try walking the same route you walked when you had your thought.

Nurture your ideas

Usually when ideas come to you, they do not come fully formed. Think of them as tiny seedlings: although sun and rain help them grow, too much of either too soon will kill them. Sometimes what you need is a greenhouse, where all outside influence is carefully controlled. As soon as your seedlings grow robust enough, they can be transplanted outside and exposed to the elements. Ideas, too, need time to mature and ripen before they can be fully integrated into your work.

When your ideas are at this infant stage, they are very vulnerable and must be handled with care. Sometimes this means protecting them from external threat. So, even though a very important part of research is to familiarize yourself with other scholars' thoughts, at this crucial stage you may have to close yourself off to such input. This is because when you are deep in the throes of the creative phase, other people's voices – either indirectly in the form of existing scholarship or directly in the form of feedback from peers – can drown out your own voice. Doing additional reading at this point can throw you off track. At this stage, when you look at what other people have done, it is natural to think, 'How could I have not thought of that myself?' So you quickly integrate it into your work, and before you know it, you have smothered your own points with points that other people have already made.

Sometimes ideas need a chance to grow before they are ready to stand on their own

Likewise, in the vulnerable creative phase, criticism carries too much weight. For creativity to flow, you need confidence that what you are doing is important. You might even need a heaping portion of naïveté with a side order of arrogance to carry you through the difficult times. Even a seemingly helpful comment can leave you feeling deflated and rob you of important momentum.

Getting feedback and doing additional reading are unarguably an important part of the creative process. But timing is key. There are times to engage in these activities and times to avoid them. When you are trying to nurture your fledgling idea so it can fly on its own, it is time to stick your fingers in your ears to shut out the sound of others. In Chapter 8 you'll learn how to get the most out of feedback, but here it is enough to say that there are times when feedback and external input may hurt you more than help you. Most ideas need a bit of solitude to grow to full strength.

Take advantage of deadline pressure

Many writers find that pressure makes writing more difficult, but many others depend on it. They cannot get anything done until the deadline is imminent. There are several possible reasons for this, but the most likely one is that severe deadline pressure can release you from some of your own demands for perfection. You can always say to yourself, 'It would have been better if I had had more time, but this was the best I could do under the circumstances.' This permission to be less than perfect may be exactly what you need to let the words flow (see Figure 2.2).

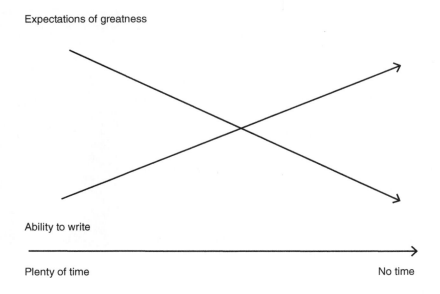

Figure 2.2 The relationship between perfectionism and output

Sometimes your ability to get words on paper increases as you run out of time and lower your expectations of perfection

People who need deadlines to get any sort of writing done at all thrive in environments where deadlines are constant – such as in journalism. Academia, even in an applied research environment, has a much slower pace. If you are a PhD student, for example, waiting until the last few months of your fellowship before you start writing anything will truly get you in trouble. If you seem to need deadline pressure to get started, then you can try pushing up your deadlines or creating additional deadlines (that is, instead of having one deadline for the whole project, you make deadlines for each part). It is important here to make real deadlines, because if you know your deadlines are fake, you will not take them seriously. But if you give yourself deadlines that have to be met, you may be able to get started earlier than you would have otherwise.

One way to set earlier deadlines is to make agreements with others. If you are a student, for example, you can make (binding) agreements with your advisor for submitting drafts of various sections. If you are a scholar, you can make agreements with an editor or your peers.

But perhaps the most useful way to give yourself earlier or additional deadlines is to schedule a presentation of your work. (For more about presentations, see Chapter 9.) For example, sign up to attend a scholarly conference where you can present your work either orally or in poster form. Or agree to hold a less formal presentation for your colleagues. In either case, you will be forced to prepare something for the presentation, which gives you a kind of deadline. In this context, the actual presentation is less important than the preparing for it and the potential feedback. Preparing for the presentation will require you to put your ideas into words, which is in effect another form of rough draft. Even if you write down only key words, you will be forced to speak more or less in full sentences – and in terms of discovering strengths and weaknesses in your work, you will come just as far as you would have done had you written a complete first draft. In addition, the feedback you get will help you further with your writing: the questions and comments you get not only give you a better understanding of your audience, but can also reveal areas that might need some more work or underscore the importance of your endeavour. Sometimes, there is nothing more stimulating to the writing process than meeting with an enthusiastic (or even critical) member of the audience who wants to discuss your ideas.

LEARNING TO STOP

Knowing when you are finished and ready to submit is also a skill that takes some time to develop. One of the biggest mistakes novice writers can make is to polish their work so much that they actually also start rubbing out the parts that are good. As a rule, we are terrible judges of our own work – which is why we see so much bad academic writing (see the text box 'Signs of bad academic writing' in Chapter 1). Sentences that we think crackle with life may be completely incomprehensible to others. Ideas that we think we have expressed so clearly that there is no possible room for misunderstanding may well be completely misunderstood by readers. The opposite is also true. Things we think are boring or mundane might seem revolutionary to others. And, unfortunately, the more you know about your subject matter, and the longer you have been working on something, the less likely you will be able to look at it as an outsider. So, for some people, knowing when they are finished depends on what others tell them: they need peer feedback before they can submit (see Chapter 8).

Regardless of how or when you are able to get feedback, you need to develop a sense of 'good enough'. It is a bit of a paradox: if you try to aim for excellence from the get go, you might not be able to write a single word. (Imagine right now starting to write a paper if you think to yourself, 'This has to be the best thing I've ever written in my life and will change the shape of the academic discourse forever.' Good luck with that first sentence!) But if you aim for 'good enough', you might end up with something excellent – simply because you were able to get words onto paper and then work with them. Aiming for 'good enough' means letting go of the idea that you can write something perfect. You will *always* be able to think of something to do that could 'improve' your paper – but, ironically, these very things can also make it worse. For example, adding more theory can make your argument more robust, but perhaps also make it harder to see your contribution to the discourse. And, in any case, perfection is in the eye of the beholder: what would be perfect for me as a reader might not be perfect for you. So aiming for perfection will always be an exercise in futility.

So, what constitutes 'good enough'? As the main body of this book will explain, you need to ask a question, answer it, and provide justification for your answer. You also need to explain how the question is a relevant one for the audience you've picked, and how it fits into the larger discourse. In essence, you need to identify a conversation, make your point and back it up, and trust that the other participants in this conversation will be able to carry the conversation further: it is not your job to shut down the conversation once and for all.

Tip

Make yourself do at least one thing outside your comfort zone each year. Terrified of making a presentation? Sign up to speak at a conference. Afraid of writing in English? Target your next article at an international journal. Learning to confront and manage fear of failure is an important part of being an academic. Aiming to eliminate this fear completely is not only unrealistic, but also undesirable: a small dose of fear is what inspires us to try a little harder. We just need to make fear work for us, and not against us. In the scholarly dialogue, thinking twice keeps you honest; overthinking keeps you silent.

IDENTIFYING AS A WRITER

Perhaps the most important step we can take to develop good writing habits is to make the mental shift required to identify ourselves as writers. Many of us find this difficult: no matter how much time we spend writing, we rarely think of ourselves as *real* writers. Real writers write Literature. They wear a lot of black, drink a lot of espresso and smoke too much. Worst of all, they can publish one slim volume at a vanity press and think of themselves as writers, while we publish 15 articles in scholarly journals and four books and still say, 'Oh, I'm not a *real* writer.'

Writing is about getting an idea, refining it and communicating it on paper to the rest of the world. Scholars struggle just like other writers to come up with the perfect image to describe an idea. We stare into space and try out words to see if they work in the sentence we're writing; we swirl them around in our mouths like a good cognac – even if the word is something like 'municipal' rather than, say, 'diaphanous'. We've even been known to hurl a rough draft across the room because it just isn't working. In other words – we *are* real writers.

Identifying as a writer does not mean you have to wear black turtlenecks and corduroy. It means that you view writing as serious business. It means that you use writing as a way of developing your ideas, not just recording them. It means that you set aside time for writing, and create an environment that nurtures your writing skills. And, most of all, it means that you derive satisfaction not only from thinking a thought, but from getting it down on paper.

Remember

You *are* a real writer, and you can use the writing process to help you get closer to what you want to say. Learn to temporarily turn off your critical voice, and find out what best stimulates *your* creative mind. But don't expect ideas to just come by themselves: schedule time to write.

FURTHER READING

- Becker, Howard S. (2008) *Writing for Social Scientists: How to Start and Finish Your Thesis, Book, or Article*, 2nd revd edn, Chicago, IL: University of Chicago Press. Warm and engaging, the book is particularly strong in describing the struggles with finding your voice and revising.
- Elbow, Peter (1998) *Writing with Power: Techniques for Mastering the Writing Process*, 2nd edn, New York: Oxford University Press. Generally acknowledged as the father of 'free-writing', in sections I and II Elbow describes a wide variety of ways to get words on paper.
- Goldberg, Natalie (2005) *Writing Down the Bones: Freeing the Writer Within*, expanded edn, Boston, MA: Shambhala Publications. Too often we think of scholarly writing as being a completely different species than creative writing, but the difference is smaller than you think. Goldberg's book, aimed at fiction writers, has ideas and exercises that are also useful and inspiring for the academic writer.
- Murray, Rowena (2013) *Writing for Academic Journals*, 3rd edn, Maidenhead: Open University Press. Murray talks specifically about various ways to approach the writing process, including strategies such as 'snacking' and 'binging'. She has some very useful suggestions for goal-setting.
- Murray, Rowena and Moore, Sarah (2006) *The Handbook of Academic Writing: A Fresh Approach*, Maidenhead: Open University Press. One of the few books that truly seems to understand the dilemmas and challenges faced by academic writers, it explores not only different ways of conceptualizing academic writing, but also practical advice for developing strategies that will work for you. Particularly relevant here are the chapters describing different types of writing groups, writing programmes and writing retreats.
- Silva, Paul J. (2007) *How to Write a Lot: A Practical Guide to Productive Academic Writing*, Washington, DC: American Psychological Association. Chapter 2 on 'Spurious Barriers' systematically (and quite humorously) rips to shreds all the typical excuses for not writing, and chapter 3 focuses on ways to motivate yourself. I dare you to not schedule regular writing sessions after reading this!

THREE

The 'I' in (social) science

Objectivity, transparency and argument

At its positivistic roots, science is supposed to be objective. It seeks a Truth, one that can be measured and identified, and is utterly independent of the beholder. The researcher in pursuit of this Truth is meant to be a neutral, value-free recorder of events about which he has no opinion and preferably no involvement: 'Who, me? I was just standing here minding my own business when suddenly these two chemicals leaped out of their containers and combined themselves in a Petri dish. Fortunately, I was present and could record the event as it transpired. I have no idea why it happened and dare not guess what it means. But I can tell you precisely how many bubbles it produced.' Although many, if not most, researchers today find this view antiquated – or at the very least, lacking in nuance – it still permeates the way we approach scholarly writing. Most of us still think our writing should be free of any opinion. And we think this because we still, perhaps only unconsciously, cling to a utopian view of research where fact and opinion are easy to distinguish from one another and opinion is unwelcome. Even in the social sciences we echo this belief: somehow, after we carefully transcribe interviews with informants, themes 'emerge' all by themselves, and we simply note them down for the convenience of the reader.

But as tightly as we cling to the notion that our work should not be contaminated with our own opinions, scholarly inquiry would stagnate if it were not. There are good reasons why research is carried out by human beings and not computers. It isn't just about facts; it's about ideas – and thus very much about perception. It's about putting facts together and trying to discover what they mean. Anyone who has collected and analyzed data knows that the hard part is not gathering the information, but rather making sense of it all. This is why there is debate and discussion in every discipline. Someone gathers facts and draws a conclusion. Someone else looks at the same facts and draws a different conclusion. A third person questions how the facts were gathered in the first place, and casts doubt on the conclusions of both researcher one and researcher two. A fourth person looks at both the method and the conclusions and argues that researchers one, two and three have missed the point entirely and that the research question should be turned on its head. This is how scholarly thinking progresses. This is how the frontier of knowledge is pushed forward every time a scholar proffers an idea. But the frontier cannot be pushed forward unless other scholars can identify the choices that were made, the steps that were taken, the conclusions that were drawn and the logic that binds them all together. When we write for other scholars, we cannot clarify these steps without clarifying our own involvement: explaining exactly what we've done and what we think it means.

This is particularly true for the academic disciplines and methods where the lines between external evidence and the perceptions of the scholar are at their most blurred. When data or observation is based on something that is concrete and measurable, it is much easier to see where observation stops and interpretation starts. Reporting how students scored on a particular test is an observation. Determining whether or not these students have learned what they are supposed to have learned is an interpretation based on the observation. The more what is being observed is abstract, difficult to describe and difficult to define, the more difficult it is to draw that line between observation and interpretation. Recounting an anecdote about teenagers posting party pictures on the net can make a very smooth transition to generalizing about threats to privacy posed by Facebook, and not even the author is clear about where observation starts and interpretation begins.

The question is, then, where exactly does the 'I' go in (social) science? When is it appropriate to bring in our own thoughts, and when is it not? And how exactly do we deal with this when we're writing?

OBJECTIVITY REVISITED

The idea that we might exercise our own judgement – let alone trumpet this judgement to our readers – makes many of us nervous. It seems to contradict the principle of objectivity, the very cornerstone of science. How can we reconcile the idea of making choices and exercising judgement with the principle of distancing ourselves from our own personal opinions? To answer this question, it is important to understand what 'objectivity' really means.

Objectivity refers primarily to the extent to which the scholar relies on *external* criteria, facts or evidence (including theoretical arguments) in making a choice or reaching a conclusion. Subjectivity refers to the extent to which the scholar relies solely on *personal* thoughts and feelings. So objectivity is not related to whether or not you have exercised judgement, but rather to what you have based that judgement on.

Say I want to test whether good-looking people get better jobs. I could simply flip through a pile of pictures, divide the subjects of the photographs into two categories – good-looking and not good-looking – and rank their jobs on a scale of one to five, according to how much I would like such a job myself. By any standard this would be a very subjective evaluation. If I wanted to exclude my personal opinion, I would have to take an entirely different approach. I might refer to a study that finds that most people think that people with symmetrical facial features are good-looking (and the more symmetrical, the better looking); I could then use facial symmetry as a criterion for measuring good looks. And instead of ranking the jobs on the basis of how much I coveted them, I could pick a criterion such as salary. You might disagree with my choice of method – perhaps discovering some flaws in the study on facial symmetry, or in the way I've measured symmetry in my study, or in the assumption that higher-paid jobs are necessarily better than those that don't pay as well – but you cannot claim that my own personal opinion has skewed the classification process. I might have a preference for prominent Roman noses, but since I was measuring good looks on the basis of facial symmetry, my own opinion would not matter. In categorizing my subjects, I have relied on external measures. Where my judgement comes into play is in my choice of criteria: symmetry and salary.

There is no question that objectivity, in the sense of relying on external criteria to make judgements, is still, and probably always will be, central to scholarly inquiry. Your challenge as a writer is to demonstrate the objectivity of the choices and interpretations you've made, to reveal to the reader how you got from A to B.

TOWARD TRANSPARENCY

The necessity of making your choices and interpretations clear in scholarly inquiry means that clarity supersedes all other measurements of quality in writing. It is more important than eloquence or wit – or even brevity. While clarity certainly depends to some extent on how well the author can put together a sentence, it relies far more on how transparent the author has made his or her choices to the reader. Because judgement is involved in making these choices, each or all of them may be disputed: our research question can be called irrelevant, our methodology or approach unsound, our analysis inadequate, our data set insufficient or incomplete or faulty, and our criteria unrepresentative or biased. The only way to counter these attacks

What's obvious to you is not always obvious to the reader. Transparency means showing your reader your reasoning, step by step

is to make explicit not only our choices, but also the rationale behind them, so that the reader can be convinced by our reasoning. And the more we move from the realm of facts to the realm of ideas, the more important choice and judgement become – and the more important it is to show the reader the logic behind these choices and the reason that governs our judgement. If we are able to achieve this level of explicitness, then when we finally come to our conclusion, the path that we have taken to get there will be visible and – hopefully – beyond reproach (see the text box 'Revealing your funders').

Revealing your funders

Being explicit about where your funding comes from is particularly important if the research has been funded by a party with a potential interest in the outcome of the findings. Although this is more of a pressing issue in medicine, particularly with medical research funded by pharmaceutical companies, this is becoming an increasing issue in the social sciences. Any reports that have a clear policy recommendation should also be equally clear about who has sponsored the research. And many journals now *require* you to explicitly state your funding sources. The greater the risk that you might be accused of bias, the more important transparency is.

Thus, writing a good scholarly paper begins as early as the research design or planning stage. This is when you make your important methodological decisions – decisions you will later have to explain and justify to your reader. Why did I pick my particular case? Why did I choose a survey method instead of interviews? Why did I decide to focus on the period 1850–1900? Why am I reviewing only the early works of Toni Morrison? So, keep your reader in mind from the very beginning. Design your research project in a way that sounds logical to you, then try explaining it on paper to a reader.

One particular concern, especially in the social sciences and humanities, is that research not be designed in such a way that only one outcome is possible. Ask yourself how you would design your research if you wanted to prove the *opposite* of what you suspect. If you want to argue that the characters of Hamlet and Ophelia represent Jung's conceptualization of animus and anima, what would constitute evidence *against* such an interpretation? If you want to argue that the use of social media is gendered, what would you expect social media patterns to look like if they were *not* gendered? At the very least, any argument we put forward should be possible to disprove or at least refute.

A related concern is that your method not be unconsciously chosen to favour your argument. Perhaps you want to compare Corntown and Cappuccinoville and argue that people in rural communities are more likely to perceive wolves as a direct threat, whereas urban residents are more likely to perceive wolves as a natural part of the ecosystem. If you ask the farmers questions like, 'Don't you think it's awful when wolves kill your sheep?' and 'Would you shoot a wolf if it were running right toward you?' while asking your urban population, 'Don't you think the wolf is a natural part of the ecosystem and has just as much right to live as any other indigenous species?' you will have a foregone conclusion, not research. But if you give each group the same list of questions, formulated in more neutral terms, you might just find something entirely different. You will also get a different result if you ask only yes-or-no questions or multiple-choice questions, compared to open-ended questions. Yes-or-no or multiple-choice questions constrain the possible range of answers considerably. This makes answers easier to compare (53 per cent said 'yes'; 4 out of 5 said that they were 'somewhat concerned'), but will allow little room for nuance. Interviews will generate more nuanced answers, but it will be more difficult for you to make generalizations.

Once you have settled on the basic issues – what will be compared with what, what will be the subject of analysis, what tool will be used for analyzing, and so on – you can begin to fine-tune your theoretical and operational definitions. (Definitions are covered in Chapter 6.) How will I define 'democracy' and what indicators will I use in categorizing the countries in my study? What exactly do I mean by 'regime theory'? And so on. The more you do this at the planning stage, the easier it will be for you in the writing stage.

During the writing stage, there are three places where transparency is particularly important: in justifying your choice of method, approach or theoretical anchoring; in explaining how data or external sources were used in your reasoning; and in interpreting your findings or analysis.

Choice of method, approach or theoretical anchoring: Just because a method, approach, or theory might be well established and respected doesn't mean that it is the most effective for your particular study. You need to explain how your choice was the best option for answering your particular research question. For example, 'We analyze the relationship between scholars and university presses in the perspective of actor–network theory because it allows us to see their interaction as a network made up of equal actants.' This may also entail explaining why other relevant approaches, methods, or theories are not being used. For example:

> We conduct in-depth, non-structured interviews with only a handful of specially selected subjects instead of distributing surveys to a large number of randomly selected subjects because the selected subjects were most likely to have been affected by the phenomenon under study, and since so little is known about this phenomenon, we did not want to constrain the scope of their responses during the interview.

Or:

> We do not use the common Finkelstein method to measure skin colour because it was developed for use on primates and we are looking at frogs.

Data or external sources: If you are using concrete, empirical data, you need to show that your data are both accurate and representative – and will help you answer the question you are asking. For example, if your question is about how convicted felons adjust to life outside prison and you are using employment records and welfare statistics to answer that question, you need to show that these records and statistics are not only complete for your sample, but that together they will be sufficient for answering your question. If you have a largely theoretical or qualitative discussion, you need to show that you have interpreted other theoretical contributions in a reasonable manner and applied them justifiably. For example, if you are planning to use Marx's theory of class struggle to explain the development of the US Constitution, you need to show how applying his theories in this context is both relevant and fruitful. If there are competing data and theories, you need to defend the choices you made, such as, 'The data from Parker et al. cover only the years 1981–82, while our focus is on the years 1995–2005.' Writing 'I did not take into account any theory published after 1985 because I can't be bothered to keep abreast of developments in the field' may well increase your transparency, but is not likely to count in your favour. Your reasons should be good ones, based on the constraints of your research question.

Interpretation: This is where your judgement plays the greatest role. In answering the question 'What does it mean?' you pull together the main elements of your research and make sense of it. And because your personal judgement plays such a strong role, you have to be meticulous about making your thought processes transparent, especially with respect to how they connect to any external findings or sources. Consider the statement: 'It is clear that a new law is needed.' It baldly states what the best course of action *should* be. But it does not explain *why*; it simply asks the reader to trust the writer's judgement. Trust is not enough in scholarly writing. Transparency requires that the premises on which the statement is based be visible: 'Given that the conflict is based on differing interpretations of current legislation, future conflict could be resolved if the text were less ambiguous.' (See also Chapter 5 for more detail about supporting your claims.)

In many fields that focus on the study of people and human interaction, such as anthropology and women's studies, the notion of transparency is taken even further: to revealing possible biases of the author. The premise is that while some degree of objectivity may be possible when you study, say, rocks, objectivity at any level becomes impossible when you are looking at a social system of which you are a part. If a process is to be truly transparent, then the reader should also be made aware of *all* the factors that might be influencing the way the scholar thinks – including the strictly personal: 'My urban upbringing, white skin and longtime residence in Great Britain almost certainly affected my relationships with these subsistence farmers in Central Africa.' Rather than denying the researcher's subjectivity, it is simply recognized as another factor to be considered, analyzed and interpreted. It becomes, in essence, another form of input. So, while transparency is a goal for all scholarly inquiry, exactly *where* we draw the line at revealing our choices and their contextual background is a function of the disciplines in which we operate.

FAUX OBJECTIVITY AND THREATS TO TRANSPARENCY

Scholars establish their objectivity by making both their criteria and their judgement transparent. Unfortunately, because many of us are unclear about what 'objectivity' really means, we strive for the mere appearance of objectivity in our writing. When the appearance of objectivity becomes equated with actual objectivity, the result is often what I call 'faux objectivity' – that is, something that may convince the untrained eye but is in no way the real thing. The danger of faux objectivity is not simply that it isn't genuine, but that it threatens transparency – which means that it can have the opposite effect to what the author intended.

I think that open plan classrooms are an abomination
Open plan classrooms are considered by many to be inefficient.

If you have an opinion that you cannot back up with argument or evidence, 'fixing' the language does not fix the problem - and may make things harder for the reader.

Demonstrating an 'open mind'

Objectivity involves more than striving for the absence of personal opinion and bias in scholarly work; it also involves an absence of preconceived ideas. But while we all agree that having an open mind is a good thing, we may disagree on what that means in practice. No scholar ever begins with a completely blank slate – and it would make little sense to do so. New knowledge is built on existing knowledge. What we know shapes the way we approach our study. Few would dispute this. Opinions might diverge, however, on how much we should let this previous knowledge shape our expected findings. In society at large, there is a romantic notion that scholars start every new study with no preconceived idea of what their findings might be. This might sound good in theory, but not only does it happen very rarely, it may not even be desirable. Usually, we have at least a hunch that x may be related to y, although we might not be sure of how much or why. We may suspect that a composer's creative development was influenced by a certain historic event, but we don't know how or to what extent. These 'preconceived ideas' are what make the research idea interesting in the first place.

Pretending these hunches do not exist is a type of faux objectivity that harms both the research and the writing. During the research process, excessive concern with keeping an open mind can rob us of the ability to distinguish between significant and insignificant input. We become like first year university students underlining every sentence in our textbooks. Not only do we give undue attention to insignificant input, but more important, we risk missing what is significant. When we have a clear idea of what we *expect* to find, findings that are not consistent with our expectations will stand out – and these findings are potentially the most important. Surprise is a valuable emotion for a researcher: it means, 'Pay attention! Something is going on here that you did not expect!' So, if you think that being a researcher means completely ignoring all your emotions then you lose out on some potentially powerful tools. Just know that these tools alone are not enough: the rest of the job means critically examining these 'surprises' and relying on evidence other than your own feelings to convince your readers that you truly have found something interesting. Being objective does not mean that you have no idea how the research will turn out. It means that you are willing to change course if the evidence points in an unanticipated direction.

Likewise, when writing, we do our readers no favour by refusing to distinguish between significant and insignificant details. Presenting all the facts and letting readers decide for themselves might sound like a good idea in theory, but in practice it makes the end result excruciating to read. 'Boring' doesn't even come close to describing the exquisite torture of being presented with every little detail, no matter how small, while simultaneously being denied any access to the scholar's train of thought to make sense of it all. As writers, we need to think of ourselves as guides through previously uncharted territory: our readers might want to know about the detours, roadblocks, pitfalls and other horrors we endured on our journey, but they don't necessarily want to experience them all for themselves. Giving our readers a map of where we are heading, of where we think the points of interest are along the way, does not force them to accept everything we say. On the contrary, it gives them the tools to evaluate the evidence we are presenting, which is essential for transparency. Readers cannot evaluate the evidence unless they know what it is supposed to be used as evidence *for*.

Expunging the pronoun 'I'

The pronoun 'I' is the simplest way for us to refer to ourselves, but if we are under the misapprehension that we personally should not be involved in the design, implementation or even interpretation of our own research, we will go to great lengths to expunge it from our writing. I cannot blame this solely on the individual researcher's ignorance: it is ingrained in our scientific tradition – albeit in some disciplines more than others. The natural sciences are famous for their disdain of 'I', but the first person singular is far more accepted in the humanities and occasionally in the social sciences. Although use of 'I' is a perfectly valid grammatical choice, some journals, and some journal editors (but certainly not all), won't allow it. Even though it seems entirely reasonable to acknowledge that it was indeed you who carried out the interviews, many still feel that it makes your work *sound* less objective.

Avoiding 'I' often leads to some painful grammatical contortions, the most egregious of which is the use of 'we' to refer to a single author (often called the 'academic we' or the 'editorial we'). Oddly enough, while the first person singular ('I') is often considered non-academic, the first person plural ('we') usually is not – perhaps because it suggests a group of bearded men in white lab coats solemnly reaching consensus based on a careful weighing of the evidence. But unless you are the king or queen of an actual recognized country (or a certifiable multiple personality), using 'we' to refer to just yourself makes no sense.

I'm not saying that it is never all right to use 'we' when you are a single author. It is legitimate any time you use it to refer to you and another person. Sometimes 'we' might logically encompass you and your reader. If you write, 'How are we supposed to understand Jones in the light of Smith?' you are doing the equivalent of sidling up to your reader, flinging your arm around his shoulders and directing his gaze to Jones, whereupon the two of you can contemplate the significance of Jones's work in the light of Smith's contributions. Similarly, if you write, 'We saw a pronounced decrease in interest rates between 2001 and 2004', the 'we' refers to you and your reader and is based on the assumption that both of you were alive and paying attention to interest rates between 2001 and 2004. You might also use 'we' legitimately to refer to yourself and your colleagues, even if they are not co-authors of the particular paper you are writing: 'In the Working Group established to carry out the surveys in Nigeria, we found that the survey developed by the European Working Group was inappropriate for the respondents we were aiming for.' Here, it is clear that the 'we' refers to the author and his fellow Working Group members.

When it is *not* all right to use 'we' is when you mean 'I' but are afraid to say 'I' because you think it sounds non-academic. For example, 'In this paper we discuss the nature of kinship systems' or 'We argue here that non-governmental organizations are more effective than international organizations.' Exactly who is the 'we' supposed to include? There are no other authors, and the reader is neither discussing nor arguing; the reader is just reading. This is no different – and no less irritating – than a nurse patting a patient on the head and saying, 'How are we feeling today?'

Perhaps the most common way of avoiding 'I' in scholarly writing is to eliminate mention of the agent (the person performing the action) by using the passive voice: 'It is argued that there is a significant correlation between alcohol abuse and domestic violence.' Such use of the passive voice is another example of faux objectivity. The passive voice is no more than a grammatical choice (see the text box 'Legitimate use of the passive voice'), and is therefore unrelated to the degree of actual objectivity that exists. 'Informants were interviewed' is not inherently more objective than 'I interviewed the informants.' They are both simple statements of fact, and the only real difference between the two is their transparency: the latter tells you who actually performed the research, while the former leaves it to your imagination. Perhaps it was the principle investigator of the research team. Perhaps it was some research assistant who was recruited from another project and had absolutely no idea what the interview was trying to accomplish. Who knows?

Legitimate use of the passive voice

It's not just scholars who ascribe magical powers to the passive voice. Editors do it, too, but they often take the opposite view: they believe the passive voice invariably drains the life out of a sentence. Many – if not most – writing guides will urge you to purge your writing entirely of the passive voice. But the passive voice is not an invention of the devil; it is simply a grammatical option. Using it does not automatically make you a bad writer any more than it automatically makes you objective. It serves a useful purpose by putting the focus on the object of the sentence rather than the subject: 'The ball was thrown' draws attention to the ball, and perhaps the throwing of it; 'Bob threw the ball' calls attention to Bob. Sometimes the ball, or the act of throwing, is simply more important than Bob. For example, if you are writing about the history of a bill's journey through the Senate, you might quite naturally write, 'Finally, the bill was passed in 2003.' Because you have already made it clear that you are talking about the Senate, you do not need to write, 'The Senate passed the bill in 2003.'

Because the passive voice does not magically transform something subjective into something objective, using the passive voice will not rescue you from bad research choices. In my study of good looks and job success, if I had classified subjects according to my own personal taste, writing 'Subjects were divided into categories representing their external appearance, and their appearance was compared with their job ranking' would have represented a futile effort to mask the essential problem. Not using the pronoun 'I' does not change the fact that I used subjective sorting criteria – it merely hides it from the reader. I have done nothing more than dangle a little pine tree air freshener over a garbage dump.

What is important here is the potential threat to transparency. Using the passive voice detracts attention from or eliminates mention of the agent from the particular sentence. (See the text box 'Anthropomorphism as an alternative to "I"' for a different option.) If you have already made it clear who or what the agent is, the passive voice poses no threat to transparency and can be a useful grammatical option. But the more you use the passive voice, the harder it will be for the reader to discern who did what.

Anthropomorphism as an alternative to 'I'

Anthropomorphism is the ascribing of human qualities to a non-human object or animal. Some editors will tell you that this is frowned upon, but a variation of it is becoming more and more accepted in scholarly writing. Expressions such as 'this article argues' or 'this section discusses' attribute human characteristics – here, the ability to argue or discuss – to a manuscript. It is difficult to understand the objection: if you can write, 'the illustration shows' or 'the document states' – or even 'this study shows' – why is 'this article argues' problematic? The meaning is very clear: 'The following argument is presented in this article', or 'I argue in this article.' I believe that if using 'I' is ruled out, this option is far superior to the ludicrous academic 'we' or the potentially evasive passive voice.

Treating opinion as fact

Because many wrongly believe that scholars should not deal in opinion but only in fact, we have fallen into a third form of faux objectivity: the habit of disguising opinion as fact. Instead of writing, 'I found the poor voter turnout disturbing', which is clearly opinion, we write, 'There was a disturbingly poor voter turnout', which sounds like fact. We may even write, 'Many claim that there was a disturbingly poor voter turnout', which, in pushing the responsibility for the subjective evaluation over to other people who do not actually exist, transforms a merely subjective statement into an outright lie. (See the text box 'How many is "many"?')

How many is 'many'?

The 'many claim' technique threatens transparency even when it is not an outright lie. Although 'many' may indeed have objected to the voter turnout, what's not clear is (1) how many, and (2) whether they have any credibility or not. Hundreds of people may be making the claim – that's 'many' enough for some people – while tens of thousands are claiming the opposite. And tens of thousands of people may claim that everyone who wanted to vote, could vote, but if they're all white people and we're talking about Alabama in the 1950s, the claim doesn't mean much. Do not say 'many' unless you back it up with references.

The antidote is not to stop having opinions. Scholars and researchers bring their expertise to their research, and scholarly inquiry would be very limited indeed if they were not allowed to exercise their expert judgement and share it with the reader. The solution lies in learning to recognize normative or value-laden statements and increase their transparency. Instead of merely writing, 'It is interesting', explain why: 'It is interesting because it clearly shows the discrepancy between theory and practice.' Usually you will find that if you provide a good answer for *why* something is interesting (or important, necessary, disturbing or what have you), then you no longer need to tell readers how to feel about it: 'This clearly shows a discrepancy between theory and practice' is enough to stimulate their interest. 'Show, don't tell' is a very common piece of advice in books on writing: show your readers why something is interesting; don't just tell them that it is.

Unfortunately, scholarly discourse is so riddled with value-laden words treated as fact that we have a hard time noticing them. Consider: 'This paper discusses five important contemporary poets.' What makes them important? Are they the most famous? Included in the most anthologies? Won the most Pulitzer Prizes? Been reviewed in the *New York Times* most often? Have the most friends at Harvard? Most of us let the word 'important' just slip by unnoticed. The threat to transparency is obvious: treating any form of opinion as fact absolves us of having to make explicit the values, premises and assumptions that lie behind the opinion – thus making them inaccessible to the reader. The answer to 'Why is this important?' becomes 'Because I said so' – which is no more satisfying coming from another scholar than it was when it came from your parents. But once you get used to the idea that the challenge you face as a researcher is not to mask your opinion but rather to explain it, these faux objective words and statements will become easier to see.

SCHOLARLY ARGUMENT AND RHETORIC

The goal of transparency is to convince your readers that your reasoning is sound by showing them exactly what you did and how you were thinking. To achieve this goal, it is useful to think of scholarly writing as a form of argument. Not the kind of argument where you stubbornly stick to your position and try to bludgeon your opponent into agreeing with you, but rather the kind that resembles a mathematical proof: you establish a set of givens, define a question and lay out the proof, in which each step is logically derived from the one before it. The actual answer matters less than how you got there.

Developing an argument that will persuade researchers and scholars is no simple task. As a group, we are not easily impressed. When we hear bells and whistles, our first reaction is not usually 'Isn't that neat?' but rather 'Why is that noise there?' Because the first response of our readers will be to pull things apart to see how they work, our arguments have to stand up to dissection.

Fortunately for us, this is not a new concept. The ancient Greeks and Romans spent centuries studying logic and the art of argumentation. This knowledge is concentrated in *rhetoric*, the study of effective and persuasive speaking and writing. Unfortunately, many people believe that rhetoric is nothing but cheap verbal tricks – it's what politicians and televangelists do to sell a ridiculous idea to an unsuspecting and naïve public. For us as serious researchers and scholars, the idea of 'tricking' a reader into believing what we write is unconscionable: we want our readers to recognize the intrinsic value of our work. For this reason, researchers and scholars have been reluctant to adopt rhetorical principles in their work. Yet we have done so without realizing it: the classic rhetorical structure is reflected in modern scholarly writing (see text box 'Elements of structure from classical rhetoric'). Like the ancient Greek or Roman orator, we have to capture the interest of our audience, establish our credibility and a shared understanding of the state of current knowledge, have a specific thesis and the evidence to back it up and offer a conclusion that will indicate what it all means (see Chapter 6 on elements of structure). The most important lesson scholars can draw from rhetoric, and one that permeates this book, is that we must understand our readers if we want to formulate an argument and marshal supporting evidence that will convince them.

Elements of structure from classical rhetoric

Exordium (introduction)
The first thing the speaker has to do is to pique the interest of his audience and establish his credibility: 'Friends, Romans, countrymen. We are gathered here on this side of the river unable to cross, while lush green fields wait on the other side. I have swum those fords, and seen those fields.'

In scholarship, piquing the interest of your reader often means putting your finger on a gap or contradiction in our cumulative knowledge, and establishing credibility means demonstrating that you came to your conclusion through research: 'Roberts argues that women are more risk-averse than men. Findings from our four-year study suggest otherwise.'

Narratio (background)
Next, the speaker must establish a connection with the audience: 'I, too, know hunger and dream of cropland that will feed us all.'

In scholarship, establishing a connection with the audience means connecting them to your work through reference to the larger discourse: 'Roberts (1998), building on work by Ryan (1995), argued that when faced with a challenge, women were more likely than men to opt out, even when they were equally competent.'

Propositio (thesis)
Then the speaker makes a proposal or a contention: 'I say we build that bridge!'

In the academic world, the thesis identifies a relationship and sometimes a cause: 'We argue that the observed risk aversion in women comes from a superior ability to realistically judge the likely outcome of a given situation.'

(Continued)

(Continued)

Argumentatio (argument)

The speaker then offers reasons or evidence to support his proposal or contention: 'Building the bridge will allow us to use the cropland on the other side.'

In the social sciences, valid reasons or evidence come from either building logically on ideas or by direct observational evidence: 'We observed both men and women attempt to cross busy intersections without a pedestrian crossing, and men were six times more likely to be injured or killed.'

Peroratio (conclusion)

Finally, the speaker ends with a call to action. This told the audience what was expected of them: 'So pick up your shovels! Every man, woman, and child!'

The concluding call to action in a scholarly work is often a call for future research: 'Our findings suggest that the role of perceived outcome is far more important than previously thought. Future research could look at differences in how women and men not only perceive the outcome of a given situation, but also the importance of this outcome.'

Because our readers are scholars, they will be best persuaded by objective arguments – that is, by judgements based on sound reasoning and established knowledge. The challenge of convincing our readers that our judgement is sound – that the choices we made were reasonable ones – becomes insurmountable if we are simultaneously trying to deny that any judgement was exercised at all. The more we attempt to distance ourselves from our own research and obscure the choices we made, the more we hinder the reader from truly being able to judge the value of our work. And drowning our readers in facts or background information while simultaneously giving them no idea of how to interpret it, hiding our own involvement in our work by avoiding the pronoun 'I', and disguising opinion as fact all get in the way of objectivity in the long run.

Our audience doesn't need us to pretend we weren't part of our own research. What it needs is exactly the opposite: for us to make our role and our train of thought transparent by being clear about the values, assumptions and premises we brought to bear on our research, as well as the choices and value judgements we made in our work. There is, after all, an 'I' in science.

Remember

What makes an argument scholarly is that it is based on sound, objective reasoning or observation. The best way to convince your reader that you have been objective is to be as transparent as possible about what you did, how you did it and why.

FURTHER READING

- Graff, Gerald and Birkenstein, Cathy (2014) 'They Say/I Say': The Moves that Matter in Academic Writing, 3rd edn, New York: W.W. Norton & Company. This book goes into detail about how you can position yourself in a conversation – how you refer to others and how you develop your own voice. Although aimed at students, it is relevant for scholars at all levels and should be particularly helpful to non-native speakers.
- Lloyd, Keith (2005) 'The uses of Uses of Argument: Feminist critique and adaptation of the Toulmin model to written arguments', in David Hitchcock and Daniel Farr (eds), The Uses of Argument: Proceedings of a Conference at McMaster University (May 2005), Ontario Society for the Study of Argumentation, Hamilton, Ontario: McMaster University Press, pp. 316–25. Lloyd presents an alternative metaphor for argumentation, and thus alternative stances on objectivity and transparency.
- Schostak, John and Schostak, Jill (2013) Writing Research Critically: Developing the Power to Make a Difference, London: Routledge. The authors of this book challenge the ability of facts to speak for themselves. They explore how authors can develop a critical understanding of their material and communicate it to readers.
- Thody, Angela M. (2006) Writing and Presenting Research, London: Sage. In addition to being a good all-round book on scholarly writing and publishing, this book does an exceptionally good job at highlighting the different challenges of building arguments on different types of data: qualitative, quantitative and narrative – each with their own demands for transparency. It also addresses the debates about alternative ways for researchers to present their work, and what this means for voice and stance.
- Toulmin, Stephen E. (2003) The Uses of Argument, updated edn, Cambridge: Cambridge University Press. Toulmin's philosophical analysis of how arguments are supported shows the importance of transparency: not only does the reader need to see the factual basis for the argument, but also the warrants, the ideas that put the facts into context.

FOUR

Who are you talking to?

Defining your audience

Imagine you have met the person of your dreams and you cannot wait to tell everyone you know about your newfound happiness. When you call your best friend, you gush about your transcendent experience on the dance floor. But when you call your mother, you start reeling off your beloved's impressive work experience and academic credentials. Are you talking about the same person? Of course. You have simply shifted your focus according to who you were talking to – probably without even realizing it. In both cases your goal was to convince the listener that you have found Person Right, but you adopted different strategies based on what you knew about the listener. The same is true in scholarly discourse: you want to make your point as clearly as possible, but the best path to clarity depends very much on your audience. Sometimes it's merely a matter of adopting the vocabulary of the people you want to reach; at other times, it may be a more complex matter of reframing the issue you're discussing. This suggests that the sooner you define your target audience, the more likely you will be able to tailor your writing to reach it most effectively.

THE NATURE OF THE READER

As readers, we usually get an immediate sense of whether the text in front of us was written with us in mind. But when we write, we tend to forget that different readers need different things from us, and we end up writing with no clear idea of our audience in our mind. In fact, we end up writing for our computers. We look at our introduction and ask ourselves, 'Is this long enough? Maybe I should add a paragraph about legislation in other countries.' And the computer very obligingly lets you do that. 'Is it too long now?' you wonder. 'Maybe I should cut out this reference to Foucault.' And the computer very obligingly lets you do that, too. The computer will let you do anything you want to your text because it is a machine – unlike your actual audience. When it comes to your actual audience, the question is not whether your introduction is too long or too short, but whether it was written with them in mind. There is no such thing as the perfect paper for every audience. Writing for everyone generally means writing for no one.

Try this: Framing your work to suit your audience

Think of the general topic of your study. Explore how changing your intended audience will force you to reframe the issue.

Other Scholars
What do you have that will appeal most to another researcher? What is this scholar's discipline? How would you change your approach for a scholar in a different field?

User Groups
Think about what the 'real-world' user group for your field might be: practitioners (such as lawyers, doctors, psychologists or teachers)? Decision-makers (local, national or international)? Business and industry? What is it about your work that would be most interesting to this group?

The general public
What about the general public? If you were to write an opinion piece based on your work for your local paper, what would you focus on?

The objective of this exercise is to pinpoint which aspects of your work appeal to whom. This will help you avoid the problem of trying to please everyone (by helping you sharpen your focus). It may also open your eyes to other possibilities and alternative audiences!

If we are to change from writing for no one to writing for someone, then we need tools for understanding just who that someone is. Two of the most useful ways to identify an audience are by how much they know about your subject (the knowledge dimension), and by how likely they are to accept your premises (the value dimension) (see Figure 4.1).

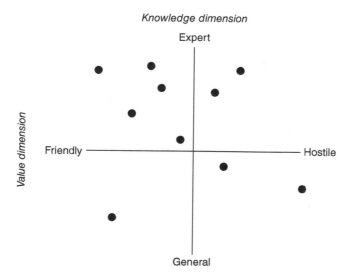

Figure 4.1 Knowledge and value dimensions: where does your target reader fit?

Try this: How much does your audience know?

Find a partner. First, spend about 3-5 minutes explaining your work as if your partner were a colleague. Note your use of technical terms and assumptions about method.

Next, spend another 3-5 minutes explaining your work as if your partner were about ten years old. Note how much background material you need to explain and how your technical terminology no longer helps you. Do you make greater use of metaphor? Does drawing pictures help?

The objective of this exercise is to demonstrate how much you shape your explanation based on your assumption of how much your audience knows. Most people find that speaking to a ten-year-old is far more difficult than speaking to a colleague. Some find it virtually impossible. This is precisely why this exercise is useful: it will force you to explain your work in terms other than the ones you use on a daily basis.

Knowledge dimension: 'I don't know. Tell me.'

An expert audience knows a lot about the subject matter. Note that I'm not talking about how smart they are, but rather about how much they know about your particular subject. If your subject is sixteenth-century Hungarian poets, an expert audience might be expected to know a lot about the topic, and you don't have to spend a lot of time identifying each poet and explaining the terminology you use. The people you present your findings to at an academic conference

What kind of background information to put in, and what to leave out, depends entirely on the audience you are aiming to reach and what they are already likely to know: 'I picked up this article because I'm doing research on incarceration of political prisoners, but I don't know anything about Tajikistan. Fill me in.'

probably represent a reasonably knowledgeable audience, as do many of your colleagues (although they will not necessarily all be knowledgeable in the same way – some may know a lot about sixteenth-century Hungary but not necessarily about its poets; others may know a lot about sixteenth-century poetry, but not much about Hungary, for example). A general audience of, for instance, family members, newspaper readers or high school students knows little about the subject matter. For such an audience, you may have to spend more time explaining your terms and filling them in on the background of your work.

This is worth thinking about if you intend to translate your work from one language to another. The easy part is getting it into another language. The hard part is thinking about what the new audience needs to have explained. For example, if a Norwegian researcher wanted to translate an article on reforms in the *barnehageloven* into English, it is not enough to call it the 'Kindergarten Act': *barnehage* and 'kindergarten' are not at all the same thing, so the author will also have to explain how they differ, which she would not have to do for a Norwegian audience. The same is true if you are keeping the same language but moving outside your local context. For example, take the word 'sheriff'. Most people know what it means, and if you are writing a novel, you probably wouldn't need to say more than 'the sheriff moseyed into town'. But say you are writing about local government: even among English-speaking countries the position of sheriff implies different responsibilities.

Value dimension: 'I'm not convinced. Persuade me.'

Now look at the value dimension. In the previous chapter, I talked about how you make a number of informed choices during your research process – including choice of research question, method, approach, data set or theory. Some or even much of what goes into making these choices are assumptions, many of which are related to values: what makes good research, which methods are reliable, which theories are salient, what are the relevant questions and so on. A friendly audience agrees with these assumptions at the outset, whereas a hostile audience disagrees (or is at least very sceptical). Note that a hostile audience is not necessarily directly antagonistic toward you or what you are saying; here, 'hostile' means simply that they will not be able to accept your assumptions without some persuasion. The value dimension has a methodological and epistemological element (approach), a political element (priority) and a practical element (purpose).

Approach: In the philosophy of science, we learn that both inductive reasoning (making generalizations on the basis of concrete observations) and deductive reasoning (using arguments to move from accepted premises to conclusions) are just two among many valid approaches to research. But within a given discipline – or methodological orientation within a discipline – usually a much smaller range of approaches are embraced. Some favour top-down (deductive) reasoning, while others favour bottom-up (inductive). A few are comfortable with both. Others favour different approaches entirely. This is especially evident across disciplines, but even within a discipline,

A hostile audience might not even hear your ideas because they are so sceptical about what you are doing or how you are doing it: 'That's not how we did research in my day. A typewriter and a box of highlighters, that's all we needed.'

some scholars have a more positivist leaning and tend toward the quantitative methods, while others espouse a social-constructivist philosophy and use more qualitative and interpretive methods – and these are not always a friendly combination: 'That's not science, that's storytelling!' says the quantitative political scientist to the anthropologist. 'Well, you've missed every important nuance there is with your over-simplified coding and have no idea what you are talking about. You haven't even *been* to any of these countries in your database!' responds the anthropologist. The question here is *not* whether one method, approach or philosophy is better or more 'correct', but rather to what extent your audience shares your assumptions about what constitutes good research or good scholarship. See the section below about addressing interdisciplinary and mixed audiences.

Priority: Is it better to buy a diesel car or a gasoline-driven car? Well, it depends on what your value set is, and how you understand 'best outcome'. Are you more concerned about your household budget, or about the environment? And if the environment is your primary concern, are you more worried about air pollution or about climate change? Applied research is largely about solving problems: How can we prevent teenagers from taking drugs? How can we improve the agricultural production of Boomtown? Would policy X be more effective than policy Y? The preferred solution to any given problem will always be a function of the underlying value structure. Policy X may well be more cost-effective than policy Y, but if your target group values political feasibility and fairness above cost-effectiveness, then policy Y might be their preferred solution. Like any value set, this one is often implicit. And for scholars, it often comes as a result of their academic background: economics virtually by definition is concerned with finding the most cost-effective solution, for example. For scholars carrying out applied research, understanding both their own value set and the value set of their target audience is essential (for more about problem-solving research questions and recommendations, see Chapter 5). If your recommendation is based on cost-effectiveness and your audience places a higher value on, say, political feasibility, then you will have to show not only that your solution is cost-effective but also that it addresses feasibility concerns.

Purpose: Research on different learning styles in children might well be aimed at teachers who want to improve their skills. But it might just as well be aimed at scholars in the field of learning theory. No matter how practical the topic, research aimed at other scholars is often incomprehensible to practitioners. And research aimed at practitioners might not seem useful to scholars. The question here is: Are your findings meant to add to cumulative scholarly knowledge, or are they meant to be useful in the 'real world', such as for policy-making, clinical practice or technology development? And, most important, how likely is your target audience to share your understanding of your purpose? In an applied science setting where scholarly publishing is also encouraged, a scholar is always juggling what is interesting to, say, policy-makers with what is interesting to scholars – and with what is interesting to scholars interested in policy-making. If you are presenting the practical aspects of the issue to an audience that is interested in the practical aspects, then you have no problem. But if you want to present the practical aspects to an audience that is primarily interested in the scholarly, you will have to treat the audience as hostile: not only do you have to explain the practical aspects, but you also have to persuade readers that these matter in a scholarly context. For example, say you study trends in urban planning, specializing in how the designs of schools are changing. Your research has uncovered that architectural trends favouring steel and glass have made modern schools difficult to teach in because of the lack of wall space to hang things on and acoustics that carry sound from one classroom to the next. You decide to aim your article at a journal of urban studies whose audience is 'social scientists with a concern for the complex, changing roles and futures of cities and regions'. If you plan to conclude, 'thus architects need to take into account the needs of teachers', then you will miss your mark. The journal's audience is not architects, but rather other scholars who study building trends. If you want to make that argument, you will also have to argue why it is important for scholars to understand this. The reverse is also true: if you are aiming for an audience of practitioners, make sure that your academic points will make sense to them.

Make sure your audience can use your work for its intended purpose: 'I commissioned that report so I would have a better idea how to spend our tax dollars. Now what exactly am I supposed to do with "$\forall i, x_i \in S_i : f_i(x_i^*, x_{-i}^*) \geq f_i(x_i^*, x_{-i}^*)$"?'

Try this: What kind of assumptions do you make in your work?

It is often very difficult to spot assumptions in our own work. This exercise works best with a partner who has a very different academic background.

Go through your own or your partner's paper. Try to find at least three assumptions each about existing knowledge (e.g., different learning styles exist), method (e.g., single case studies are generalizable) and values (e.g., small classrooms are a good thing). Which assumptions do you think might be controversial? And to whom?

The objective of this exercise is to reveal the kinds of assumptions you take for granted in your writing and raise your awareness about your audience's possible reaction to them. Your audience probably won't disagree with you on every point, but it is not unrealistic to expect that they may disagree on at least one. The question that you need to ask yourself is which points are the most important and worth fighting for (in terms of using valuable space to explain yourself) and which you are willing to let slide (either drop or not spend time explaining). You might also want to ask yourself how this would change if you switch to an entirely different audience.

Note that the degree to which your audience shares your value set is not necessarily related to how much the audience knows about the subject matter. Your audience may know a lot about your subject matter and still disagree with your general approach or your conclusions. Or you may have an audience that knows practically nothing about your subject matter but is open to whatever methods you use to say something about it. Or you may have an audience that has simply read a few paragraphs about the subject in a newspaper and has formed a seemingly unshakeable opinion sceptical to your viewpoint. In scholarly writing, however, most of us tend to write for friendly audiences that have extensive knowledge of the subject matter – unless we venture into interdisciplinary work (see the next section). But even if your audience is relatively knowledgeable and relatively friendly, it is a fairly safe bet that they aren't quite as friendly or as knowledgeable as you think they are. Unless you are boldly going where few scholars have gone before (again, see below), your best bet is to treat your audience as only somewhat friendly and somewhat knowledgeable.

Writing for hostile, interdisciplinary or mixed audiences

Writing for an audience with a different disciplinary background than your own poses special challenges in both the knowledge dimension and the value dimension. An academic discipline – such as sociology, geophysics, biology, English literature, history or anthropology – embodies both a shared body of knowledge and shared assumptions about methodology, relevant research questions, epistemology, ontology and basic relationships between units of study (e.g., agent and structure). The same can also be said for subdisciplines within a larger discipline, such as feminist literary criticism within the larger discipline of literary criticism.

This shared body of knowledge is often reflected in shared terminology that acts as a kind of shorthand. A given term has a very specific meaning to scholars in a particular field; no other single standard English term can be substituted for it. But a term that is readily understood by and simplifies communication among scholars of a similar background may be incomprehensible jargon to others. Social psychologists are no more likely to understand 'radiative forcing' than atmospheric chemists are to understand 'cognitive dissonance'. Thus, writing for audiences from other academic backgrounds requires sensitivity to terminology – knowing which terms can be used without definition, which should be defined, and which would be best avoided altogether.

This is particularly true when words from standard, everyday English take on a special meaning in a scholarly context. Take the word 'gender'. For the general public, it is mostly a more socially acceptable way to say 'sex'. But for a psychologist, it represents a social identity separate from a biological identity. In gender studies, a 'gender perspective' is one that can be applied to almost any kind of phenomenon or idea; it has distinct political implications. And for a linguist, it can describe a class of nouns. Even obviously technical terms can have different meanings for different disciplines. The term 'carbon leakage' is used in climate change research; but in geophysics, it refers to the leakage of carbon from a geological storage area; and in the social sciences, it refers to the indirect impacts of climate change policy, specifically the displacement of emissions from one source to another. Reaching across disciplinary barriers means taking the time to make sure that you and your audience are talking about the same thing.

The challenges related to the value dimension are more complex because values regarding what makes good science are often implicit, leading scholars to distrust 'different' approaches without necessarily being able to give a good reason why. The only way to handle this is to make your assumptions explicit (more transparent) when you are trying to reach beyond the boundaries of your discipline, either to a lay audience or to experts in other fields. (Transparency is discussed in Chapter 3.) For example, if you are an economist, you are quite likely to say somewhere near the beginning of your article something like, 'Assume perfect information and no transaction costs.' Other economists will nod and move on to the rest of your argument. A political scientist, on the other hand, may well be brought up short, sputtering, 'But there's no such thing! Apart from, maybe, breathing, every exchange has transaction costs!' To reach the political scientist, you will have to backtrack a bit and explain: 'In order to isolate the one particular variable we are interested in here, we will have to keep all other variables constant, even if this is unrealistic in real life. We call this *ceteris paribus*.' One of the main challenges here is to identify your own assumptions. When we write within any discipline long enough, its assumptions often become so fully incorporated into our thinking that we aren't aware of them: we unconsciously classify these assumptions as 'something that should be treated as fact'.

The easiest way to keep track of what you should be defining, justifying or explaining is to keep a particular person in mind when you write. Think of someone who represents the kind of audience you want to read your paper, and write for that person. Instead of agonizing over every term and every assumption, ask yourself, 'Would Burt require an explanation?' With an image of Burt firmly planted in your mind, you will be better able to anticipate and avoid problems: 'Burt is such a rationalist. If I am going to borrow any theory from the constructivists, I'm going to have to tread carefully.'

Treading carefully means first figuring out the nature of the hostility. What exactly will they object to? Are you taking a concept from one particular field and introducing it to another, one that already has a similar concept that dominates? Then you will have to explain exactly what is gained by abandoning the traditional conceptual framework and introducing a new one. Are you presenting qualitative research to a predominantly quantitative audience? Or vice versa? Then you will have to show them that you understand the contributions of the other, but also show that every method has natural limitations and that your perspective can bring the discussion a bit further: 'The quantitative research on faculty research productivity shows that attendance at international conferences is consistent with high levels of productivity, but we do not really understand why' or 'The qualitative interviews suggest that the female informants took reviewer feedback more personally than the male informants, but we do not know to what extent this can be generalized.'

Once you map out where you think the objections will lie, you can start addressing them one by one. Go back to a point where you and your audience are likely to agree, and then each time you introduce a potentially explosive point, deflect the expected criticism by beating the reader to the punch. If you say it before they have a chance to formulate the thought completely, then they will not only feel like you understand them, but also that their concerns are taken into account: 'Nobody likes paying taxes. And introducing a new tax when we already have trouble seeing the benefit of the taxes we are currently paying would seem like political suicide.' The author has now indicated that he understands the audience's perspective, laying the ground for introducing a sentence that says something like, 'But what if I could show you that introducing a new tax on sugar would save the average taxpayer considerable amounts of money in the long run?'

In an academic context, it is all about showing your audience that you know where they are coming from, and that you have respect for their viewpoints (even if secretly you do not):

A lot of important research has shown that climate change is likely to increase political violence. Blather and Dither (2008) convincingly demonstrate how scarcity of resources leads to increased inter-group inequalities. The question here is whether this picture becomes more nuanced when we also take into account state fragility.

Here, the author does not say that Blather and Dither (2008) have missed the point entirely and have no idea what they are talking about. On the contrary, he says that their research is good – he merely introduces a new variable. Disarming your hostile audience means knowing where they keep their weapons, so you know when and how to draw yours.

It's one thing to write for a uniformly hostile audience – at least you know where you have them. But many of us, for one reason or another, have to write for more than one audience at the same time. Sometimes, this is because we are writing for more than one discipline. Sometimes, you are taking knowledge that has been gained from an interdisciplinary environment and presenting it to a single-disciplinary environment. Sometimes, we are writing for both the expert and the non-expert. So, writing can be a lot more difficult when you the political scientist are not just writing for Burt the rationalist economist, but also for Anna the biologist. And perhaps for Mary the government advisor as well. By trying to make all of them happy, you will probably end up making none of them happy. At this point you need to ask yourself: What am I really trying to accomplish here? Is my goal to bring several disparate groups together in mutual understanding? In that case, I'll have to strive to explain everything in language they'll all understand and use plenty of examples. Or is there perhaps one particular group that is more important to me than another? Maybe I can afford to irritate the natural scientists by oversimplifying my descriptions of the ecosystem because the ones I really want to reach are the decision-makers – the ones who hold the chequebooks.

The key to writing for a mixed audience is to remember that not everyone will read your manuscript in the same way, and not every manuscript needs to be read in full from beginning to end to be of value. It is possible, for example, to reach both experts and non-experts by making your abstract, introduction and conclusion as simple as possible – avoiding or explaining technical terms and making sure you explain the general relevance of your point. You can then be as technical as you like in the middle sections. The non-experts will not read this part anyway, and as long as they can get the gist from the other parts, they will be happy. This also means that you should make your headings as clear as possible so readers can navigate appropriately.

The strategy you pick as a writer should be based not just on what your audience needs from you, but also on your ultimate purpose, and your choice of journal should reflect that purpose. Are you reaching out primarily to other scholars? If so, the journals that will be most receptive to your work will most likely be those that focus on theory or pure science. Are you talking primarily to practitioners? If so, you'll want to focus instead on journals that address the practical applications of knowledge. The questions you are now facing are: How do you find the journals that are right for your work? How can you tell? Before you can answer these questions, it helps to understand a little bit more about scholarly journals in general.

THE NATURE OF ACADEMIC JOURNALS

Like individual readers, all journals are different, and necessarily so; the scholarly dialogue is far too expansive to be sufficiently covered by a handful of journals with similar profiles. To help sort them out, keep in mind that, like readers, journals have a knowledge dimension (theme) and a value dimension (discipline) (Figure 4.2).

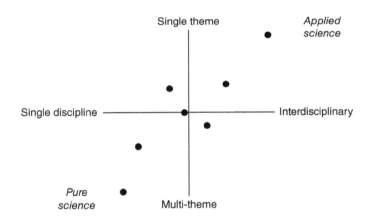

Figure 4.2 Locating scholarly journals along thematic and disciplinary dimensions

Thematic dimension: The thematic dimension is the degree to which a journal concentrates on a single subject. For example, *Climatic Change* is a journal that limits its subject matter, not surprisingly, to climate change. You can expect readers of such a journal to know quite a bit about climate change in general, and you probably will not have to explain what the Kyoto Protocol is. But this is a theme that interests not only meteorologists and atmospheric chemists, who may look at the physical mechanisms of climate change, but also economists, who may look at the socioeconomic repercussions of both climate change and climate-related policy; political scientists, who may consider how science is translated into international policy and what makes international agreements effective; and individuals from a wide range of other disciplines. The breadth of subject matter, however, is not always easy to tell by the journal's title. The title of *International*

Organization, for example, suggests that the journal focuses on international organizations. While this may have been true many years ago, the journal now looks into virtually any area of international relations.

Disciplinary dimension: Disciplinary dimension in this context refers not to *which* discipline the journal focuses on, but rather to the extent to which it attempts to appeal to scholars from more than one discipline. A *single-discipline* journal, such as the *American Journal of Economics*, covers a variety of themes within a single academic discipline. An *interdisciplinary* journal embraces more than one discipline and aims to present material that is equally accessible to all the disciplines represented. Technical terminology may be used, but it must be understandable to all readers; likewise, methodologies have to be explained to a much greater degree, and values made explicit. The level of ambition here can vary significantly. Sometimes 'interdisciplinary' means joining two or three very closely related disciplines, such as sociology and political science; sometimes it means joining disciplines as different as biology and economics. The more the disciplines differ and the more disciplines that are included in the journal's target audience, the more 'interdisciplinary' it is.

Unlike individual readers, who can be found almost anywhere on the map (as depicted by the randomly placed dots in Figure 4.1), journals tend to concentrate themselves along a diagonal line (see Figure 4.2). This is because if a journal has a strong focus on a single theme, it also tends to be associated with interdisciplinary research with an emphasis on applied science. A single-discipline journal generally has no particular thematic focus but a greater emphasis on pure science. The reasons for these associations are fairly simple: journals that are strongly issue-oriented tend to focus on problem-solving (or at least problem-diagnosing), which usually requires input from more than one discipline and tends to attract the attention of non-scientists as well (e.g., decision-makers). Journals that are interested in pure science focus on building cumulative knowledge and theory development; any empirical observations have to be generalizable to be relevant.

The implications are pretty clear: if you want to appeal to a single-discipline journal, you need to emphasize theory-building and cumulative knowledge; if you want to appeal to an issue-oriented journal, you will probably need to emphasize the practical applications of your work – what it has to do with real life. To illustrate: if you are a social psychologist writing about how the current building trend in Western countries of integrating the kitchen area into the living room area makes it difficult for certain groups of Asian immigrants to buy homes, you have a lot of choices. You can focus on the social psychological aspects of building design and ethnic identity and submit to a social psychology journal. You can focus on the more practical aspects and submit to a journal on modern architectural practice. You could also appeal to an interdisciplinary journal that covers issues related to immigration. Each of these choices will have ramifications for how you present your research and the terminology you use (see the section on writing introductions in Chapter 6). The more closely the focus of your work matches the focus of the journal in terms of theme, discipline, theory and observational data, the friendlier your audience is likely to be. The converse is also true: the more your work deviates from the focus of the journal, the more you will have to treat your audience as potentially hostile.

LOCATING YOUR AUDIENCE

Most of us prefer a friendly and knowledgeable audience – after all, it takes some of the burden off us when it comes to explaining and justifying everything. But some of us are braver (at least some of the time), and see it as our mission to introduce a topic to a new audience or get a normally hostile audience to consider a different perspective. Either one of these routes is valid, as long as we know what we are getting ourselves into, but both of them depend on our ability to locate the audience we want to reach. How can we find out what kind of focus a particular journal has?

The first, and most obvious, place you can look is the mission statement, usually located on the inside cover or on the journal's website. All journals have (or should have) a mission statement describing their purpose and intended audience. The mission statement from *Foreign Policy Analysis*, for example, reads as follows:

> Reflecting the diverse and multidisciplinary nature of the field, *Foreign Policy Analysis* provides an open forum for research publication that enhances the communication of concepts and ideas across theoretical, methodological, geographical and disciplinary boundaries. By emphasizing accessibility of content for scholars of all perspectives and approaches in the editorial and review process, *Foreign Policy Analysis* serves as a source for efforts at theoretical and methodological integration and deepening the conceptual debates throughout this rich and complex academic research tradition. Foreign policy analysis, as a field of study, is characterized by its actor-specific focus. The underlying, often implicit argument is that the source of international politics and change in international politics is human beings, acting individually or in groups. In the simplest terms, foreign policy analysis is the study of the process, effects, causes or outputs of foreign policy decision-making in either a comparative or case-specific manner.

This mission statement tells you that the journal is interdisciplinary (which means you will have to be careful with your terminology and how you explain your method). The theme is fairly narrow – foreign policy analysis – but presumably you can write about any type of foreign policy (generalizability will thus be an issue). Theory development seems to be more of a priority than concrete application (despite the interdisciplinary nature of the journal and its relatively narrow thematic focus), and the preferred empirical approach is clearly qualitative.

The second place you can look is the 'Instructions to Authors' or 'Author Guidelines'. These have been traditionally located at the back of the journal, but now virtually all journals publish their author guidelines on the Internet instead of in the journal. (Sometimes the print and online versions differ; one is more current than the other. See Chapter 10 for a fuller discussion of author guidelines.) The guidelines will often explain in more detail than the mission statement what kind of research the journal is looking for.

A third place you can look, and probably the most helpful, is the table of contents. Look through a few back issues of the journal you are interested in and skim the table of contents. Is a wide range of topics covered? Are several disciplines represented? Does the journal favour qualitative research over quantitative, or vice versa? Theory development or real-world applications? In other words, does it look like your article will feel at home in this family?

SELECTING A JOURNAL

Once you've settled on what kind of audience you want to write for, and located a selection of journals your audience is likely to read and where your work is likely to fit in, how do you decide on a particular journal?

One thing you can do is to ask colleagues in your field. They can tell you about not only the general reputability of a certain journal and the quality of the editorial board, but also their own personal experiences: 'The journal is good, but it took two years before my article was published,' or 'This journal is excellent because they use five peer reviewers, so you get very useful feedback on your work.' They will also be able to tell you whether authors communicate directly with the editor or through a secretary, and whether the editor appears to exercise any independent judgement (or whether he or she relies solely on the reviewers). (See the text box 'Journals are people, too' for a discussion of how journals differ behind the scenes.)

Journals are people, too

When we look at a journal, we see glossy paper covers or a webpage filled with words. It seems impersonal, and increasingly sophisticated electronic submission systems do nothing to dispel this image. We forget that behind all this print and electronics are actual humans who read and make decisions. Like people in general, journal editors have different opinions and prejudices – and different degrees of awareness of how much these opinions and prejudices affect their decisions. They also differ with respect to how much time they have to devote to their work on the journal, and how much this work matters to them. And like everyone else, they have good days and bad days – and little pet peeves that set them off. Before you decide to submit your work to a journal, take a look at who the journal editor is, and who is sitting on the editorial board.

You might also want to think about whether or not you want to publish in an open access journal or a journal with an open access option for specific articles. At the time this book went to press, open access has been rapidly gaining attention, but both publishers and authors are still wary. Normally when you submit an article to a journal, you pay nothing – unless you want colour figures (see Chapter 7), or you pay for your own copy-editing. Publishers make their money by charging readers, either through subscriptions (usually to libraries) or one-time fees for downloading individual articles. Open access means that the reader can freely access the article, even without a subscription. Since publishing a journal is tremendously expensive and the journal has to cover the costs somehow, open access requires pushing the cost over to the authors. While this certainly makes published work more accessible to everyone – especially those not connected to a university library – it may make it more difficult for some to publish, if the costs are prohibitive. Much of the debate is about different cost models. Another concern is journals that are fully web-based and open access: it is not always easy for an author to tell the difference between a legitimate, peer-reviewed online journal and one that is predatory (see the text box 'Beware of predatory publishers!').

Beware of predatory publishers!

Do you get unsolicited emails inviting you to submit your work to a journal you've never heard of? If it sounds too good to be true, it probably is. While some of these new journals are legitimate, many exist only to take advantage of scholars desperate to get their work published. Hiding behind a rhetoric of 'open access', these publishers are not actually interested in furthering academic debate, but only in taking your money. Signs to look for include the following:

- High processing fees (NB: don't confuse this with the legitimate fees charged by reputable open access publishers)
- No identifiable editor or editorial board
- No clear routine for peer review or quality control

Jeffrey Beall on the *Scholarly Open Access* website has detailed information about what makes a publisher predatory, and which journals are currently questionable ('Beall's List'). See: http://scholarlyoa.com.

Another thing to consider is the ranking of your potential journals. Lists of every flavour abound – perhaps one is kept by your own department or research institute – but perhaps the most comprehensive is located on the ISI Web of Knowledge. The ISI Web of Knowledge provides three criteria for ranking: impact factor, immediacy index and cited half-life. The basic assumption is that there is a relationship between the quality of an article and the number of times it is cited.

The impact factor is considered the most important and measures *how frequently* the average article from that journal has been cited in a given year. The immediacy index shows *how quickly* (e.g., within the same year of publication) the average article in a given journal is cited. The cited half-life shows *how long* the majority of articles from a given journal are cited.

But as with any ranking system, *caveat emptor*: quality and number of citations may not necessarily be related. Moreover, the way these statistics are generated creates biases in the results. First, each journal's impact factor is calculated on the basis of how often its articles are generally cited – but different disciplines have different traditions when it comes to citation, with some citing far more than others. And a specialized journal with a smaller target audience may be cited less frequently, giving it a lower impact factor despite its having a significant impact in its field. Second, the immediacy index will clearly be affected by how often a journal comes out. And, third, the more a journal is oriented toward pure science, the greater its cited half-life will be in comparison to more applied journals. Anything that relates to theory-building is relevant for a far longer time than something specifically tied to one particular problem, case or question.

This type of ranking system favours single-disciplinary journals (particularly in the natural sciences) that lean toward pure science. It may also tend to give 'trendy' research an unfairly high rating. Like any ranking system, this one should be approached with caution. The built-in biases of the system mean that it is unsuitable for comparing journals from very different disciplinary backgrounds, or for comparing theoretical (pure science) journals with applied journals, and so on. It is most useful if you want to compare a handful of journals that fall into the same category with respect to thematic focus, discipline and theoretical orientation.

How important are these rankings anyway? There is no doubt that the merit systems used by most universities and some research institutes reward scholars who publish in the more highly ranked journals. The reputational effect of publishing in higher-ranked journals can help you achieve promotion. But another equally relevant question for most writers is whether you've communicated what you have to say to the people you want to reach. Publishing in the more prestigious journal may not always be the best way of reaching your target audience.

We need to ask ourselves not only 'Where would I like my work to appear?' but also 'Which journal cares about what I have to say?' If we return to the metaphor of scholarship being a dialogue that takes place in a gigantic conference hall with small groups of people discussing various subjects, our chances of being listened to increase significantly if we direct our comments to people who are actually talking about the same things we are. The most relevant question you can ask yourself when you are trying to locate your audience may be: 'Where is the dialogue that I want to get involved in taking place?' If the discussion that fascinates you most, and to which you have something to contribute, is happening in a far corner of the conference hall, being in the centre of the room, even if that's where the big crowd is, means you won't be heard – no matter how loudly you shout.

If you want to find out where your dialogue is taking place, look at your own reference list. What publications did you reference in your work? If you notice that one particular journal shows up again and again, you are probably working on something that is relevant for that particular journal – and that's where your most interested audience will be.

Tip

Get to know 'your' journal editors. Many larger conferences regularly offer panel or roundtable discussions featuring journal editors from some of the relevant journals for the conference theme. Attending these sessions gives you tremendous insight into how different journal editors think.

MISSING YOUR TARGET

Submitting your paper to a prestigious journal instead of one that covers the subject matter you are interested in is an egregious example of missing your target. Most likely your work will simply be rejected, even before it goes to peer review. But even if it is accepted (perhaps with major revisions) by the journal of your choice, it may not be read by the people you want to reach. Perhaps your target audience doesn't generally read that journal, or even worse, perhaps the changes you made to suit the preferences of the journal mean that it no longer seems relevant to them.

You can also miss your target by underestimating what your audience knows about your subject matter, and thus devoting pages and pages to informing them about what they already know. This may result in your readers being so bored they simply refuse to read further. And if you overestimate how much they know, you may leave them confused.

The same holds true for getting it wrong with respect to how much they agree with you. If you spend time and effort trying to convince those who are already convinced, they will get impatient. And if you assume that your audience agrees with you when no such assumption is warranted, you will anger your audience. You can also stumble unwittingly into a political hornets' nest: your emphasis on the scholarly nature of a problem might blind you to its more controversial aspects.

Getting it wrong in either the knowledge dimension or the value dimension will alienate your audience. The audience will feel that you are not talking to them, and they are less likely to get something useful out of your work – that is, if they can be bothered to read it at all.

RECALIBRATING YOUR WORK

Sometimes when you miss your mark, the fault lies less in the writing than in your perception of who your audience should be. It may not be a question of *whether* your research is useful, but rather a question of *to whom* it is useful. You may simply have to ask whether your work is more useful for a different type of audience than you originally had in mind. Audience plays a huge role in determining both the soundness of your method and the relevance of your topic (see Chapter 1) – the two most important criteria for acceptance in a scholarly journal. What is irrelevant for one audience may be very relevant for another. And what may be considered pseudo-science by one discipline may well be a perfectly acceptable methodology for another. If your work has merit, there is a home for it somewhere – even if it is in the *Journal of Groundless Speculation* or *Obscurity Digest*.

But most of the time when you face rejection, it is not enough to send your work to a different journal. You will have to go back and rework your material – particularly with respect to the introduction, conclusion and relationship to theory – to more closely meet the needs of your audience. This means reassessing how much your audience knows, and how much they may share your assumptions. Here, feedback from a colleague can be very valuable (see Chapter 8).

Recalibration is also required when we 'repurpose' existing material for oral presentation (see Chapter 9) or for publication in a different medium – for example, when we convert a journal article into a book chapter (or vice versa), or a commissioned report into a journal article. Repurposing is often touted as an effective way to extend the lifetime of your research or, to the more cynical, pad your publications list: instead of simply publishing one journal article, you can publish journal articles in very different journals, write a book chapter and make a presentation. This does indeed give you a much greater chance of reaching a wider audience, but most people seriously underestimate the work involved.

In applied research institutes, for example, it is fairly common for a research project to result in both a report to the funding agency and a journal article. Many researchers convince themselves that they can first prepare a report, and then shorten it for publication in a scholarly journal. But it is not just the length that distinguishes a report from a journal article. The two audiences – those who commissioned the research and your fellow scholars – have very different needs and expectations. The usual, and unfortunate, result is that the report is too academic to suit the funding institution, and the journal article is too case-specific and not generalizable enough for the academic community. The obvious solution here is that if you want to meet the needs of two different audiences, then you need to budget time for two different forms of output, and not just assume that two birds can be killed with one pile of paper. And it is possible that the funding institution might not need a detailed report and might be far happier with an oral presentation accompanied by a brief summary, in which case you will have more time to write a journal article.

Switching from journal article to academic book chapter in an edited volume, or vice versa, is a more subtle move. The audience in both cases is scholarly, so it is tempting to think that no real changes must be made. But these are very different media, and each imposes its own demands.

Adapting an academic book chapter to be a journal article obviously requires recalibration to fit the structural requirements of the journal. Most book chapters are longer than the average journal article, so they most likely have to be cut – which means you will have to focus and tighten your argument. More important, while a book chapter is meant to be read in the context of the other book chapters, a journal article is generally expected to be read in isolation. This means it has to stand on its own to a far greater degree, and you may have to incorporate some of the background material from other chapters for your work to make sense by itself. And what might well be the deal-breaker is that journals require that you submit work that has not been published earlier, which means that you have to change it enough to satisfy the journal that it now constitutes new and unpublished work (see Chapter 10). This will be far easier for those working with more theoretical arguments than those presenting empirical data.

The issue of book context is equally relevant when you are recalibrating a journal article for inclusion in a book. While copyright issues are certainly involved, it is not uncommon to gather previously published articles into book form. To make your work relevant for the book, you need to find out what the rest of the book will be about. What is the common theme of all the chapters? That is, what does your work have in common with the rest of the book? And, likewise, what sets your chapter apart? You may want to play down the sections that are sufficiently covered in other chapters, while further developing the sections that are unique. These concerns are equally relevant if you are collecting your own work: Do the chapters work together as a whole? Does each make a unique contribution?

Whether you are adjusting your work to suit the needs of your audience or rethinking your audience to suit your work, your ability to communicate your message also depends on your knowing exactly what that message is. Developing and fine-tuning your core argument is the subject of the next chapter.

Remember

To make sense in the scientific dialogue, tailor your argument to your audience: How much do they know about your subject? How likely are they to accept your premises?
  To be heard, pick a journal aimed at those you want to reach.

FURTHER READING

- Belcher, Wendy Laura (2009) *Writing Your Journal Article in 12 Weeks: A Guide to Academic Publishing Success*, Thousand Oaks, CA: Sage. The chapter on 'Selecting a journal' includes some good advice about how to avoid the wrong journal and other questionable publishing outlets.
- Curry, Mary Jane and Lillis, Theresa (2013) *A Scholar's Guide to Getting Published in English: Critical Choices and Practical Strategies*, Bristol: Multilingual Matters. Curry and Lillis tailor their discussion of audience to the non-native speaker of English and also include discussions about using conferences to explore the conversation and get to know the audience.
- Murray, Rowena and Moore, Sarah (2006) *The Handbook of Academic Writing: A Fresh Approach*, Maidenhead: Open University Press. Chapter 4 on disciplinarity is particularly relevant to thinking about audience.
- Reid, Natalie (2010) *Getting Published in International Journals: Writing Strategies for European Social Scientists*, Oslo: Norwegian Social Research (NOVA). One of the few books to target non-native speakers of English, Reid explains Anglo-Saxon argumentation and style of writing. Her section on journal analysis is detailed and extremely useful.
- Thody, Angela M. (2006) *Writing and Presenting Research*, London: Sage. Chapter 3, 'Adapting to audience: Adjusting for their aims', looks specifically at the issue of audience.

FIVE

What do you want to say?
Forming your core argument

They say that to sculpt a bird, you start with a block of marble and chip away everything that does not look like a bird. Sounds reasonable enough, but it presupposes that you have a very clear idea of what a bird looks like. Scholarly writing involves a similar process: we always possess far more information than we need, and writing is a process of sorting through all that information until we get something that looks like what we want to say. Again, this presupposes that we have a very clear idea of exactly what that is.

But that kind of clarity is not always with us at the outset. To draw out the sculpting analogy a bit more, when you get the block of marble, you may not be sure you want to make a bird out of it. Sometimes, you just chip away until you see a shape that intrigues you. Other times, you might have a general idea – some sort of winged creature? Or you know you want a bird, but not what kind of bird. Or you know what kind of bird, but aren't sure what pose you want it in. Scholarship is likewise always a work in progress, and papers evolve significantly as we write them.

This is all the more reason to step back every now and then and ask ourselves what we've got in front of us – and what we want to end up with. Whether we are sculpting birds or writing a scholarly paper, at some point we need to develop a clear vision of what we are trying to do if we are ever going to satisfactorily complete our project.

YOUR CORE ARGUMENT: ASK A QUESTION, THEN ANSWER IT

Strip away everything else, all the tables and figures, all the references, all the discussions, and the essence of scholarly writing is asking a question and then answering it. Everything you do in the paper justifies, supports, clarifies or explains either the question or the answer (see Chapter 6). So the clear vision you need to have in your mind – the one that will allow you to chip away everything that does not look like a bird – is made up of your research question (the question you ask) and your thesis statement (your answer to the question).

The research question is perhaps the most undervalued part of any scholarly work: the real secret of good scholarly writing lies not in coming up with the right answer, but rather in asking the right question. First of all, a good question will capture the reader's attention, no matter what the answer. But a good question does more than just grab our attention; it directs analytical focus in a fruitful direction and pinpoints meaningful gaps in our collective knowledge. Asking a truly good question is an art, and one at which few novices are proficient. A keen knowledge of your field is required before you can look around and see not only where the gaps are, but also how you might go about filling them. And a good question will entice your readers to join the quest with you. This ensures that they read your work, and might even tempt them to follow up with research of their own.

The question you ask (your research question) and the answer you provide the reader (your thesis statement) make up the core argument of your entire paper: everything else - the rest of the apple - either justifies the question or helps explain the answer.

If the research question is the most undervalued part of scholarly writing, then the thesis statement is the least understood. You don't have to worry that your thesis statement must provide the ultimately correct and final answer to the research question. It doesn't. A thesis statement is merely the summary of what your particular work contributes toward an answer. Many of the questions that we ask in academic inquiry are difficult, if not impossible, to answer in a single paper. Some can't be answered at all. Your thesis statement merely sums up what you intend to say about the question you asked. It does not matter if your thesis statement is: 'The evidence is insufficient at this time to see any clear correlation'; what matters is that you have a clear idea of the point you want to make. As a writer, you need this 'answer' to your question *not* because it represents the final word on the matter, but because it provides a destination for your argument.

Your research question and thesis statement form the starting point and end point of the journey you want to take your readers on. Together they form your *core argument*.

FORMING YOUR RESEARCH QUESTION

The most important thing about your research question is that you have one – one that ends in a question mark. One of the reasons that most of us fail to appreciate the importance of having a specific question is that in the final product, the published journal article or book chapter, the question often appears not as a question but as a stated objective or a hypothesis to be tested. This can give the impression that a question isn't necessary. But the question has a crucial role to play both for your reader and for you.

For your reader, the question functions as a kind of contract: 'I promise to devote some time to reading this article (or book) if you answer this question.' When your reader then diligently ploughs through your entire article and you do *not* answer the question you dangled so enticingly in the title or introduction, the reader is justifiably disappointed, maybe even angry. It is, after all, a breach of contract. You made a promise and did not deliver.

And for you, the question acts as a reminder of what it is you are supposed to be doing in this piece of writing: when in doubt about whether or not to include a particular point, you need to ask yourself, 'How does it help me answer the question I'm asking?' If the answer is 'It doesn't, but I just thought I should throw it in there because it shows I read Foucault', then you should probably drop that point.

Scholars making the transition from writing reports (or even books) to writing articles for scholarly journals frequently stumble here because reports (and sometimes books) do not necessarily require a research question; a topic will often suffice. Unfortunately, our earliest exposure to academic writing does not prepare us for appreciating the difference between a question and a topic. In elementary school we are taught to write reports that are little more than a random selection of facts: 'My paper is on tigers.' The more facts you can come up with about tigers (what they eat, where they live and so on), the more likely you will get a gold star – and the less likely you will develop the ability to distinguish between information that is important and information that is inconsequential or merely interesting.

The topics that we write about as scholars – the ethics of war, non-governmental organizations in Estonia, definitions of sexuality among today's youth – are much more specialized than they were in elementary school, but making your topic more specific is not enough. 'Remittances from Pakistani migrants' is no more a research question than 'tigers'. Even 'conceptions of family obligation among migrants from Pakistan and remittances to Pakistani family members' is not a question. A question is an inquiry: who, what, when, where, how or why. And unlike a topic, a question needs a verb, an action, which serves to specify the relationship between the specific elements of the topic:

- Who receives remittances from Pakistani migrants?
- How do remittances sent from abroad shape the local economy in Pakistan?
- How is the conceptualization of family obligations reflected in remittances made from Pakistani migrants to relatives in Pakistan?

You might be asking yourself, 'But what's the difference between saying, "I'm going to write about the remittances from Pakistani migrants", and asking the question "Who receives remittances from Pakistani migrants?"' For your reader, there may not be much difference at all. But for you, formulating a question specifies the scope of your inquiry in a way that stating your topic does not. In this case, you are to stick only to describing who the recipients of the remittances are, and not wander off into how the money affects the local community, or how the amounts are determined on the basis of conceptualizations of family obligation. The logical boundaries of your inquiry seldom become clear until it is stated in question form.

Asking questions is important in all disciplines – even those that might eschew the formal research question. From the reader's perspective, the question marks the line that you draw between what you are presenting as background material – and thus asking your reader to accept as a given – and what you intend to argue. Consider the theme 'Visual interpretations of Islam in European textbooks in the 1990s'. If you simply start talking about the topic without letting us know what specific question you intend to answer, we will have a very hard time seeing what *your* contribution to this discourse actually is. It will read more like a coffee-table book, or at best a textbook, rather than a scholarly argument. Making the question clear – even if it is not posed in question form in the final draft – helps us see your unique contribution more clearly. For instance:

- *Which groups of Muslims are depicted in religious studies textbooks in European middle school?* This question suggests that previous work grouped all Muslims together, whereas your discussion will shed new light on the distinction, or lack of distinction, between various groups of Muslims in these textbooks.
- *Has the visual representation changed character between 1990 and 1999?* This suggests that previous work has not looked at the dynamic nature of visual portrayals, and moreover that something has happened, or should have happened, in this time period that could affect how Islam is visualized. The reader would expect you to make a new connection between, for example, social change and change in visual representations of Islam.
- *How is Islam represented visually differently in various European countries?* This suggests that previous work might not have taken into account how European countries differ with respect to how accepting they are of Islam, and that you will make some sort of argument about how and why visual portrayals differ even within Europe.

A specific question, no matter how broad it is, will always give you a better guideline for writing than a mere topic. If you do not have a specific question in mind when you are writing, what you will end up with is just a more exotic version of an elementary school paper on tigers: a regurgitation of everything you know about the subject, in no particular order, with no particular aim.

That said, the reality is often (or usually, for many of us) that you discover your research question as you write. That's fine. But the final draft should make it look as though that was the question you intended to answer all along. So, if you discover you have been writing without a specific research question in mind, it is not too late. There are several ways to go about forming one, and making the effort to do so will help you considerably in the revision stage. If you are lucky enough to know where you want to end up – if your thesis statement is fairly well developed – you can make a research question through back-formation: take your answer and put it in question form. For example, if what you really want to say is that the portrayal of Islam in European textbooks has changed considerably over the last ten years as a direct result of increased immigration, you could ask either: 'How has immigration affected the portrayal of Islam in European textbooks?' or 'What has caused the change in the portrayal of Islam in European textbooks?'

Try this: Brainstorm research questions

Think of a couple of different topics – say, the modern family and adaptation to climate change. Come up with at least three research questions for each topic. For example:

- How does the modern family differ from the traditional family?
- How does the makeup of the modern family reflect social change?
- What do we expect the modern family to look like in 50 years?

- What are the benefits of focusing on adaptation to climate change rather than mitigation of greenhouse gas emissions?
- What are the institutional barriers to implementing adaptation policy?
- How can adaptation policies take into account other pressures on society?

The objective is to see that any given topic can branch out in any number of different directions depending on the research question you choose.

Using back-formation to create questions sounds easier than it is. Although both of the questions asked about portraying Islam in European textbooks could end up where you want to end up, they approach their destination from two completely different starting points. This means that they will generate very different papers. The question that is right for you, the angle that you want to take, is not always clear from the beginning – and it may depend very much on your specific audience. You will probably have to reformulate your research question several times while you are writing; perhaps you will wind up changing the very type of question you are asking. There are many different ways of categorizing research questions, and there is no such thing as a definitive list. Here are five different types, illustrated with sample research questions that all stem from the topic 'Fathers and infants'.

Descriptive questions: Descriptive questions seek to describe a current or past phenomenon. They generally presume that a certain relationship exists, but aim to quantify or qualify its extent – to find out exactly how much or to what degree. For example:

- How much time do infants spend with their fathers compared to with their mothers?
- In what situations do infants spend time with their fathers?

Descriptive questions can be answered in isolation from theory or as a way of testing, illustrating or expanding on theory. In isolation, they are perhaps most useful in an applied research setting and often have a high degree of relevance for policy-makers or practitioners. If they are explicitly related to theory in some way, they can also have a high degree of relevance for the scholarly dialogue.

Analytical questions: Analytical questions take description a step further and look for patterns, trends, mechanisms or causal relationships. For example:

- How has the pattern of contact between fathers and infants changed over the last ten years?
- What are the socioeconomic mechanisms that encourage fathers to spend more time with their children?

Analytical questions are often stated as hypotheses, if they can be formally tested with empirical data. For example: 'As women become more involved in the workforce, men will spend more time with infant children.' As with descriptive questions, the relationship between the observations and existing theory will determine to what extent these questions are most relevant for an applied or pure science audience.

Predictive questions: Predictive questions take their point of departure in existing theory and attempt to forecast the likelihood of a phenomenon given a specific set of circumstances. For example:

- Will fathers elect to spend more time with their infant children if they are compensated financially?

Like analytical questions, predictive questions are also frequently stated as hypotheses if they are tested using empirical data. For example, 'In accordance with Little's theory of family economics, men will spend more time with their infant children if they are compensated financially.'

Problem-solving questions: Problem-solving questions aim to alleviate a given social problem or improve a given condition. They are often, but not exclusively, used in the social sciences. For example:

- What steps can state governments take to encourage fathers to spend more time with their infant children?

Problem-solving questions are, by their very nature, most relevant in an applied context and virtually always conclude with a recommendation of some sort.

Theoretical questions: This type of question is specifically designed to push theory development forward. For example:

- What questions should developmental theory be focusing on to better understand the relationship between fathers and infants?
- What can developmental theory learn from feminist inquiries into relationships between fathers and infants?

These questions are clearly most relevant for the scholarly dialogue and are seldom interesting in an applied context (unless the author can argue for their practical relevance).

Note that these types of questions are *not* ranked in order of their importance to the scholarly dialogue. Depending on the context of your inquiry, descriptive questions can be more important than questions aimed at theory development. If you want to 'upgrade' the category of your question – make it more interesting, more fruitful, more challenging – do so on the basis of the material you have to work with and the context of the scholarly dialogue, not because of a misconception that descriptive questions aren't good enough.

Try this: Rethinking your research question

Take a look at the paper you are working on. Focus on the general topic of your paper and think of at least four other research questions you could ask. Try formulating a question to fit into each of the categories above. How does the ideal audience (interdisciplinary vs single discipline; applied vs pure science) for your research question change as you reformulate?

FORMING YOUR THESIS STATEMENT

A thesis statement is a one- or two-sentence summary of your main conclusion. It is the logical destination of your paper. Everything you write should lead up to that point. Formulating a good thesis statement means being able to concisely express exactly what it is you want to say – what it is you want to contribute to the conversation you aim to be part of.

The challenge here is that the longer you have been working on a certain project, the more likely you will lose perspective on what your specific contribution to the discourse is. And, ironically, the harder a time you will have explaining what you mean because the more you know about something, the harder it is to imagine what it is like to not know that thing (this is a real thing called 'the curse of knowledge' – look it up!). Chances are you will feel that whatever you are working on is obvious (because it makes sense to you) and you have nothing new to offer at all – maybe just a different way of interpreting Robert Frost, or a historical review of the concept of 'public television broadcasting'. But remember that knowledge is accumulated piece by piece, and major insights are often the result of many small pieces put together. That historical review of public television may not seem like much to you, but it may end up providing evidence of a significant shift in cultural programming. Collecting, summarizing and translating the household accounts of a meticulous but obscure late nineteenth-century farmwife from the Loire Valley may eventually become a key piece in another scholar's economic history of France. If your work adds to our cumulative knowledge, even by looking at something old in a new way, then it's a contribution. It's not always about coming up with a whole new theory.

Putting your finger on your particular contribution means asking yourself: 'What do I know that no one else knows? What can I talk about that no one else has talked about yet?' Even if your answer to this question seems inadequate to you, it will ultimately be your best point of departure. For example, say you were an observer at a historic summit meeting. While you may not have anything new to contribute to theory development, your observations are likely to prove invaluable to other researchers who can carry the ball further. If what you have to offer is a description, then offer that description and do it well. Do not try to offer an analysis or a theoretical contribution if you do not have adequate material to do so.

If you still feel that you have nothing new to offer, you can ask yourself, 'Why did I start this research project in the first place?' Research projects are initiated to fill in gaps in our collective knowledge. As the project progresses, its focus may change, but when it comes time to write, a useful question is always: 'What was it I wanted to find out in the first place, and why?' And remember: *not* finding a change and *not* finding a relationship between A and B are also findings – and sometimes important ones, especially when they go against established thinking. Both researchers and journals have a bias against so-called negative findings. That is, we tend to think that research projects that end up with something like, 'Well, we thought we would find something but we didn't', are failed projects and not worth publishing. But failure to publish negative findings can, in the long run, lead to a distorted body of knowledge. Say four out of five projects that look at maths performance in children observe no differences between boys and girls (but since they did find that other variables mattered – like parents' educational background – they could at least publish something). Since nothing 'interesting' was found when looking at gender, gender was ignored or downplayed in the published work. But one out of these five projects *does* find a significant difference between boys and girls, and suddenly an article is published claiming that boys and girls have different abilities in maths. If this pattern is repeated enough times, there will be a large body of published research showing gender differences – but an even larger body of research that remains unpublished showing no gender differences. When you search for literature on 'gender and maths ability', you will get hits for only the tip of that iceberg. So, you build your research design on the basis of an assumed difference between boys and girls, and much to your disappointment, you don't find any.[1] But instead of writing an article that screams 'Hey! I didn't find anything, even though I really expected to!' you let the results quietly die, and the pattern continues for the next researcher – who was not able to read about your experiences and thus repeats the same effort to no avail. Daring to publish that you found nothing at all might then be less of a 'failure' and more of a step towards correcting the existing literature.

Once you have a general idea about what you are going to say – even if it wasn't what you were hoping you would be able to say – you can then force yourself to be precise. The aim of a thesis statement is to condense the main point of your work into a single sentence (or maybe two). It may comprise your findings or your discussion of what they mean. It is what you would say if you had a gun to your head and only 15 seconds to explain yourself, the one thing you hope your reader will remember a week after reading your article. The more concise you can be, and the less you rely on technical terminology, the easier it will be for you to get a sense of your destination and purpose of your article:

> Throughout Western Europe, the Industrial Revolution changed popular attitudes about what constitutes a 'good marriage' because inherited wealth was no longer a prerequisite for prosperity.

Of course this feels artificial: if you could squeeze your argument into one or two sentences then you wouldn't need to write a 10,000-word article. Keep in mind that the function of a thesis statement is not to provide the complete answer to the research question, but to specify the *destination* of your paper. Knowing this is your destination, you can then map out your strategy: 'How will I show that it was this new access to wealth that changed attitudes about what a "good marriage" is, and not something else – like the changing role of religion?'

A formula for analyzing your argument: 'X is Y because Z'

Sometimes you need to take a step back and ask yourself what you are really doing in your paper. The formula 'X is Y because Z' can help you ask the questions you need to think critically about when you are trying to figure out what your argument actually is.

---

[1] See Cordelia Fine's excellent book *Delusions of Gender: How Our Minds, Society, and Neurosexism Create Difference* (2010) for more examples of the dangers of not publishing negative findings.

'X' stands for your *topic*: What is this a conversation about? And what are you asking a question about? Civil war? The duration of civil war? The duration of civil war in conflicts in geographical areas with certain topographic features? There is seldom one correct answer to this, but deciding what the conversation is about will help you formulate both your research question and your introduction. For example, if the conversation is about civil war in general, you would talk about why it would be useful to look at the duration, as opposed to, say, its intensity. If there is already a vibrant conversation on the duration of civil war, you would not have to explain (much) about why it is useful to look at duration, but you would have to justify why it would be useful to look at topographic features of the landscape as opposed to all the other features that might affect how long a conflict persists.

'Y' stands for your *claim*: What is it you have to say about X? What are you contributing to the discourse? For example, you might want to claim that 'the duration of civil war is likely to be longer when insurgent groups are located far from the centre'.

'Z' stands for the *support* for your claim: On what basis do you make your claim? The word 'because' in this formula makes a lot of researchers nervous because they think it means they have to state a 'cause'. But what I mean here is simply: 'What can you show the reader to make your claim convincing?' Pretty much the only thing you cannot use here is 'because I said so'. Here it is helpful to take a look at the difference between *evidence* and *reasons* (see Figure 5.1) In my experience as an editor, most authors draw on both empirical evidence (qualitative or quantitative) and reasons (theoretical or logical), but usually there is an emphasis on one over the other. If you want to claim that 'the duration of civil war is likely to be longer when insurgent groups are located far from the urban centre', you could provide evidence: 'because this is a statistically significant relationship'. Or you could provide a reason: 'because distant groups are too costly to control'. Or both. To what extent the evidence or reasons become part of your main claim relate to what method you have chosen. If you have conducted a large-n study that codes for the duration of war and distance between rebel bases and urban centres, you can provide a lot of evidence, but perhaps not the reasons. To make your paper stronger, you will probably draw from a theoretical discussion of reasons to frame the hypotheses you are testing, or perhaps speculate on reasons if your discussion includes the suggestion of a new hypothesis. But the real strength of your claim should rest on the empirical evidence if that represents what you have contributed to the conversation. Likewise, if you have not conducted a large-n study but rather are exploring the theoretical literature and drawing only on other researchers' data, your claim will focus on the reasons because theory development is your main contribution.

The purpose of this 'X is Y because Z' exercise is to force you to think about what claims you are making and which of them you can actually back up through reasons or evidence or both (see both Toulmin, 2003; and Booth et al., 2008, listed at the end of this chapter under 'Further reading' for a more detailed discussion about this).

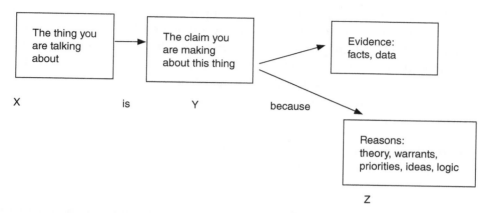

Figure 5.1 What makes a thesis statement: supporting a claim through evidence and reason

And note that the requirement to provide support for your claims holds true for every claim you make. Researchers in applied fields often follow up their main arguments with a secondary claim in the form of a recommendation. These, too, need to be supported by more than just 'Trust me, I'm the researcher.' Usually, recommendations are supported through implicit reasons, which are in turn based on underlying priorities (see Chapter 4); the trick is to make them explicit (see Chapter 3). For example, in a research paper on the impact of an aluminium factory, the researcher could easily conclude with a recommendation – keep it open or close it down. But if you treat the recommendation like any other kind of claim, the researcher then has to make the support for that claim transparent through reasons or evidence:

- *Given that the aluminium factory is harming the livestock and the livelihoods of the local farmers*, the factory should be closed down.
- *Given that the aluminium factory is crucial to the international competitiveness of the country*, the factory should remain open.

If you want to put it in the form of 'X is Y because Z', it would be 'The factory should be closed down because it is harming the livestock and livelihoods of the local farmers' or 'The factory should remain open because it is crucial to the international competitiveness of the country.' For both of these claims, the author can support through evidence (statistics about livestock death or profit) and reasons (arguments about the importance of farming or economic competeveness). The actual phrasing here is less important than your ability to analyze the parts of your core argument. The sentences that result from trying to formulate your argument in terms of 'X is Y because Z' are unlikely to appear in your final paper (with the possible exception of your abstract). The exercise is merely meant to make you think all the way through your core argument.

Again, I stress that it is not about discovering the one true thesis statement that is waiting to be revealed. It is about looking at your material and asking, 'What can I say about this?' and 'In which conversation would this be an interesting point?' Sometimes the direction you should take will be far from clear. Say you have been looking at the role of the Intergovernmental Panel on Climate Change (IPCC), and are using regime theory as a theoretical framework. Consider the following research questions:

- How does regime theory explain the role of the IPCC in climate negotiations?
- How *well* does regime theory explain the role of the IPCC in climate negotiations?

There is only one word that differentiates these two questions, but if we start trying to figure out the rest of the core argument, they suddenly become very different. The 'X' of the first question appears to be 'the role of the IPCC' and my claim (the 'Y') might be something about how the IPCC is an 'arena for negotiations'. My introduction thus makes it clear that the topic is the role of the IPCC, and that regime theory is a tool to help me say something about that topic:

> In 2007, the IPCC was awarded a Nobel Peace Prize for their efforts to lay the foundations for measures that could counteract climate change. But what is it that the IPCC actually does, or is capable of doing, to help build these foundations? Regime theory helps shed light on state actors on the international stage, and I will draw from regime theory to help explain both the potentials and limitations of the IPCC in international climate negotiations.

The second question, however, is completely different. The 'X' here is actually 'regime theory'. My discussion about the IPCC is only to illustrate the main point I want to make about regime theory, which might be that: 'Regime theory fails to account satisfactorily for the role of any international organization because it fails to understand how different organizations are from states.' My introduction might be something like this:

> In international relations, regime theory is used to explain how states cooperate through institutions, or regimes, despite a system of anarchy. However, it is unclear how well regime theory is able to understand how *international governmental organizations* are able to act. Here, I will use the example of the IPCC to explore the limitations of regime theory in the context of understanding how intergovernmental organizations behave.

Here, I've switched the focus: instead of using regime theory to help me understand the IPCC, I'm using the IPCC to help me understand regime theory. Without an explicit thesis statement (and research question), I could well write something like this: 'This paper is about the IPCC and regime theory. The IPCC is an important organization in international climate negotiations. Regime theory is an important theory in political science.' I could yammer on for a hundred pages or so without ever making explicit the relationship between the two. Worse, I could make a shift without even being aware of it – starting out intending to evaluate the role of the IPCC in international climate negotiations, and ending up making pronouncements about the fruitfulness of regime theory. (This type of shift is covered in the section 'Answering a different question than you asked on p. 95.)

So when you formulate your thesis statement, you need to be very clear about the difference between what is being explained and what is providing the explanation, between what provides the backdrop for the analysis and what is being analyzed. What makes this particularly difficult is that this may change over the course of your research. It is very common to use a theory as a tool to explain a particular phenomenon, and then during the course of the research discover an important flaw in the theory – which makes it tempting to draw some conclusion about the efficacy of the theory itself. It is also common to have a broad subject of analysis that over the course of the writing becomes narrower. In the process, aspects of your subject move from being something you actively analyze to something you simply describe or establish in your background material.

MAKING SURE YOUR QUESTION MATCHES YOUR ANSWER

Even more important than having a pertinent research question and a well-formulated thesis statement is having a question and an answer that actually fit with each other. Your thesis statement has to answer your question, your whole question, and nothing but your question. It's surprisingly easy to fail on any of these points. Not only can you fail to have a question at all (which I talked about above), but you can also ask more questions than you answer, answer more questions than you asked, or answer a *different* question than you asked.

Asking more than you answer

Failure to answer a research question in full is almost always the result of an over-ambitious research question rather than an inadequate thesis statement. Like the road to hell, the overambitious research question starts off with good intentions. The effort to ask the good research question, the pertinent inquiry that will change the very course of social science as we know it, often results in a question that is too broad for any one paper to handle. Most scholars realize this as soon as they go to work operationalizing their concepts. What started off as 'What is the cause of poverty?' ends up being 'What are the socioeconomic driving forces keeping low-income, inner-city families in the southern United States from entering the middle class?' Limiting the scope of inquiry is not problematic; it is simply a natural step to take. What

The scholar's oath: Do you solemnly swear to answer the question, the whole question, and nothing but the question?

is problematic is limiting the scope of inquiry while keeping the original research question and offering no explanation for the disparity.

An inability to answer your research question in full may also spring from having simply *too many* research questions, even if each one is specific and well defined. My discussion so far has presumed that each paper has only one research question, but it is not uncommon to have two or more. There is no rule prohibiting the multi-part research question, but common sense discourages it. For every question you need an answer, and for every answer you need a supporting argument. Journal articles are not very long. Most are 8,000 words or less. In those 8,000 words (which usually include footnotes and references), you have to explain the background to your inquiry, establish its relevance, update your readers on current scholarly thinking, and explain how you came up with your conclusions. The more questions you have, the less space you can devote to answering each one. And the more complex your questions and answers are, the more they will suffer. Either you will treat each one superficially, or you will not answer some at all.

There are at least three different strategies for dealing with an overambitious paper:

- Split it into more than one paper.
- Unite multiple questions with an umbrella question.
- Emphasize one part more than another.

Splitting up your paper

Many problem papers are actually two or more papers trying to share living quarters. Just as there comes a time when your teenager really should move out of the house and find his own place to live, there also comes a time when your secondary research question must move to a different paper if it is ever to mature. The separation process can be painful, but usually everyone is the better off for it.

However, it seldom happens that both parts of the paper are equally mature. If you focus your paper on the primary question, you may have to set the secondary question aside. This will hurt, but remember that it does not mean you are disposing of your secondary question for good. It is quite common for scholars to go off on an interesting tangent in their research. If it eventually has to be cut out of the current project, it may well go on to be the seed for the next. The beauty of viewing scholarship as an ongoing discourse is that you need not feel pressured to make every contribution you make 'the final word'.

Finding an umbrella question

If you honestly feel that you are not ready to kick your secondary research question(s) out into the big world all alone, and that your primary and secondary research questions are indeed so closely linked that separation would do a disservice to both, then you need to make that link between the questions as clear to your readers as it is to you. Strive to find one question that unites all the other questions you want to ask. You may still have an overambitious question, but you can at least give the reader the impression that you have one united paper, not two or more papers jockeying for place in a single article.

Emphasizing one part over another

Another way you can keep your multiple questions is to redistribute the weight of your argument so that you answer only one of them properly, and intentionally relegate the other(s) to background or discussion material.

A classic example of this is the 'diagnosis–cure' article, which often results from a problem-solving research question. A diagnosis–cure article is one that identifies and describes the nature and causes of a certain problem and then proceeds to solve it. It is very difficult for a single journal article to support an argument for both a diagnosis and a cure.

First there is the space problem. Consider the hypothetical compound research question: What causes illiteracy in inner-city children and how can we alleviate it? The author needs to provide separate answers for each part of that question. For the sake of argument, let's say her answer to the first part is 'lack of access to reading material', and her answer to the second is 'build more public libraries'. Sounds simple enough, but look more closely at what she must do. For the first question, she will now have to place herself in the landscape of illiteracy research and provide a convincing argument that the main cause of illiteracy is the lack of access to reading material. This is a fairly major undertaking. She will have to describe her method in great detail, and how she was able to pinpoint this particular cause among all the other potential causes. Now she has to move on to the 'cure' section. Granted, she can start where she left off: with the diagnosis. If the cause is the lack of access to reading material, then presumably the solution will be something that addresses the lack of access. She wants to argue that building public libraries is the solution, which means she has to consider this solution in the context of other solutions that may have presented themselves, weigh the pros and cons, discuss the feasibility of the solution and so on. It is hard to imagine how she will be able to squeeze all of this (including notes and references) into a short journal article.

Space is not the only problem, or even the most serious one. A bigger problem is that these two main sections involve such different rhetorical strategies. For the diagnosis, the author usually presents a description of a certain phenomenon and explores potential causes, making an argument for what she believes to be the main explanatory factors. The author's stance is *descriptive*. For the cure, the author suddenly has to make an argument based on values and make assumptions about what goal is desirable. The author's stance is now *prescriptive*. These two stances are seldom comfortable in the same paper, but they can coexist if one is allowed to dominate – which will also solve the space problem.

Allowing one question to dominate means making one your main question and the other a subquestion or simply part of your background or discussion. In deciding which question to demote to a subquestion, you need to pinpoint your main contribution to the scientific dialogue. Have you provided an innovative and groundbreaking diagnosis? Then consider making that the focus of your paper and only touching on a possible 'cure' in your discussion. Our author could argue along these lines:

> Although it has long been known that there is a high rate of illiteracy among inner-city children, the cause has been unclear. By using my extraordinarily innovative method, I argue that the cause is simply the lack of exposure to reading material. In my discussion, I propose that a reasonable solution would be to consider improving access, for example through the construction of more public libraries.

Or, if the diagnosis is fairly straightforward (perhaps it has been made before), you can emphasize the cure. Our author could argue as follows:

> There is a high rate of literacy among inner-city children, and one of the causes that have been put forward is the lack of access to reading material. Given that this is an important cause, I argue that an effective cure would be to build more public libraries.

Note the wording 'Given that this is an important cause'. This relieves the author of the burden of having to prove causality: she can simply refer to other research that does that particular job for her. She also stipulates that her conclusion is only valid insofar as that cause is valid; she leaves open the possibility that if the cause is later disproved, then her argument may no longer hold.

Answering more than you ask

Who among us has not gotten carried away? We may start out doing a good job restricting the scope of our research question, but then when we get down to answering it we can't help ourselves, and the 'while I'm at it …' attitude possesses us. It may feel harmless enough – after all, what's wrong with a little extra knowledge? But once readers start asking themselves, 'Why are they telling me all this?' we are in danger of losing them entirely. For most readers it is not enough that your material be interesting, or even fascinating: it must go directly toward answering the research question. If it doesn't, then it doesn't belong in your paper. If you find that your discussion takes you to places that are not covered by your question, you have two choices: cut those parts out, or enlarge the scope of your question.

Enlarging the scope of your question is not a step that should ever be undertaken lightly. Scholars very seldom err on the side of having too little to say about anything; usually they struggle to restrict the scope of their inquiry to a manageable size. Nevertheless, there may be times when it is recommended, particularly if you began with a simple 'yes or no' question. Most 'yes or no' questions demand a 'why' component to make them interesting.

Answering a different question than you asked

You know those pictures that, if you stare at them long enough, the subject will shift from a goblet to the profiles of two people, or shift from a young woman to an old crone? Sometimes, when you work too long or too closely with your material, your perspective will shift and you won't even know it happened. Without even realizing it, you may end up answering an entirely different question than the one you asked at the beginning.

This does not mean you are a terrible scholar; it is simply a by-product of academic inquiry and the scholarly mind. Let's say I am conducting research on what makes some academic writers more productive than others. I assume that some behaviours and strategies will be more associated with high levels of productivity, and other behaviours and strategies will be associated with lower levels of productivity: my task is simply to identify these behaviours and strategies. But then as I dig deeper into my material, I discover that measuring productivity at the individual level is very problematic because the indicators are designed to measure at the institutional level. This causes me to dig deeper into indicators of productivity. Suddenly I have an 'Aha!' moment and realize that indicators of productivity are based on assumptions that do not hold for all types of academic writers. A critical exploration of indicators of productivity is a completely valid subject of a paper, and I can be forgiven for wanting to pursue this. What I cannot be forgiven for is starting my paper with a research question about individual strategies for productivity but answering with a critique of productivity indicators. If my readers decided to devote more than their usual five minutes to this paper, it is because they were under the impression I was going to talk individual strategies and behaviours. When I do not, they will probably want to cast the paper aside with great vigour. They won't care if a critique of indicators is perhaps interesting to the academic discourse *in general*. They want something that will be relevant for them in particular, and they were looking for something on individual strategies and behaviours.

Clearly, a problem of this sort requires that you revise either your research question or your thesis statement – or both. Chances are you have ended up in this situation because your research has taken you in an exciting but unexpected direction. While you may want to continue in the new direction, you might feel obligated to stick with the original question because that was what was in your project description. However, the reader has no idea what your original proposal stated, only what it is now – and a mismatch between the research question and the thesis statement thwarts the reader's reasonable expectations.

Try this: Identifying your core argument

Even though your research question and thesis statement may not appear in your paper as such, it should still be possible for the reader to identify your core argument within a few minutes of looking at your work.

- Without looking at your paper, write down your research question and your thesis statement. Now pick up your paper and see whether you can identify them in your writing. Pay especially close attention to whether your core argument has been revised in your mind but has not been revised on paper.

Or:

- Ask a friend or two to spend no more than five minutes skimming through your paper to identify your core argument. Ask them to underline what they think might be your research question and thesis statement. See whether what they found reflects what you had in mind.

What is obvious to us is not always obvious to the reader. If a reader cannot locate your research question and thesis statement in five minutes, or if she has a different understanding of your aims and findings than you do, you have some revising to do.

In the example above, I could have changed the research question to 'What do indicators of research productivity assume about academic writing and publishing?' or 'Why do indicators of research productivity favour some academic writers over others?' and nobody would have been angry. Or I could have saved the whole productivity indicator thing for another paper, and just answered the question about behaviours and strategies. The problem here, though, is that it is not always easy to see when and if you have gotten off track. In this example, it is fairly easy to see the difference between behaviours of writers and indicators of productivity. It is not always so obvious. The difference between, say, categories of sexuality and perceptions of sexual identity is far more subtle.

USING YOUR CORE ARGUMENT AS A WRITING GUIDE

The beginning of this chapter compares writing to sculpting, arguing that both require a clear vision of the end product. This is an important similarity. But there is also an important difference: it is far easier to change direction in your writing than it is to glue bits of marble back on to the block because you decided you wanted a bird in flight rather than a bird in repose. I described above how changing direction can work to our disadvantage – when we go off track without realizing it. The advantage is that when we're aware that our direction is changing, our writing can accommodate the shift. In writing we can make room for the inquiring mind.

The challenge is to allow your thoughts to develop without getting hopelessly lost. The answer is as simple to say as it is difficult to do: use your research question and your thesis statement as a guide to the writing, and dare to revise them on a regular basis.

As I stated earlier, your core argument lays out the path of your writing. It gives you a point of departure and a destination, defines your scope of inquiry, and specifies what belongs and what does not. Each time your thought processes lead you to wander into the wilderness off your chosen path, you have the opportunity to ask yourself whether you want to get back on your previous path, or whether you want to map out a new course. If you have your research question and thesis statement written out and visible to you (for example, taped to the wall), it will be easier for you to make this decision. You can look at what you've written, compare it to what you thought you were going to write, and ask yourself which is the most fruitful direction. If what you've written is more fruitful, then you revise your core argument, paste the new version on the wall, and carry on until the next crossroads, when you make the decision again. If you decide that what you've written is just a sign that you got momentarily lost, having your core argument visible makes it easier to see where you went astray and get back on course. If you decide that your tangent was off course but you want to file it away as a possible route to take at a later time, then you open a new document, put your thoughts in it, and save it so you can get back to it later.

Serving as a guide to writing is probably your core argument's most important function. Indeed, unless they're in your abstract, it is unlikely that either your research question or your thesis statement will be spelled out so explicitly in your paper. Not many articles state, 'My research question is blah blah and my thesis statement is yada yada yada.' As will be described in the following chapter, your research question should appear in your introduction, but it will likely appear in the form of a statement: 'This article aims to …' or 'Here, we seek to …' or something similar. A thesis statement often begins with statements like: 'This article argues that …' or 'We posit that …' But it may even be more difficult to identify than your research question, since your conclusion is likely to be spread over several paragraphs.

Even if you never revise your core argument, having it present and visible at all times will make it easier for you to connect the details of your work to the whole.

An occupational hazard for scholars is an inability to see the forest for the trees – or an inability to realize you are even looking at a tree (let alone a forest) because you've become so bogged down in describing each and every leaf. Sometimes, we get so lost in the details of our work that we forget why we are doing it in the first place; thus, we become unable to show our readers how the detail fits into the larger picture. Having a clear – and ever present – idea of your destination makes it easier for you to keep the connection between the parts and the whole explicit. In particular, it makes it easier for you to keep track of the role each section should play in developing your argument and structuring your paper. The structure of your paper is the subject of the next chapter.

Remember

Make your research question or questions explicit – if not to your reader then at least to yourself.

For every question you ask, you need to have an answer – where you answer the question, the whole question, and nothing but the question.

For every answer (thesis statement), you need to provide support in the form of empirical data, theoretical/logical argument, or both.

Revise your research question(s) and thesis statement(s) as needed over the course of the writing process.

FURTHER READING

- Belcher, Wendy Laura (2009) *Writing Your Journal Article in 12 Weeks: A Guide to Academic Publishing Success*, Thousand Oaks, CA: Sage. The chapter on 'Advancing your argument' looks at some of the main reasons that articles are rejected and how you can adjust your core argument (and structure) accordingly. Her discussions about moving from topic to argument and writing an argument-driven article are particularly strong.
- Booth, Wayne C., Colomb, Gregory G. and Williams, Joseph M. (2008) *The Craft of Research*, 3rd edn, Chicago, IL: University of Chicago Press. Section II 'Asking questions, finding answers' and section III 'Making a claim and supporting it' are particularly relevant in this context. Booth et al. provide a good detailed discussion of the difference between 'reasons' and 'evidence', and the various types of claims researchers make.
- Sloane, William (1979) *The Craft of Writing*, New York: W.W. Norton & Company. I include this book because it was my very first introduction to the idea of a thesis statement – to the idea that I had to back up my claims with something other than 'because I say so'. Short and well written, this book gave me a whole new perspective on argument and still influences my thinking.
- Toulmin, Stephen E. (2003) *The Uses of Argument*, updated edn, Cambridge: Cambridge University Press. Unlike most of the other books that I've suggested for further reading, this is not a book on academic writing. It is more a philosophy book, but section III 'The layout of arguments' describes in detail what has come to be known as the 'Toulmin model of argumentation', which has been exceptionally influential in the thinking around arguments in academic writing.

SIX

How are you going to say it?
Developing your structure

Want to make a toddler laugh? Try blowing up a balloon until it is almost ready to burst, and instead of tying off the end, just let it go. Make bets about how long it will take before it runs out of air. Try to guess where it will end up! Want to make your reader cry? Try writing your paper the same way. Unlike toddlers, readers seldom derive pleasure from having no idea what's going on. But very much like toddlers, they will leave if they can't get it their way.

Structuring your writing gives you a flight plan, making it easier for one idea to lead logically to the next. If you want your readers to stick with you, you need to have a structure that reflects your core argument. This chapter describes in more detail the specific role each structural element plays not only in making your argument comprehensible, but also in conveying its relevance and credibility.

ACADEMIC WRITING AS STORYTELLING

Before you start thinking about what kind of structural elements to include, it is helpful to take a step back and think about the overall story – the beginning, the middle and the end. In fairytales, the beginning starts with a variation of 'once upon a time' and a description of a setting that is usually quite wonderful except for one thing: someone gets into trouble. The middle part is the hero's journey:

a description of how the obstacles (usually three) are overcome. The end is how the hero breaks the spell, kills the dragon, releases the princess, or something like that, and then everyone lives happily ever after. The beginning creates a tension, the middle describes a journey, and the end is a resolution: each part motivates the next. In structuring your academic writing, you, too, need to tell a story – one that is told to a specific audience and focuses on your core argument. Your beginning will set up the problem that your question is designed to address; your middle part will tell us the researcher's journey – what you did and what you found; and the end will bring resolution by putting it all together, developing the thesis statement in full. Like all good stories, each part needs to add something new and keep the momentum going to hold the listeners' interest. And like fairytales, the way you do this is a combination of following convention and bringing in your own individual voice and contribution. The remainder of this chapter focuses on the structural conventions of academic writing and their rhetorical purpose.

Try this: Tell your story

In a group exercise (or on paper by yourself) take turns telling your stories as fairytales:

Once upon a time, there was a country called Somalia. A terrible curse fell over the country and people ran away. But what they ran to was often worse than what they left behind and many died. Yet, they kept coming. 'Why?' wondered the brave young researcher, 'would these families risk their lives this way?' To find out, she set out upon a perilous journey of her own ...

THE DIFFERENCE BETWEEN RULES AND CONVENTIONS

Academic writing and publication is brimming with conventions disguised as rules – and you need to be aware of the difference between the two. 'Rule' implies that one way is right, and all the other ways are wrong. For example, in the US it is a rule that you drive on the right side of the street. In the UK, it is a rule to drive on the left. In neither place would breaking these rules be a particularly good idea, and in fact you would be fined heavily (if you managed to get caught before killing yourself and other motorists). 'Conventions' imply that there are certain ways of doing things that we are used to. For example, we are used to a Santa Claus costume being red with white trim. There is no law against having a Santa outfit in green with black trim, but the only kids climbing up on your lap will be the colour-blind ones. We are used to seeing place settings with forks on the left and knives on the right; doing it differently can – depending on your panache – make it seem like you are an ignorant slob who was raised in a cave or that you are bold and daring. Conventions exist to ease social interaction and communication by presenting things in the way we are used to seeing them.

Academic writing has few rules, but many conventions. Conventions permeate academic writing at every level: from how you list your references (see Chapter 10) to how you, the author and researcher, refer to yourself in your writing (see Chapter 3). Many of these conventions differ considerably between disciplines and methodological orientations – not to mention countries. When writers follow the conventions you are familiar with, you assume they are competent researchers. When they do not follow convention, you start to wonder if they know what they are doing – and by extension, what they are talking about. Because the world of academic writing regularly crosses disciplinary boundaries and national borders – and, like anything else, changes over time – researchers are regularly being accused of being incompetent because they have made different choices than their readers are used to seeing, such as using 'I' to refer to themselves. Until you have established yourself as a researcher and published scholarly writer, you might want to show that you can master the basic structural conventions before you start challenging them to any substantial degree. Moreover, having a basic idea of structure – what the reader expects from you – can help you avoid the types of bad academic writing described in Chapter 1.

When it comes to structure, the broad conventions for the genre of the journal article are fairly consistent across disciplines: we expect the abstract to be followed by some introductory remarks, we expect the introductory remarks to be followed by some sort of background describing the state of knowledge and what's missing, we then expect the main body of the paper, and finally we expect it to end with some kind of conclusion. While it is likely that some of the articles that stick out in your mind the most might be ones that specifically challenge these conventions, the point of these conventions is that they facilitate scholarly communication much in the same way that it is easier to talk to someone from your own culture who does not encroach on your personal space or in any other way distract you from the content of the conversation by inadvertently appearing rude or strange.

Within these broad conventions, however, there is far more latitude in structure than most researchers are aware of. In the humanities and social sciences, you will see both essay style and IMRAD (*introduction, method, results* and *discussion*) – and many different things in between. Indeed, rather than thinking of essay and IMRAD as two distinct categories, it is perhaps more useful to see them as outer points on a scale; you might see the 'purest' examples of essay written by philosophers (a continuous argument, without section breaks) or those who develop theory in any of the other disciplines, and the 'purest' examples of IMRAD written by anyone doing quantitative research, but most social science research seems to fall somewhere in-between (see Figure 6.1).

While I don't think I have ever seen a philosopher use IMRAD, even pure quantitative researchers often have structural elements that resemble essay (such as in their introduction). The truth is that academic structure is far less constraining than many would believe – just take a quick look at some of the articles you have on your desk. Although some journals have specific preferences and some disciplines or methodological approaches have particular traditions, the range of possibility is far greater than you would expect.

Figure 6.1 The structural continuum in social science

With that in mind, the next section revisits the structural elements that comprise the IMRAD format: not because they are the only structural elements available to us, but because in my mind they represent the bare minimum of what you need to communicate to your reader before they will understand what you are trying to say. Somewhere, at some point, no matter how theoretical or abstract your research, your paper has to explain:

- What you are trying to do
- How you set about doing it
- What you found
- What it means

IMRAD: THE LOAD-BEARING BEAMS OF STRUCTURE

IMRAD gives us four sets of questions that mirror the bare minimum of what the reader needs to understand to appreciate the point you are trying to make:

Like the load-bearing beams in your house, the basic elements of structure in your article need to be strong or your argument will collapse.

- *Introduction*: What is your question, and why is it a good one? How does your question fit in to a larger conversation? How is it relevant?
- *Method*: How did you go about answering your question? What tools did you use? Through which conceptual lenses did you view your material?
- *Results*: What did you find? What is new here? How does this support your argument?
- *Discussion*: What does all this mean? How are you pushing the conversation further?

This is why it is useful to think of IMRAD as four sets of questions, rather than a recipe for organization. A religious philosopher won't need a whole methods section to explain how he set out to find an answer to his question about how Thomas Aquinas defines a 'just war', but he does need to explain to us which Aquinas texts he was looking at and how he interpreted what he found – and this might well be integrated into the introduction. Most qualitative researchers do not separate the presentation of their findings from the interpretations of their findings, so those sections might be merged – but they do need to do both of these things somewhere.

The point I want to make here is that, regardless of your discipline or methodological approach, regardless of the journal you publish in, these basic functions of IMRAD correspond to the basic questions any reader will ask of your work in order to understand what you are saying – and, more important, what it means. Each element of structure, its function and its significance for the reader are discussed below.

Abstract

Although not included in the IMRAD acronym, the abstract is an essential part of your structure. The abstract is the only part of your structure that is expected to function as a self-contained unit (which is probably why it is left out of 'IMRAD'). Many scholars underestimate its importance. This is a mistake. The abstract condenses your work into its smallest possible form so that the reader can decide whether or not your paper warrants further reading. Sometimes, if not most times, this is all the reader will ever see of your work. Abstracts are often posted on the Internet or other places where scholars can access them. If the article sounds relevant, they may choose to download or order the full text version. Unlike the abstract, the full text is unlikely to be free of charge. Readers may have to subscribe to the journal or pay a fee to obtain a copy. Or they may have to track it down at their university library. The decision of whether or not to take that extra step rests on the strength of your abstract.

For this reason, the abstract is not a place to be coy. It is not a place to say, 'We found something interesting but we won't tell you what it is unless you make the effort to find and read the whole article.' At the very least, the abstract needs to contain your entire core argument: both your research question *and* your thesis statement, both your aims *and* your findings.

Beyond that, what you decide to include depends mostly on the conventions of your discipline and the constraints and preferences of your target journal. Some journals allow lengthy abstracts of up to 300 words. Others allow only a miserly 150. For some journals and disciplines, a sentence about your method is mandatory. For others, method is inconsequential unless the method itself is the main point of the article.

When you write your abstract is also something to consider. Some people prefer to write it early and use it as a kind of outline (which is not unlike pasting your core argument to the wall next to your monitor). Others prefer to write it after they have finished writing the article. But no matter when you write it, make sure that it is the last thing you *revise* before you send your work off. The abstract is the closest the reader will ever come to seeing your research question and thesis statement in their purest form. Because you may have changed direction while you were writing, you have to make sure that your abstract accurately reflects the core argument of your paper *now*, not as it was when you first wrote the abstract. If you have been diligent about updating your research question and thesis statement regularly, this will be a simple task (see Chapter 5).

Introduction: What is your question, and why is it a good one?

While the introduction may not feel like the most difficult section to write, it is by far the most difficult to write *well* because it requires you to stop thinking so much about what is in your own head and start thinking about who your readers are and how you can get them to pay attention to you and the story you want to tell. Its function is relatively straightforward: if a journal article represents your contribution to a larger scholarly conversation, then the introduction lets your audience know where you fit into that conversation. It sets the stage for the main part of your story. This is a three-step process. First, you indicate *which* conversation you are participating in; second, you demonstrate a knowledge gap in that conversation; and, third, you show how answering your research question will help fill that knowledge gap. These steps are described in more detail below.

Step 1: Indicate which discourse you are participating in

The more involved you are in your research, the more banal and obvious it may seem to you – especially the background material. What's hard to remember is that the reader is not in that same place. To get a feel of what it is like for your reader, imagine sitting in your office when someone suddenly bursts in and blurts out, 'Twelve!' Your natural reaction will be some variation of 'Huh?' But if they knock first, allowing you time to divert your attention from whatever is keeping you occupied at the moment, and then kindly provide some background, like 'Remember you were asking me how many people had signed up for the seminar next week?' you will be able to put 'Twelve' into its proper context. You can then respond more appropriately: 'Thanks, Bill! I'll make sure I have enough handouts.' Leaping right into your findings – or sometimes even your research question – is the equivalent of barging through the door and shouting 'Twelve!' at someone. They cannot possibly grasp the significance of what you are saying until they have some context to put it in. Almost any scholarly finding is incomprehensible out of context ('My frogs are blue!'), and it is the job of your introduction to supply enough context so that the reader says, 'OK, I see where you are going', instead of 'Huh?'

Sometimes pinpointing the discourse you want to participate in is more difficult than you might expect; your topic may be relevant for several different discourses (see discussion in Chapter 5 about finding your 'X'). Say you are trying to argue that the reason carbon capture and storage (CCS) technologies have not kept pace with, for example, mobile phone technologies is that CCS has the characteristics of a public good – which means that everyone is hoping someone else will do the work of developing the technology that everyone will benefit from. For you to decide which discourse you want to take part in, you have to have a clear vision of who you are talking to. If you are talking to economists, the context for your argument may be public goods theory. If you are talking to decision-makers, the context for your argument may be post-2012 climate agreements that focus on technology development rather than abatement. If you are talking to social anthropologists, who normally distrust the top-down approach economists take, you can still take a point of departure in public goods theory, but your point of departure will be *introducing* public goods theory rather than embracing it and exploring its finer points.

Likewise, if you are looking at the dominant metaphors in the films of Ingmar Bergman, your point of departure could be either the general discourse on cinematic metaphor, or the discourse on Ingmar Bergman, or even the discourse on the social history of postwar Europe – depending on your audience and the specific scholarly discourse you want to participate in.

Step 2: Demonstrate a knowledge gap

When you are providing the background for the discourse that frames your research question, it is important to remember that not all background is created equal. In scholarly discourse, the background that matters the most is that which demonstrates a gap or tension in our cumulative knowledge. Perhaps there is a lot of existing theory but few concrete observations. Perhaps there are many observations but little existing theory. Maybe there is a discrepancy between observation and theory, or between what two different theorists have argued, or between what two different sets of observations show. In other words, demonstrate your knowledge of the field with a focus on pointing out an inconsistency or a hole in what has already been established, and explaining why this hole or inconsistency is *important*. This is what Swales calls *carving out a research space* (CARS) (see the list of 'Further reading' at the end of this chapter). We not only need to see the puzzle, but we also have to feel motivated to find the missing pieces. It is not enough, for example, to say, 'We know how many left-handed people live in California; we also know how many people have bought a car in the last year.

What we don't know is how many left-handed people bought cars, and if it is proportional to the percentage of left-handed people in the general population.' Most readers will be thinking, 'So what?' Your job is to show why filling this particular knowledge gap matters.

Try this: Tailoring your introduction to your audience

More than any other section of your paper, your introduction has to be specifically tailored to your audience based on how much they know, what they are likely to be sceptical about, what they will use your writing for, and what they are interested in. With your current research in mind, look at the portraits of the people below and imagine yourself explaining your work to each of them. How will you get them interested? How does changing who you are looking at change the way you would frame your argument?

Describing a knowledge gap to your readers means you have to start by giving them an overview of the current state of knowledge. Explaining the current state of knowledge gives novice writers no end of trouble, particularly when it comes to deciding how many references to include and how much detail is necessary.

The problem with references can be traced back to when we were students, when our underlying motivation was to convince our professors that we had actually done the required reading. The incentive was to cite absolutely every book and journal we had ever read plus a few more we felt like we ought to have read. Or perhaps we took the rebellious route: citing no one else at all because we believed our argument should rest on its own merit and we did not want to play the name-dropping game. Both of these strategies miss the point entirely. It's not about impressing the reader with what you have read; it's about locating your argument in an ongoing scholarly discourse. In a real-life conversation, you don't need to repeat what the person before you just said because there is no lapse in time, and presumably everyone in the room heard it as well. In the scholarly conversation, a year or two (or ten, or more) may elapse between the time someone says something and the time someone else responds to it. If you merely pick up where the others left off, your readers will feel as if they have walked in on the middle of someone else's conversation. So some recap is necessary: 'Smith says A, Jones says B, I will argue C.' What makes this more complex is that Smith and Jones may not have even been talking to each other: they might be from different disciplines or sub-fields, but the points that they make are both relevant in the context of your research, so you bring them together and show how they each contribute a piece of the puzzle. You do not need to cite every source you've read – only the ones that specifically help you draw the shape of the puzzle for your reader, where the different pieces fit in and which pieces are still missing.

The same can be said about how much background detail you should provide in your introduction: just enough to show the reader the contours of the puzzle. You will always have more detail than you can use. If you are showing a discrepancy between something one theorist has argued and the observations you have made, you do not need to give your reader the entire history of everything the theorist has ever argued, nor do you have to report every single one of your observations. Stick to the ones that are the most relevant. It is understandable that some of this detail will have been difficult to come by – but your readers don't care that it took you two weeks to track down a particular fact. They only care whether it makes the context clearer or not. If you uncritically put in everything you know, you will quickly fall into the background trap and drag your readers down with you, making it impossible for anyone to see the main point.

Keep in mind that while it is important to demonstrate a gap, overstating its size (or importance) will not help your cause. If you bombastically state that 'no research on this has ever been done before', your readers might be less inclined to believe you've unearthed a completely new topic and more inclined to suspect that you do not know how to use a library. And if it is true that absolutely no research has been done on that topic before, you will have to answer the question of why this is the case. An utter absence of research on a particular topic could indicate that it is not all that interesting (for example, I found no existing research on the correlation between shoelaces and college aptitude), in which case you will have to argue the relevance. On the other hand, it could also indicate that something has happened to suddenly make such research possible – such as a discovery of new archives or development of a new measuring instrument. More likely, you have simply been unable to find existing research – perhaps because it is not published in the languages you are familiar with. In any case, you are better off not claiming that 'nothing has been done', but rather showing how your work builds on and extends the conversation, and suggesting areas that need further exploration: rather than saying 'Nobody has ever done any research at all on how school children in Colombia imagine their futures', say 'This study builds on the work of Robinson (2005) but looks at school children in Colombia rather than North America. This will help shed light on the importance of the cultural and socioeconomic context in creating frameworks for imagining our future selves.'

Step 3: Show how answering your research question can help fill that gap

Once you have presented an important gap in established knowledge, your reader will be ready to hear how you intend to fill that gap. Knowledge gaps are generally too big for a single research question to fill, so your job is not to convince your reader that you will provide a definitive answer. Just as it is important to not overstate the gap itself, you need to restrain yourself from making the claim that answering the question you ask will fill the gap so completely that everyone can pack up and go home because this conversation is now over. Just show how your contribution fits into the puzzle, and why your particular piece matters. Take us down the logical path you took to get from the broader knowledge gap to your particular research question. To continue with the above example:

> We know a lot about the role of elementary schools in shaping how children imagine their future selves. Robinson (2005), for example, conducted an influential study on how school children think about and imagine their futures. She argues that their 'menu of possibilities' is shaped by their sense of self-efficacy as students. However, little is known about the role that cultural and socioeconomic background plays. Robinson's study looked only at children in North America, and although they came from different parts of the US and had different racial backgrounds, they were all American citizens with the United States as a point of reference. This study looks at school children in Colombia, and explores how a completely different frame of reference influences the 'menu of possibilities'.

The logic here is that there is no way a single study can address all the possible cultural and socioeconomic variations in every region of the world. Here, the authors have to explain in what way the Colombian case would add to this discussion, and they need only make the argument that the Colombian context is different, and that this context could explain a different 'menu of possibilities'. The aim is not to come up with the 'correct' menu and suggest that the case of Colombia is the right way of seeing things, but only to suggest that changing the context could change the menu – and hence that this case will shed light on the broader question of the role of culture and socioeconomic background. They open up for other authors to continue the conversation by adding cases from different countries.

Once you have demonstrated that the answer to your question will help fill an important knowledge gap, you face the dilemma of whether or not you should reveal your answer in the introduction or wait until the conclusion. It is tempting to go the Agatha Christie route: keep the reader in suspense until you reveal the answer at the very end in a sudden and stunning twist. But we are not writing a mystery novel, and it is a mistake to think that your readers will only continue to read as long as they are kept in the dark. When we read as scholars, we generally want to get the essential information as quickly as possible and with minimal exertion, and we keep reading because we want to see in more detail how it all hangs together. Your thesis statement is not like a football score: it won't ruin the game by knowing it in advance. Scholars are unlikely to stop reading if the introduction tells them: 'We argue that the real cause of the Second World War was a pasta shortage in Italy.' On the contrary, this is likely to make them sit up and pay attention. Knowing where the author is headed allows readers to sort the incoming information into useful categories: 'important', 'useful', 'background', 'transition' and so on. This will allow them to read more actively: 'Aha, she's going to argue that fluctuations in the pigeon population in New York City can be explained by similar fluctuations in the stock market. I wonder what kind of evidence she will use.' We can only evaluate evidence when we know what it is supposed to be evidence *of* (see Chapter 3 'Demonstrating an "Open Mind"').

A similar dilemma is to what extent you should reveal to the reader the organization of your paper. It is common at the end of your introduction to provide a sort of map for the rest of the paper: what the remaining sections will cover. But, here, you have the choice between offering the obvious ('First, I will introduce my topic and provide some background. Second, I will describe my method, followed by my findings. Finally, I will conclude with a conclusion'), or giving the reader something a little more useful – an understanding of not only where we are going, but why. Many authors balk at providing such information so early. But as with keeping your reader in the dark about your thesis statement, withholding from your reader the motivation for the organization of your paper is more likely to create frustration than suspense. To illustrate: if your research question is 'How does the role of science affect how we understand ourselves in the universe at a mythological level?' you could write:

> First, I will look into the ancient mythologies; then I will explore the budding science of the Early Modern period. Finally, I will look into the development of science as we know it to explore our perception of our world.

Not only does this seem to promise one of the world's longest papers (since you have not explained what your focus will be in each of these broad categories), but you have not explained how these steps are connected: it is merely a table of contents in sentence form. While many readers expect little more, it is possible to stretch a bit further – to use this paragraph to outline your argument itself. You do this by concentrating not just on the general role of each section (such as 'method' or 'findings'), but on the main point that particular section makes, and how it contributes to your overall argument. Drawing from the same example above, we can get something like this:

> The discovery that the earth revolves around the sun has dramatically changed the way we perceive ourselves in the universe. First, I show how ancient mythologies placed the Earth at the centre of the universe. I then show how Galileo's heliocentric view of the universe changed the very way we perceive ourselves in nature. I argue that science and myth are not two separate universes, but are in fact very much interrelated.

It may take a few more words, but it gives your reader an idea not only of where you are going, but also why.

Method: How did you get to your answer?

Remember when you were in school and the purpose of maths changed from having the right answer to showing the teacher how you got that answer? The method section is much the same. It's one thing to have an argument, another thing to show the reader how you got there: the approach you took, the tools you used, and the conceptual framework that helped you make sense of what you were seeing in your data. Just as your introduction has the main responsibility for establishing the relevance of your inquiry, the methods section has the main responsibility for establishing its *credibility*. Before a reader can decide whether or not to believe your findings and conclusion, he or she has to know how you got there. You need to describe the elements that will convince your reader that the steps you took were the right ones – the most logical and fruitful approach under the circumstances.

The challenge in writing a methods section is to describe your research design to someone else. After you have worked on a project long enough, the choices you make, the terminology you use, the theory you draw from all seem obvious. But they aren't obvious to the reader. Chapter 3 discusses in more detail some concerns about research design; here, I look at the kinds of things your reader needs to know about your work to be able to judge its soundness.

If your research is empirical in nature, and particularly if it is quantitative, then describing your method is fairly straightforward. Your main concern will be reproducibility. For example, if you have discovered that longevity can be predicted by the number of pets a person has owned, then what you need to do is to explain exactly how you defined 'pet' and how you measured 'longevity'. This makes it possible for other researchers to try the same thing to see if they get the same result. It also makes it easier for others to see how they can take your research a step further.

If your research is qualitative, describing your method may be a little more difficult. Qualitative research typically uses such methods as case studies, interviews and observation. While complex quantitative work often includes a description of a type of method that might be unfamiliar to the reader ('We used the Prestrud method, which implies dividing the subjects alphabetically into six groups, dividing the median age of each group by the cross sum of the oldest group member's birth date, and then comparing the chi-square across groups'), the methods used in qualitative work are more well known. This means that your readers seldom need a description of the method per se; what they need is a description of how exactly you implemented the method in your study. For example, if you have used a case study approach, you do not need to write 'a case study is an in-depth examination of a particular individual or situation'. What you do need to write about is your particular case or cases: How did you pick your cases? Why did you decide to compare Brazil and Finland? Are they supposed to be very different or very similar? Why not more countries? Or why not just one? What kind of data did you focus on? What is the unit of analysis? What kind of information did you look for? The same goes for other common methods: you do not need to explain what an interview is; you do need to explain who you interviewed and what you asked them. How did you pick your informants? What kind of interview guide did you use? How long did the interviews take?

The most difficult methods to describe are those used in non-empirical research – that is, research that is more theoretical or philosophical in nature. Many scholars associate the word 'method' with formal statistical analysis, so those working primarily with ideas often don't even think they have a method: 'We just read stuff and think about it.' But even 'reading stuff and thinking about it' should be methodical. You make very active decisions about, say, the period you will be looking at, the theoretical material you consider relevant, the various approaches you could choose from, and the concepts that are likely to play a key role in your analysis. This is what your reader needs to know. So, when you do non-empirical work, describing your method focuses not on the concrete activities you carried out (as would be the case in experimental work), but rather on the train of thought for your analysis and the lenses through which you view your subject matter. For example, you do not write, 'I went to the library and checked out all the biographies of Shakespeare. I read them all and then went to a café. As I was drinking my forty-seventh double-espresso, I had a revelation: Shakespeare had to have been a woman.' Rather, you write something along the lines of: 'Here, I analyze what is known about Shakespeare's education and economic status and interpret it in the light of the gender roles of the time.' You will then elaborate on what you mean by education, economic status and gender roles, and what criteria you used to classify what you found.

Keep in mind that in your method section you describe not only how you gathered the data, but also how you analyzed it. Just telling us the computer program you used is not sufficient. 'I analyzed the data using NVivo' is about as informative as saying 'I wrote my paper using Microsoft Word.' *How* did you analyze the data? What were you looking for in your data? What codes did you use? Did you count instances of things people said, or were you looking for a range of themes? Were you only interested in things that most of your informants said? What if a particular viewpoint was expressed by only one person? How did you know what you were looking at? Likewise, it is singularly unhelpful to tell your reader that 'themes emerged' in the data you were coding (whether you used software or not). Themes 'emerge' because you are looking for something. Sometimes you find things that you did not expect to see, and here it is very tempting to say that the themes just popped out entirely on their own. It is far more helpful, however, to explain to your reader how you directed your gaze. For example:

> While interviewing the ICU nurses about how they manage stress, I looked for how they saw their own responsibility. I noticed that the women seemed to blame themselves for unfortunate outcomes whereas the male nurses tended to blame others. I then recoded the interviews looking for instances of 'self-blame' and 'blaming others' and actually found that self-blame seemed to be more related to seniority than to gender.

In this case, the issue of blame might not have been on the radar in the initial interview, but it became visible because the researcher was looking for the extent to which nurses felt responsible for making decisions.

When you are describing how you went about conducting your research – whether your research is empirical or non-empirical, qualitative or quantitative – an essential and often overlooked step is to define important terms and concepts. Scholarship is filled with terms that are vague, have several meanings, have different meanings for different disciplines, or have a separate meaning for the layperson.

Consider the following sentence: 'We found that juveniles from non-traditional family structures were significantly at risk for displaying habitual criminal behaviour.' This is a sentence that most of us think we understand. But if we start checking around with one another, we might find that we all have different interpretations. For you, 'juvenile' might mean anyone from age 6 to age 19, whereas I might have a more limited definition that only includes ages 13 through 16. And what's a 'non-traditional family structure'? A hundred years ago it was common for a household to include in-laws, grandparents or other more distant relatives. The nuclear family – a father, a mother and their children – as a basis of a household is a fairly modern concept. And today, while we may consider the nuclear family to be the norm, a good percentage of households consist of single parents, or parents who have remarried and brought children from a previous marriage into the household, or single-sex parents, or children being raised by grandparents, adoptive parents or foster parents. While we're at it, just what exactly do we mean by 'criminal behaviour'? Felonies? Misdemeanours? Antisocial behaviour? Does it count if you are not caught? And how many times do you have to do it before it becomes 'habitual'? What about 'at risk'? Finally, the word 'significantly' is worth looking at: what is significant in one type of method is not significant in another. The author of this sentence will have to define what each of these problematic terms means *in the context of her paper*. She does not need to trace the history of the concept of criminal behaviour and describe at length every possible way to interpret it. She need merely write something along the lines of the following: 'In this paper, "criminal behaviour" is understood as any activity that is considered punishable by fine or sentencing by law.' If your particular choice of definition could be considered controversial, you need not take up space in the body of your paper discussing the implications. It is sufficient to include a footnote that says something like: 'See Smith 2004; Jones 2005; and Johnson 2005, for a discussion of alternative definitions. Although they make good arguments for expanding the definition to include disruptive behaviour, constraints on data collection limit us to the current definition.'

Many of your terms may also have to be operationalized. This means that you are going to have to explain how you intend to identify or measure a concept that is so abstract that it cannot be measured directly. Say you want to ask whether children from loving families perform better in school. How are you going to identify 'a loving family'? How are you going to measure the child's performance at school?

Because your method section is so intimately connected with research design, the earlier you can start writing it the better. Often, a definition or a method of operationalization will seem precise enough in the design stage, but when you face the challenge of writing it down so that someone else can understand it, you discover weaknesses. This is particularly true in the social sciences, the humanities or any kind of analytical or theoretical research.

Results: What did you find?

The results section is perhaps the least problematic of any section, particularly for quantitative research. This is where most researchers feel the most confident. Your goal is to describe faithfully what you found, the evidence on which you will base your argument. In other words, you answer the question: 'What results did my method generate?' Here, there are three main challenges.

First, you need to sort the important from the interesting or merely existing findings. If you have conducted a complex empirical study, you may have far more findings than you can fully do justice to. Not all findings are of equal importance, and you may have to decide which ones are worth spending some time on describing. Note that there is a big difference between 'most important' and 'best support your hypothesis'. I argued earlier that the desire to appear objective often tempts scholars to include every single fact, regardless of its importance (see Chapter 3). A comprehensive array of facts does indeed show diligence, but it has the unfortunate side effect of drowning important findings in a sea of less interesting ones. Your job as a conscientious and objective scholar is to select and present the findings that are the most important, whether they support your hypothesis or not.

Your second challenge is to present your findings in an order that makes sense, particularly given the logic of your core argument (and your point of departure in a scholarly discourse). Say you are looking at images of women in the US media from 1920 to 2000. You want to argue that the more conservative the political climate, the more traditionally feminine women appear in advertising. You could present your results as follows:

> In 1950, the climate was conservative and women's breasts were large. Hair was generally longer in 1940. In 1920, hair was short and women had just got the right to vote. In the 1980s, when Reagan was president, large shoulder pads were popular. Women's hips have generally been portrayed as slimmer relative to their waist since the 1970s.

All of these findings are interesting, but the order in which they are presented is confusing. They have nothing to do with each other and are not easy to interpret in the light of the core argument. Several approaches are possible, but regardless of which one you settle on, pick an organization principle that makes sense for your general argument. For example:

> The peak conservative periods identified in the study were the 1950s and the 1980s (in particular during Ronald Reagan's two terms as president). During both periods, the ratios between breasts and waists and between hips and waists were relatively high. That is, a more hourglass figure was portrayed. In the 1920s (when women received the vote) and the 1970s, which were considered peak periods of women's activism, female figures in the media were far more androgynous, with slimmer hips and smaller breasts relative to their waists. Trends in hair are more difficult to interpret: short hair was popular during the liberal 1920s, but during the similarly liberal 1970s long hair was popular.

The third and perhaps greatest challenge in presenting your results is to make clear the distinction between what you found and what you think it means. The reader needs to know exactly where your interpretation comes into the picture (see Chapter 3). Consider the difference between these two sentences:

'We found that 42% of the respondents were depressed', and 'We found that 42% of the respondents demonstrated at least three out of five of our indicators for depression.' In the first, the author leaps straight into the conclusion; in the second, the author states the results from which he will draw a conclusion.

In quantitative research, the results are usually presented in a different section than the interpretations of the results; in qualitative work, they are usually woven together, which can make the difference between them difficult for even you to see. In your head, there might be little difference between 'Jodi got angry' and 'Jodi gathered her books together, shouted that the interview was now over, and ran out of the room, slamming the door behind her.' But the former is an interpretation; the latter is a description. Writing that 'Jodi appeared angry when she stormed out the door in the middle of our interview' at least signals to your reader that you are interpreting the actions of your informant.

For non-empirical work, the difference between a result and an interpretation is even harder to see. Non-empirical work in particular is about making reasonable, logical deductions – many of which are based on other reasonable, logical deductions, not concrete facts. The onus is on you as a writer to always make clear the foundation on which your deductions are based. Say you use Freudian dream interpretation to argue that Mark Twain was a repressed homosexual. If an outraged reader is to respond appropriately, she needs to know whether to criticize your interpretation of the theory and write, 'The author clearly does not understand what Freud meant', or to challenge the theory itself and write, 'Freudian dream interpretation can be used to make anyone seem like a repressed homosexual. A more nuanced dream interpretation can be made using Jungian symbology.'

Discussion: What does it mean?

The main goals of your discussion or conclusion are to answer the question you asked at the beginning, and to place that answer in the context of the conversation you referred to in your introduction. In other words, you need to ask, 'What is the answer to my question, and what does this answer mean for the scholarly discourse?' Having a clear thesis statement gives you a specific destination and will make it easier to conclude with something meaningful, rather than just stop because you've run out of air (or reached the word limit).

If we authors get sidetracked, there is little hope for our readers. Readers have it hard enough; you are lucky if your readers remember *one* thing about your article a few days after reading it. If you have a very complex argument, filled with detailed empirical evidence, and are unable to make clear what your main point is, your readers may not be able to retain anything apart from, say, your invention of the term 'reflexive post-postmodernism' or the incomprehensible figure that looked like an octopus. But if you are able to state your overall argument clearly and concisely, then your readers might retain enough to say to themselves a few weeks later, 'Oh, yes, Gates wrote about how much conflict reduces a state's ability to reach the UN Millennium Development Goals.' They may not remember the specific details of the exact per cent by which infant mortality was increased, but because they remember the key point, they may be motivated to look it up.

A reasonable question to ask yourself in writing your discussion is to what extent you need to summarize your findings or anything else you have established earlier. Indeed, a common formula for writing scientific papers is: 'Say what I'm going to say, say it, and then say what I've said.' Certainly this is a useful rule of thumb for a longer work, like a book or a dissertation. But for a short piece like a journal article, this is less of a recipe for clarity and more a recipe for tedium. The introduction is not just about 'saying what you are going to say' but rather about 'saying why what you are going to say is important'; likewise, the conclusion is not just about summarizing your findings but also about explaining what they mean. Summarizing your key points can help you do this. But what is important here is to focus on the highlights, the main pieces of evidence or insight that allow you to draw your conclusion. Summarizing for the sake of summarizing is just as boring and pointless for the reader as it is for you – after all, the thing you are summarizing was probably said only a page or so earlier.

Once you make sure your question is sufficiently answered, your main concern is the 'So what?' factor. If your reader gets through your discussion and still sits there thinking, 'So what?' you have failed. If your introduction successfully zeroes in on a particular knowledge gap in the wider scientific dialogue and then presents your particular research question, your discussion can expand the focus again by discussing the implications of your conclusions for the greater discourse. One way to do this is to compare your findings and conclusions to those of others. If your findings are different, you can speculate about why. Another way is to suggest directions for future research. Remember that even if your findings are inconclusive, they can still be important to the scholarly dialogue. For example, you can suggest ways in which future research might improve the method or the data so that future findings can be more definitive. And if you are working in applied research you can speculate on the implications of your work for 'the real world', whether that be policy, clinical practice or what have you. (Just make sure you make the foundation for any recommendations transparent! See Chapters 3 and 5.)

When writing your concluding section, keep in mind that your final sentence and paragraph have special power. Because of their position, they will leave a stronger impression on the reader than any sentence or paragraph buried in the middle of your paper – or even in the middle of your conclusion. For this reason, try to avoid ending with a review of all the uncertainties associated with your argument. As a good researcher, you should discuss your uncertainties and limitations, and this final section is a good place to put them. But for the reader, there is a big difference between presenting your limitations earlier in this section and ending with them. Discussing them earlier will leave the reader with the impression that you have taken them fully into account, but that your main conclusion holds. If you leave them to the last paragraph, your reader will be left with a sense of doubt. Instead, use the powerful position of the last sentence to your advantage: end with a version of your thesis statement, or with a statement about what it means – and perhaps 'where to go from here'.

Tips

Don't overdo the discussion of limitations. Every study has some limitations: you can always interview more people, most of us hope for a better response rate and so on. Discuss the limitations that may have had a bearing on the outcome.

Never just say 'more research is needed'. You have just wasted four words. If you want to say something about more research being needed, be specific and connect it to the work you just did. For example, 'Based on my findings that juvenile delinquents often cited a preference for team sports over individual sports, future research could look into the relationship between individual sports and self-efficacy.'

FROM GENERAL STRUCTURE TO CONCRETE ORGANIZATION

The point I made at the beginning of this chapter is that IMRAD represents the load-bearing beams of structure for a scholarly argument: you introduce your work by showing the reader where your question fits into the ongoing discourse; you show them the lenses through which you viewed your material and the instruments you used to help you answer your question; you show them what you found; and you tell them what you think it means. How you actually organize this into sections is up to you. When you get down to the business of organizing, you need to think about what you are trying to achieve in each section. For example, I often get the question, 'Where should I put my literature review?' It is true that at some point you will have to give the reader some background on the ongoing discourse in which you are participating. But where you put this depends on what it is you are trying to achieve with that literature review. If it functions as a recap of the conversation to set the stage for the research question, then it belongs in the introduction. But if it is highly theoretical and contains concepts that you intend to use actively in your analysis, it might be more relevant to think of the literature review as a kind of method and to place it in a section called 'Theoretical framework'. In still other cases, the entire body of the paper might be a literature review. And it is possible that no separate literature review is necessary – that a discussion of previous work can be woven throughout the entire article.

Likewise, explaining *how* you set out to answer your question may not require an entire section called 'Method'. In non-empirical research, there is seldom such a section. But not having a section called 'Method' does not mean you have no method. You may choose to have a section called 'Conceptual framework' or 'Theoretical background' or something similar. You may even decide not to have a separate section at all, perhaps integrating the discussion of method into your introduction. This will depend on your audience and your research question. The only thing that matters is whether or not you have made it possible for your reader to trace *how* you reached the conclusion you reached.

What is important is that you organize your structure on the basis of what your audience expects and needs, the surrounding scholarly dialogue and your core argument. Your audience will determine how much, and what type of, background information you have to provide, as well as the particular knowledge gap you choose to identify. For example, if you are writing for an interdisciplinary, sector-specific journal, you might want to take your point of departure in a concrete finding. A single-discipline journal, on the other hand, might be more receptive to a theoretical point of departure. The rest of your structure is built around your core argument: every structural element should either justify your research question in the context of the scholarly discourse or provide evidence or support for your thesis statement. How you break down your argument and divide it up into concrete sections will depend entirely on the path you choose to take.

RESTRUCTURING: RESHUFFLING THE DECK

There is always more than one way to tell a story. A good structure makes your argument more comprehensible to the reader; and the process of developing the right structure helps you fine-tune your argument. In designing your structure, you line up your research question with your conclusions, arrange your data in meaningful groups, and see whether or not it all hangs together.

Try this: Revealing your structure

Try going systematically through your paper, asking yourself what the function of each paragraph or section is. Write each one down on a sticky note. For example: 'Here, I am trying to show the connection between A and B', or 'This is a transition from C to D', or 'Here, I am trying to make connections between the theory introduced in section 2 to the background presented in section 3.' Then read through your paper a section at a time. Is the section doing what it is supposed to be doing? Or have you gotten off track?

An alternative way to reveal your structure is to use a form of colour coding, either on your monitor or on a printout. Say you are discussing the pros and cons of something and you notice to your dismay that you talk about these pros and cons all over the place. You go back and forth so much that reading it is like watching a tennis match. To fix this, you can read through and highlight all the pros with yellow and all the cons with blue. Then you can cut and paste so that all the yellow bits are in one section and all the blue bits are in another.

Very often you will discover that it *doesn't* hang together, whereupon you have to consider alternative forms of organization. Revising your research question and tweaking your thesis statement almost guarantee that you will have to rethink your structure, and sometimes you need to reconsider your approach even if your core argument has remained stable.

The truest thing I can say about restructuring is that making the decision to restructure is usually more agonizing than carrying it out. You may be close to the maximum word count for your paper. Because deadlines are looming and you really don't fancy ripping your paper apart and starting all over again, you may repress whatever qualms you have and hope no one else will notice. You tell yourself you can just submit it as is, and if the reviewers say to reorganize, then you will think about it. You tell yourself anything you can think of to avoid having to go back and start (almost) from scratch. But reorganizing doesn't have to be that painful. Sometimes it's a tremendous relief. You wouldn't even have been considering the possibility if you hadn't suspected that something wasn't working. Deep down you know that reorganizing will give you a better paper.

Start by sketching an outline of your new structure. First, save your document under a new name, and work with that. (If the new structure doesn't work out, you can go back to your old one.) Second, cut and paste with abandon. Don't worry about the lack of transitions between paragraphs or sections at this point. Just move things around to go with your new outline. Third, give it a quick read-through. Does it work better? If it does, *now* you can go back and fix the transitions. If the structure makes more sense, then working on the transitions and gaps is likely to be a pleasure. If your deadline allows, it might help to let some time elapse before you start working on the details of your new structure, just so you get a chance to get your mind fully around your new way of thinking. Try walking around for a couple of days with the new structure in your head. This can help you refine or expand it before you get down to further revision.

One last word about structure: your structure should ultimately serve your core argument. When you are developing or evaluating your structure, you need to be ruthless at every step about what belongs and what doesn't. If you have written something (developed a point, described an example, elaborated some detail, presented some data and so forth) that does not push your article toward your destination, it needs to go. Some people call this 'killing your darlings', but it need not be as final, or as traumatic, as all that. Just because a paragraph has to leave your article, it doesn't have to leave your life. Start a new file on your computer for bits and pieces that didn't belong in the article they sprouted from. Someday they may engender a new article.

Remember

Build your paper around your core argument by making sure you fulfil all the main functions of structure:

- Introduce your research question and demonstrate its relevance by connecting it to an ongoing scholarly discourse and showing how it addresses a gap in the knowledge.
- Explain your approach to answering your question, the instruments you used, and the conceptual lenses through which you analyze your material.
- Explain your main findings or line of reasoning, and show how they help answer your question.
- Explain what your argument means for the conversation you are taking part in.

FURTHER READING

- Becker, Howard S. (2008) *Writing for Social Scientists: How to Start and Finish Your Thesis, Book, or Article*, 2nd revd edn, Chicago, IL: University of Chicago Press. Becker's chapter on being terrorized by the literature can be very helpful for writing introductions.
- Booth, Wayne C., Colomb, Gregory G. and Williams, Joseph M. (2008) *The Craft of Research*, 3rd edn, Chicago, IL: University of Chicago Press. Section IV 'Planning, drafting, and revising' is very helpful for helping you think about ways to organize your argument and tell your story.
- Hartley, James (2008) *Academic Writing and Publishing: A Practical Handbook*, London: Routledge. Hartley's view is fairly conservative and very focused on IMRAD. The book provides very good insight into the standard conventions of the journal article.
- Schostak, John and Schostak, Jill (2013) *Writing Research Critically: Developing the Power to Make a Difference*, London: Routledge. Schostak and Schostak have a very alternative view, and provide a refreshing counterpoint to IMRAD.
- Swales, John (1990) *Genre Analysis: English in Academic and Research Settings*, Cambridge: Cambridge University Press. Swales is perhaps the father of genre analysis, and his development of the carving out a research space (CARS) model of the introduction in academic writing has been hugely influential. If you want to read more about academic writing as a genre, and the more specific rhetorical moves that writers make within this genre, this source is invaluable.

SEVEN

Breaking up the grey mass
Headings, figures and tables

No matter how long we spend writing, our paper will have no more than five minutes (if that) to persuade our potential audience to keep reading. Think about all the journal articles that flood your desk, all the articles that are on your 'To Read' list. When you finally sit down to get caught up, how do you attack the pile? Do you slog through each and every one, starting from the beginning and continuing relentlessly to the end, giving each sentence and every footnote your undivided attention? Or do you first spend a few minutes looking at the title, reading the abstract, skimming the introduction, checking out the reference list to see if your name is there, and then flipping through the article looking at the headings, tables and figures? If you are like most scholars, you won't even think about reading the main body of the article until it has passed this initial test. The best way to keep readers riveted for those first crucial minutes is to make sure they can find what they need as they jump around. Few things are as daunting to a potential reader as an endless grey mass with no landmarks to catch the eye. Headings, tables and figures all function both to break up the grey and to allow the reader to navigate quickly around your work.

TITLES: FIRST IMPRESSIONS COUNT

Your title is the first, and sometimes the only, part of your work that your reader gets to see. It is also your first chance to give your reader a glimpse of your main point. If your potential readers are searching a database for relevant works, or skimming through the table of contents of a journal or book, the title is what will make them take a closer look at your work – unless your name alone is likely to stop them in their tracks. This is a very good reason for picking a title that will pique a reader's interest – the so-called sexy or clever title. It appeals to the non-expert in us, the regular human being, and evokes a specific image or feeling that should relate to the content of the article. A metaphor, allusion, quote or saying can form the basis of a good sexy title. Sometimes even a cliché or a twist on a cliché works, such as the classic 'Old wine in new bottles' or 'New wine in old bottles'. The drawback is that the clever title alone seldom reveals enough of what the article is about, which is a serious shortcoming when the main job of the title is to effectively capture the essence of your work. As a result, the reader may not realize the article is relevant and simply skip it. Worse, the potential reader might think the content is frivolous or dubious and decide to pass it by. Unfortunately, it is widely assumed that scholarly writing should be on the dull side, so a snappy title with lively imagery sometimes generates scepticism and general harrumphing. This prejudice is exacerbated if one has encountered too many instances of authors trying for snappy and ending up with silly. Finally, a title that has more imagery than content may result in erroneous indexing. If your target journal or publisher does not ask you for key words, your work may be indexed by a librarian who has nothing more to go on than your title. You may find that your criticism of new radical feminist theory that you cleverly called 'Old whine in new bottles' has been filed under 'toddlers'.

This helps explain why many, if not most, authors go for the more content-rich descriptive title, like 'Peer-group social interaction of visually impaired children'. There is nothing wrong whatsoever with this kind of title. The main job of the title is to convey to the reader what the article or book is about. And it's hard enough to come up with an effective title without having to be clever at the same time.

Moreover, when you put the most important key words in your title, search engines are likely to push your work higher up on the list of hits for searches using those key words. Thinking about key words this way not only increases the chances that other researchers will be able to find your work, but it also forces you to put yourself into the mind of the reader: what would they be looking for that would make my article useful for them? What search words would my ideal reader be likely to use?

Putting your finger on *exactly* what your article or book is about is no trivial task. Finding the perfect title is just like settling on your research question – only harder. (See the text box 'Titles: The good, the bad and the confusing'.) Unlike the formal version of your research question, which is often mostly for your own benefit, a title is the face you present to others. And deciding what this face will be will require you to consider both the preferences of your reader and the preferences of the journal. Your reader wants to know what they are going to get out of reading your work, and the journal wants titles that not only pique the interests of the readers, but also conform to whatever conventions they have established – and are likely to be picked up by search engines.

Titles: The good, the bad and the confusing

There is no magic formula for writing a great title, and what is appealing to one person may be off-putting to another. Below, I list some titles of recent journal articles – some that are purely informative, and others that combine a clever element (with varying degrees of success). The subject matter notwithstanding, which of these titles appeal to you? What separates 'straightforward' from 'dull'? What separates 'clever' from 'confusing'? Do questions work for you? Does length matter? Which ones paint a clear picture in your mind about what the author is saying? Which ones leave you scratching your head?

- Not by the sword alone: Soft power, mass media, and the production of state sovereignty
- Does immigration undermine public support for social policy?
- Small steps for workers, a giant leap for productivity
- Using freedom of information requests to facilitate research
- (Auto)ethnography and cycling
- Personal reflections on cautions and considerations for navigating the path of grounded theory doctoral theses and dissertations: A long walk through a dark forest
- Influenza vaccination campaigns: Is an ounce of prevention worth a pound of cure?
- Tenure, experience, human capital, and wages: A tractable equilibrium search model of wage dynamics
- 'Notable' or 'not able': When are acts of inconsistency rewarded?

A good place to start in your effort to appeal to your reader and give them a good idea of what they will get from reading your article is your core argument – either the question or the answer. Many academics use a more informal version of their research question as a title, although whether or not this is considered a good idea is a matter of taste and disciplinary convention. For some, the question-as-title is considered a poor choice because it makes the reader have to work too hard to find your answer. While I am absolutely in favour of stating the answer early and letting the reader know what your argument will be before you've actually made it, I'm not entirely sure I agree with the ban on questions for titles. If the question is relevant, it seems to me you will want to read it no matter what the answer is: 'Does drinking red wine improve your writing ability?' is a title of an article I think I would download based on the title alone. And if you have your answer visible even in the abstract, then your reader won't have to work hard at all. Opponents to the question-as-title approach prefer the answer-in-title approach: 'Red wine enhances (perception of) writing ability'. In my mind, either of these approaches is vastly superior to the 'noun-string approach': 'Red wine and writing ability'. The problem with the noun-string title is that the reader does not get a sense of the relationship between the nouns, and the result can be a dull, lifeless title that puts readers off. For example, 'Governance, nationhood and institutional state-building'. This might well be a page-turner once you start reading, but three weighty nouns strung together without a clue about the relationship between them just suggests that this will be a very long and incoherent paper, and certainly makes me want to do the opposite of pick it up and start reading it.

The other set of concerns have to do with the stylistic constraints set by the journal or publisher. Some journals impose a strict maximum on the number of characters in a title, which may force you to look for less satisfying short synonyms for the long words you prefer. Some journals don't allow abbreviations in titles; this can pose a tremendous problem if you're writing a paper about an international organization whose spelled-out name might take up half a page. And some journals do not like hanging titles, that is, a title or heading that has two halves separated by a colon, dash or question mark. This is unfortunate because hanging titles can often function well as a compromise between the sexy title and the descriptive title, where one half is more informative and straightforward while the other uses more imagery. For example: 'Playing by ear: Peer-group social interaction of visually impaired children'. So, before you start the final fiddling with your title, make sure you check out the restrictions set by the journal or publisher and the conventions of your subject area. Then you can focus on making sure that the title really reflects the essence of your work. It is a good idea to do this when you are close to being finished. Most likely your argument has changed, or taken on a sharper focus, in the course of the writing, and the title you picked at the beginning may no longer reflect the main point of your work. A good test is to ask someone who has not read your paper to guess what it is about simply on the basis of the title. If it is close to what you've written, then you are on the right track: the ultimate criterion for a good title is that it should give the reader a good idea of what your paper will be about.

Try this: Tailor your title to different audiences

To stimulate your creativity and brainstorm title ideas, try imagining a title for your work tailored to completely different newspapers or magazines aimed at popular audiences, such as *The New York Times*, *The Daily Mail*, *Rolling Stone*, *Time Magazine*, *The Economist*, *Vogue*, *Psychology Today*, *The New Yorker* and so on. This will help you think about not only the main ideas that you want to communicate, but also how you can package them for a given audience. You might end up with an idea you can adapt to a scholarly journal.

HEADINGS: SIGNPOSTS FOR YOUR READER

If the job of the title is to start readers off on the right track, the job of your headings is to keep them there. Perhaps no other tool helps your reader navigate your paper more easily than well-formulated and well-placed headings. But using headings to their best possible advantage takes a bit of practice. Fortunately, there are some fairly straightforward dos and don'ts.

Do make sure your headings actually reflect the content that follows them. This is not as obvious as it sounds. Sometimes a section changes so much between the first and final draft that the content no longer bears much resemblance to the original, and the heading no longer reflects the main point of the section. But this may go unnoticed by you because when you revise, you tend to skip over the headings because you are so focused on the text. Often the heading could use some adjusting to make it more accurately reflect the current version.

Don't add a heading just because you cannot be bothered to think of a good transition sentence. Ideally, your prose should follow logically and smoothly from one paragraph to the next. You put in a heading to mark a major shift or to set off a component of your argument. You do not add a heading just because you can't figure out how to get from one point to the next.

Do try to avoid breaking up your introduction and conclusion into smaller parts. Your introduction and conclusion should read as coherent essays, perhaps even well enough to stand alone.

Don't have headings with no text underneath – if you can help it. Headings are social creatures, and they work best when accompanied by text. Lonely headings are both a graphical affront and jarring for the reader. Say you want to divide your methods section into two subsections: 'Survey' and 'In-depth interviews'. Avoid writing this:

Methods
Survey
The survey consisted of a five-page questionnaire distributed to a randomly selected group of 200 university students.

Try writing something under 'Methods' first:

Methods
This study used a mixed-methods approach: a general survey of a randomly selected group followed by a small number of in-depth interviews of informants who represented specifically selected subgroups.

Survey
The survey consisted of a five-page questionnaire distributed to a randomly selected group of 200 university students.

The text you come up with is often the very text the reader needs to understand how the following parts will fit together. In the above example, the reader might have assumed that the survey was the only method used, so when she started reading about the in-depth interviews she got confused. Knowing from the beginning that there were two parts prepared her for the second part. If it feels impossible to add a sentence that explains why you are subdividing the section almost immediately, you might consider another approach: perhaps you do not need one of those headings at all – for example, an introduction divided into 'Background' and 'Theory' may not need these subheads. However, if the subheads are essential but you cannot come up with a meaningful sentence or two, then it is better to bend this 'rule' than it is to generate useless text. Your ultimate goal is to make things easier on your reader.

Do keep equal-level headings parallel in structure, if you can. This is easiest to explain through example:

Level 1:   Long, detailed heading that is not a full sentence

  Level 2: A short question?

  Level 2: Another short question?

   Level 3:   Word

   Level 3:   Word

Level 1:   Another long, detailed heading that is not a full sentence

  Level 2: Short sentence fragment

   Level 3:   Question?

   Level 3:   Question?

  Level 2: Short sentence fragment

By using a similar grammatical structure in addition to the formatting, you underscore for the reader that certain sections should be grouped logically together. Note that this does not mean that, say, *all* level 2 headings must be parallel in structure, only the level 2 headings that fall under the same level 1 heading. In the example above, the level 2 headings under the *first* level 1 heading were short questions, but under the *second* level 1 heading they were short sentence fragments. When you are working on your final draft, it is a good idea to make an outline – or use the 'Navigation' feature in Microsoft Word, or a similar feature in whatever word processing software you use – to look at just the headings with no other text visible.

This makes it easier for you to see whether the headings work well together. If you can make adjustments in the headings to make equal-level headings more parallel, then do so. But there is no reason to force your headings into the same structure if it really doesn't work. An awkward heading is a far more serious crime than an elegant heading that doesn't quite fit in with its brothers and sisters.

Do check with your target journal about whether they use numbered or non-numbered headings. Numbered headings are headings that are preceded by a number that designates the heading's position in the outline hierarchy, like so:

1.0   First first-level heading

1.1   First second-level heading in section 1.0

1.2   Second second-level heading in section 1.0

  1.2.1   First third-level heading in section 1.2

  1.2.2   Second third-level heading in section 1.2

2.0   Second first-level heading

The beauty of this system is that the reader can always figure out where he or she is in the outline, no matter how many levels you have. If you find a heading that is preceded by '1.2.3.4.5.6.7', then, in addition to knowing right away that the author is using too many levels of headings, you will know that you, amazingly enough, are still only in the second part of section 1. The main downside of this system is that it is ugly, and it also lulls authors into thinking they can have as many levels of subsections as they like. Journals that use this system often specify that you should not go past three or four levels of headings even though the numbering system makes it possible to do so.

Other journals do not let you use a numbering system, so the only thing that signifies how a section fits into the general scheme of things is the formatting of the heading. Like so:

First level may be italic, POSSIBLY IN SMALL CAPS

   Second level may be bold

      Third level may be plain roman type

There are only so many tricks you can do with boldface, italics, capital letters and other font changes before the reader loses track of where in the hierarchy the heading falls. This is why non-numbered styles are usually limited to three levels of headings, and sometimes only two. If you have written your article with four or five levels of headings, this will come as an unpleasant surprise and may entail some fairly serious rewriting. It is far better to find out early on what restrictions your target journal imposes. Then you can take them into account as you write.

In addition to the fairly concrete dos and don'ts above, there are other, more nuanced – and more important – decisions you need to make about your headings: namely, how many to use and where exactly to put them. Sometimes the answer to this is obvious. Perhaps your target journal requires a relatively strict version of IMRAD and expects an introduction, a section on methods and materials, a section on results and findings, and a final section called 'discussion'. Other journals have no such requirements, which means you have more freedom – and more decisions to make. Chapter 6 describes how your structure should reflect the logical steps of your argument. With that in mind, try to use headings to highlight these logical steps. Every time you take a (more or less) significant step toward your destination, you can mark it off with a heading that underscores the point you want to make.

Unfortunately, arguments do not come packaged in proportionally sized chunks. Sometimes one logical unit covers several pages, while another only takes a paragraph or two. So, if you use headings to mark off each logical step, you may find yourself with either too many headings or too few – or quite possibly too many in some places and too few in others. While there is no strict rule for what entails 'too many' or 'too few', too many can be jarring and give the article a chopped-up feel. More important, too many headings generally mean too few transition sentences, and the reader gets tossed into new ideas too abruptly – rather like reading someone else's outline. Too few, on the other hand, can result in the dreaded impenetrable grey mass.

A very general rule of thumb is that you should have some sort of heading roughly every 400 words, and every time you make a major shift to a new idea. But since their main function is to give the reader a road map and you already know the way by heart, this is a good time to get an outside opinion: when you get someone to look through your work before you submit to your target journal, whether it be a colleague or some kind of editor, have him also pay attention to headings and how well they function (see Chapter 8 on giving and receiving feedback).

TABLES AND FIGURES: WHEN WORDS ARE NOT ENOUGH

When readers skim over your work before committing themselves to reading it in full, one of the first places their eyes land is on your tables and figures. It's said that a good table or figure is worth a thousand words – and a bad one takes a thousand words to explain. Here, 'good' and 'bad' refer to how clearly a table or figure conveys the information you want to convey. Good tables and figures can present information or conceptualizations central to your argument in easy-to-grasp, graphical form. If they are exceptionally good, they may be reproduced by other authors, extending the lifetime of your work. Bad ones don't get your message across, and they may suggest to the reader that the rest of the article will be incomprehensible as well. There are three tests that your tables and figures should pass to ensure that they add to and not detract from your argument: necessity, appropriateness and readability.

Test 1: Necessity

The first thing you need to ask yourself is whether you really need that table or figure. Yes, it is nice to have something to break up the text, but you don't want to have a *useless* thing breaking up the text. Space in a printed publication is at a premium. Not only that, but tables and figures are far more time-consuming (and thus expensive) to lay out than plain text, and publishers are not interested in performing extra work at extra cost for no good reason.

So how do you know whether a table or figure is necessary? At the very least, you have to refer to it at least once in your text. For every single table and figure there should be at least one internal reference like 'See table X' or 'Figure Y depicts …' A parenthetical reference is sufficient: 'Interest rates dropped sharply over the last decade (figure 5).' The figure you slaved over may look great, and the table may represent hours of meticulous number crunching – but if they're not relevant enough to be referred to in the text, then they're not relevant enough to include.

The second thing you should ask is whether or not the table or figure brings something additional to the manuscript that the body text alone does not. Does it provide more detail? Does it more clearly show relationships between various elements? Consider the following:

Mice were exposed to temperatures ranging from zero to 35°C. Aggressive behaviour was observed only when the temperature was between 25°C and 30°C (see Table 7.1).

Table 7.1 Aggressive behaviour in mice as a function of room temperature

Temperature (°C)	Display of aggression
35	No
30	Yes
25	Yes
20	No
15	No
10	No
5	No
0	No

In this case, the table added nothing to what was already communicated through the text. In fact, the text did a far better job of communicating that information than the table did. Be suspicious of any table that has many blank cells or cells with the same values. Its message may be far more effectively communicated in words.

Test 2: Appropriateness

You realize that you have more information than you want in the text, and you want to put it in the form of a table or figure. How do you know what format is appropriate? If the data are not complex, then figures are almost always easier to understand than tables. They can also depict a general trend more clearly, or compare the relative magnitude of two or more measurements. But figures rarely allow a high degree of precision. For example, if it matters that the growth rate was exactly 15.7 per cent, then a table will let you specify exactly that. So if precision matters, tables are the way to go.

If you know that a figure is what you want, then the next step is to decide what it should look like. To do this, you need to identify *the most important aspect* of the message you want to convey. This is not always easy. You may need to play with several different figures until you find one that works best. For example, a line graph is good for showing the growth or decline in something over time. It often works if you have more than one entity – if you are able to clearly delineate the differences in the lines. In some cases a bar graph might work better, although it's not as effective at showing a trend. A pie chart works when you want to show a percentage breakdown of something, but it is rarely successful when you want to show absolute values.

Test 3: Readability

The most important test for any of your tables or figures is whether or not it is readable. I mean this literally: Can a reader read the table or figure out loud and get the intended message? Because you already know what you are trying to convey, you are not the best person to decide this. Ask someone else. Show them your table or figure and ask them to read it out loud, so you can hear their thought processes. For a figure, they should be able to say something like: 'This shows how decisions are made at the local government level in the country of Inertia. First, a bill is proposed by the House of Pomposity. The bill is then submitted to the Office of Relentless Bureaucracy, where it makes several rounds through the system …' and so on. If they stumble somewhere, take note. Beware of figures that you make purely for your own thought processes; these are seldom of equal value to the reader. A complex drawing of boxes with lines and arrows and multiple paths might be a good way for you to visualize your own argument, but to a reader who does not understand the argument at the outset, this is often just confusing (see Figure 7.1 as an example of such a figure). Unfortunately, one of the most common comments I give on figures is: 'I don't know where I should start looking.' There are so many elements to the figure that my eye does not settle on any of them first, and I quickly feel overwhelmed. By asking a reader to read it out loud, you can see right away if she gets the intended message out of the figure or if it is just an expensive space-stealer.

Likewise, if you have a table, ask your colleague to pick a random cell and tell you what it means. They should be able to say quickly and accurately and in a full sentence what the information in the cell represents: column headings should identify the cell contents, and the units of measurements should be easy to find (e.g., in the title of the table, the column heading, or a table footnote). If you hear something like 'OK, this says that 59 per cent – or is it 59 tons? – of methane was emitted by cows in Albania in 2004. No, wait. I mean, in 2004, 59 per cent of all cows in Albania emitted methane in tons. Hang on. Maybe 2004 tons of cows emitted 59 per cent of Albania's methane. Huh?' then you know you need to revise that table.

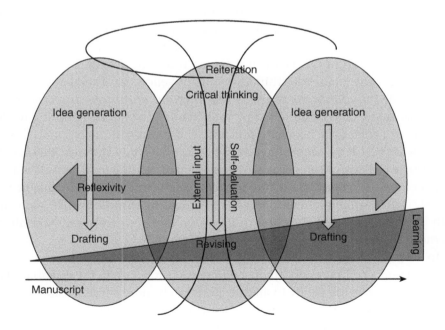

Figure 7.1   The importance of simple figures

Unnecessarily complex figures are seldom welcomed by readers, and almost never aid comprehension. Compare this non-intuitive figure with the far simpler version in Chapter 2 (creativity cycle). Does more detail help you understand more – or less?

DOS AND DON'TS FOR FIGURES

In journals, there are usually only two classifications of artwork: tables and figures. If it is not a table, it is a figure. This means that figures include everything from photographs, to line drawings, to maps, to bar graphs, to pie charts, to time lines, to flow charts. Because there are so many different kinds of figures, clear-cut guidelines are difficult. Nonetheless, there are some concerns that apply to almost all figures.

Do read the journal's or publisher's guidelines for specifications about what file types you can use (such as GIF, TIF, PDF or JPEG) and minimum standards of quality. You do not want to discover at the last minute that your hand-drawn map of village settlements is unacceptable and that getting a professionally drawn map will take several months. This is something you should find out as soon as possible. If the press has to redraw or reformat a figure for you, it may be both expensive and time-consuming.

Don't use colour if you can help it. Colour is expensive. In book publishing, you will probably have to use all the negotiation skills at your disposal for every colour map, photograph or figure you want to use – and the negotiations will have to happen very early in the process. Many journals do not allow colour figures at all. And if they do, you may have to pay for it. It probably won't be cheap, either; it'll cost enough to make you wish you had drawn that graph in black and white. This is important to remember because many software packages that draw figures for you on the basis of the data you enter use colour by default. Before you know it, you have a line graph with thin lines in light yellow, pink and baby blue. Even if you decide the colours are so pretty that they are worth the extra cost, keep in mind that many colours do not copy well. While it would be tempting to think that this will encourage people to purchase and download the original, this may not be realistic. Many people have access to journals only through libraries. And if an article or book chapter is assigned as required reading for a class, it is almost always copied on a black-and-white photocopier. If your work is unreadable when copied, it may simply remain unread. You would be surprised what you can do with shades of grey and thickness of line. Don't let your software make all your decisions for you!

Do keep your figures as simple as possible. If you are using a figure as a visual aid to present a complex concept in a different form, focus on the essentials. Lines and arrows zigzagging wildly in all directions rarely aid comprehension.

Do make sure that each figure is as self-explanatory as possible. Not only will this aid readers who are skipping around your work and jumping right to the graphics without reading the surrounding text, but it will also make it possible for other authors to use your work in theirs. A good figure is a thing of beauty and can be immortalized by appearing in many different works – properly referenced, of course.

Do make sure you have double-checked any potential copyright infringements if you intend to use someone else's artwork. Copyright law is complex, and although 'fair use' will most likely allow you to unproblematically use short passages of text and perhaps an image of a book cover in a book review, it is always smart to ask for permission when copying a figure – even if you provide a reference.

Do find out about your target journal's requirements for captions. Some journals want figures (and tables) to be wholly self-explanatory – which can lead to some very long captions indeed. Other journals do not want any redundancy between the text and the caption, which will make the captions very short and probably cryptic. If no preference is stated, make sure you provide at least enough information so that the reader has a general idea about what the figure is about and will not have to search through the text for an explanation.

TIPS FOR TABLES

Tables are useful when you need to present a large amount of dense information with precision. But don't forget that you are using this information to support your argument. There are three main steps you can take to ensure that your main message comes through:

- Arrange pertinent information in a logical order.
- Remove unnecessary graphics.
- Arrange comparable numbers so they read down and not across.

The first step is the most important because you want to call your readers' attention to the main point of the table. To do this, you remove unimportant information and arrange the rest so that readers get the most out of it. Table 7.2a presents the oil and gas reserves of four oil companies.

Table 7.2a   Crude oil and natural gas reserves of the top four oil companies

	Crude oil (billion barrels)	Natural gas (billion cubic feet)
A-OK Oil	8.8	51,000
Best Buy Oil	11.6	56,000
Crude-Is-Us	1.5	8,200
Darn Good Oil	4.8	38,000
	Crude oil (billion barrels o.e.)	Natural gas (billion barrels o.e.)
A-OK Oil	8.8	8.8
Best Buy Oil	11.6	9.7
Crude-Is-Us	1.5	1.4
Darn Good Oil	4.8	6.5

In this version, it is very difficult to see what the author is trying to convey. An initial glance shows that the oil company names are repeated, which seems odd. You then notice that one set of numbers appears twice. But if you look more closely, you see that the headings are slightly different: One says 'Crude oil (billion barrels)' and the other says 'Crude oil (billion barrels o.e.)'. 'o.e.' means 'oil equivalent', and it does stand to reason that reserves of crude oil in billions of barrels and billions of barrels oil equivalent would be the same. But putting the figures in both times seems a bit unnecessary. What is the author really trying to do here? Apparently, the goal is to show the reserves of oil and natural gas for each company, but since they are measured differently, they are converted to a common measure (oil equivalent) to make it easier for the reader to compare. In other words, the bottom half of the table is the important half. The only useful information in the upper part is the volume of natural gas reserves in billion cubic feet, which can be incorporated into the bottom half as shown in Table 7.2b.

Table 7.2b Crude oil and natural gas reserves of the top four oil companies

	Natural gas		Crude oil
Company	*Billion cubic feet*	*Billion barrels oil equivalent*	*Billion barrels*
A-OK Oil	51,000	8.8	8.8
Best Buy Oil	56,000	9.7	11.6
Crude-Is-Us	8,200	1.4	1.5
Darn Good Oil	38,000	6.5	4.8

But now it may appear that 'Billion cubic feet' and 'Billion barrels oil equivalent' are two different things, when in fact they are simply two ways of measuring the same thing. If we arrange it so it more clearly shows that we are ultimately trying to compare natural gas and crude oil, the result is Table 7.2c.

Table 7.2c Crude oil and natural gas reserves of the top four oil companies

	Crude oil	Natural gas
Company	*Billion barrels*	*Billion barrels o.e. (Billion ft^3)*
A-OK Oil	8.8	8.8 (51,000)
Best Buy Oil	11.6	9.7 (56,000)
Crude-Is-Us	1.5	1.4 (8,200)
Darn Good Oil	4.8	6.5 (38,000)

We have now succeeded in bringing out the main point, and it is easier for the reader to compare the reserves of oil and natural gas for the respective oil companies. But we could take this a small step further. So far, we have given no thought to the order in which the oil companies appear. They are in alphabetical order – probably because we gathered the information that way (that is, we had a list of companies and went about filling in the data we needed). We could arrange the oil companies in order of how big their reserves are.

And finally, we can minimize graphical noise by getting rid of any excess lines – the second main step you can take to improve your tables. Unless they include a lot of subcategories that require lines to show which elements should be grouped together, most tables need no vertical lines at all – and very few horizontal lines. There is seldom a good reason to use shading, and there is no excuse for using anything with a 3-D effect – ever. Minimal graphical noise makes it easier not only on the reader, but also on the journal's layout people: it is far simpler to add graphic elements than it is to remove them.

The final result, now that we have taken into account the size of the reserves and the elimination of excess lines, looks something like Table 7.2d. Compare Table 7.2a with Table 7.2d and ask yourself which one you would prefer as a reader!

Table 7.2d Crude oil and natural gas reserves of the top four oil companies

	Crude oil in billion barrels	Natural gas in billion barrels o.e. (billion ft³)
Best Buy	11.6	9.7 (56,000)
A-OK Oil	8.8	8.8 (51,000)
Darn Good Oil	4.8	6.5 (38,000)
Crude-Is-Us	1.5	1.4 (8,200)

The third main consideration is to make sure you arrange comparable numbers so that they read down, not across. That's just the way our minds work. We like columns of numbers, not rows. It is easier for us to digest numbers when they are lined up vertically, especially if the decimal points or separators are lined up. Consider Tables 7.3a and 7.3b.

Table 7.3a Aquaculture production

	Total	Salmon	Trout	Other
Tons	490,278	440,061	48,778	1,439
%	100	89.8	9.9	0.3
Value in 1,000 USD	1,214,340	1,090,702	117,204	6,434
%	100	89.8	9.7	0.5

Table 7.3b Aquaculture production

Type of fish	Tons (%)		Value in USD 1,000 (%)	
Salmon	440,061	(89.8)	1,090,702	(89.8)
Trout	48,778	(9.9)	117,204	(9.7)
Other	1,439	(0.3)	6,434	(0.5)
TOTAL	490,278	(100)	1,214,340	(100)

In Table 7.3a, your eyes naturally move down the 'Total' column but trip up because the numbers are not comparable. You have both absolute numbers and percentages, and both measurement in tons and value in dollars. In Table 7.3b, the total is at the bottom, where we expect it to be. The numbers in absolute value add up, as do the percentages.

Let's consider another example that combines all three of these main points: arranging information in a logical order to emphasize your message, removing unnecessary graphics, and arranging numbers so they read down and not across. Look at Table 7.4a.

Table 7.4a Longevity and urban population

City	Appleton	Boomtown	Carson City	Darbyshire	Eastwood
Population	36,000	10,000	24,000	60,000	5,000
Longevity	73	79	75	69	87

In Table 7.4a, the numbers read horizontally by row, and not vertically by column, and the items are arranged alphabetically. This arrangement makes it virtually impossible for the reader to discern any trend. Moreover, the extra lines add visual clutter. Now look at Table 7.4b.

Table 7.4b Longevity and urban population

City	Population	Longevity
Darbyshire	60,000	69
Appleton	36,000	73
Carson City	24,000	75
Boomtown	10,000	79
Eastwood	5,000	87

The new arrangement makes it much easier to see that the larger the population, the shorter the longevity. This is because the numbers appear in columns and they are in ascending/descending order. The minimalist structure also makes the table easier to read.

Once you have arranged your information in a logical order, removed all unnecessary graphics and arranged the numbers so they read down and not across, keep the three following tips in mind to make your table more readable:

Do round off your numbers to a reasonable number of places. Too many decimal places not only create extra work for the reader, but also provide a false sense of precision. Many estimates, for example, require complex mathematical calculation, but they are still estimates (often made by putting together other estimates) and should be presented as such. Saying that the economy of Bora Bora is projected to grow by 12.2568 per cent suggests that the figure is more accurate than it actually is; the figure is, after all, based on a series of estimates. Saying '12 per cent' will suffice. More important is to make sure that all entries are rounded off to the same level: if one figure is given as '2.32' and the second as '2.3', either make the second '2.30' or make both '2.3'.

Do avoid unnecessary repetition, extraneous information and empty cells. Take a look at your table. Do you have a lot of cells that are empty, contain the same information as other cells, or contain information that should perhaps be presented either in text or in another table? If so, trim the fat.

Do make sure your table is as self-explanatory as possible. As with figures, a table that can stand alone not only aids the reading of your article, but may also be more easily cited and used by other authors. Make sure units are clearly stated and abbreviations explained. This can be done in footnotes if necessary. A good title also helps.

Breaking up the grey mass of your text does more than just give your reader a momentary respite from reading long sentences. Your headings, tables and figures may well persuade your reader to read those long sentences in the first place. Moreover, everything that you include in your manuscript that is not body text has the potential to help your reader understand your message in a different way than the body text can. Where the body text is long and detailed, headings are short and concise. Tables and figures offer the reader numbers, images and single words or simple phrases. Do not underestimate the importance of appealing to different learning types: some people simply absorb information better through images or numbers than they do through written words alone. This point is developed further in Chapter 9 on giving presentations.

Remember

Headings, tables and figures help your readers navigate around your work quickly and effectively.

Make sure your title and headings reflect the content and structure of your argument.

Make sure that your tables and figures:

- add something *necessary* to the text,
- have a format that is *appropriate* for communicating their main message, and
- can be *read out loud*.

Streamline your tables to make it easier for readers to grasp the essential information: arrange information logically, minimize graphical noise, and line up corresponding numbers vertically.

FURTHER READING

- Few, Stephen (2012) *Show Me the Numbers: Designing Tables and Graphs to Enlighten*, 2nd edn, Burlingame, CA: Analytics Press. Highly informative and well presented, this book is aimed at quantitative researchers presenting statistical material clearly.
- Yau, Nathan (2011) *Visualize This: The FlowingData Guide to Design, Visualization, and Statistics*, Indianapolis, IN: Wiley Publishing. In addition to excellent advice for presenting statistics, Yau also provides good advice for maps and other types of visual presentation.
- Tufte, Edward R. (1997) *Visual and Statistical Thinking: Displays of Evidence for Making Decisions*, Cheshire, CT: Graphics Press. Tufte is highly respected as an innovative thinker in graphical presentation. He has written a kind of trilogy of books: *The Visual Display of Quantitative Information*, *Envisioning Information* and *Visual Explanation: Images and Quantities, Evidence and Narrative*. All three books are expensive and hardbound. *Visual and Statistical Thinking* is a short paperback excerpt from the third book. It is enough to give you an idea of how he thinks so that you can decide whether or not you want to invest in the other books.
- Leahy, Richard (1992) 'Twenty titles for the writer', *College Composition and Communication*, 43 (4) (1992): 516-19. This article provides some exercises to help you to think about writing your title.

EIGHT

Holding up the mirror
Giving and receiving feedback

A true story: I once took a dance class in a room without mirrors. We were simply told to watch the instructor and copy her movements. When she gracefully lifted her arms to the heavens and glided across the floor, she looked like a sprite, a nymph, a veritable goddess. When I followed her, I, too, felt the heavens at my fingertips and became the embodiment of grace.

Then we got mirrors.

Once I recovered from the horror of the revelation that I looked less like I was communicating with the gods and more like I was being held up at gunpoint, I understood something important about feedback. The most useful feedback is neither a slew of compliments ('You look fabulous!') nor a string of insults ('You look like an elephant on roller skates!'), but rather an accurate glimpse of how you actually look to the observer. Only by looking in the mirror could I actually see that if I dropped my shoulder a bit and bent my elbow slightly – like so – then I looked like I was moving out of the back alley and towards the divine.

The same principle applies to writing. The most useful feedback you can give someone (or receive yourself) is neither vague encouragement ('Good start! Keep at it!') nor scorching criticism ('Sloppy method!'), but rather an honest assessment of how the text reads. In other words, 'Rewrite your introduction because I don't like it' is not nearly as helpful as 'You start off saying you want to look at trends in functionalistic interior design, but you seem to spend most of your time talking only about the use of colour among the Bauhaus designers.' This gives the author not only insight into what is confusing the reader, but also several options for fixing it: she can rewrite the introduction either to focus on Bauhaus designers or to better explain the link between functionalistic interior design and Bauhaus designers, or she can restructure the paper to talk more about other aspects of functionalistic interior design.

MIRRORS IN SCHOLARLY WRITING

In the world of scholarly writing, we have several opportunities to have our work mirrored back to us. The most familiar one is a formal peer review. You submit your paper to a journal, and they send it out to a few anonymous reviewers who are supposed to give you feedback on where to bend, where to straighten and where to stretch so you can achieve your state of grace. You can also get feedback from your colleagues, when you ask them to give something a quick read-through before you send it off. You may also present your work orally and get feedback in the form of questions and comments afterward (see Chapter 9).

Not only will you inevitably receive feedback, but you will also be called upon to *give* it on a regular basis. You will be asked by journals to review articles submitted for publication. Your colleagues will ask you to look at their work. And if you are employed in a university setting, you will have students with endless questions and need for feedback. The scholarly dialogue depends on the quality assurance provided by peer review at all levels; without peer review, scholarly conversation would deteriorate to eccentric grumbling and unfocused babble.

Unfortunately, few of us are able to get the most out of either giving or receiving feedback. For many of us, our first exposure to feedback was as a passive, helpless recipient. We handed in a paper to a teacher, and it came back with red marks all over it and a letter grade. Feedback wasn't part of a process aimed at improving your work; it was a final judgement. Those red marks meant 'Shame on you!' Rarely did we get a chance to do something over again, to take comments into account and revise accordingly. If we did, it somehow felt like cheating – or a remedial exercise for dummies who didn't get it right the first time.

So, it's no wonder that when we finally get to the world of scholarly publishing – where we give and receive feedback on a regular basis – we are at a loss. When we get critical comments back from colleagues or reviewers, it is less natural for us to say to ourselves, 'That was edifying', than it is to wonder, 'Maybe I can still get a job at McDonald's?' And when we are called upon to give feedback, we don't know where to start. We might end up lecturing the author on how he should have cited our own work more, or desperately trying to remember grammar lessons from school so we can catch 'mistakes', or even just pasting on an insincere smile because we do not want to hurt the feelings of a colleague with negative criticism. And, by the way, giving too much feedback, especially to students, can do both you and them a grave disservice. Not only does it take an inordinate amount of time to give highly detailed feedback, but you also take away the student's – or author's – sense of ownership. Just think how defensive you would get if you got something back with so much red that you could hardly recognize your own writing. Ultimately, the author, even if they are a student, is the owner of the writing. You can give comments, but the author has to make the decisions. Students who have had too much help simply face greater problems at the next level, where they have to demonstrate even more independence.

The following sections describe steps you can take to get more out of the feedback process: how you can get feedback that actually helps you, and how you can give feedback that actually helps someone else.

RECEIVING FEEDBACK

Sometimes, the first feedback authors get on a particular piece of work is the peer review they receive after they submit an article to a journal. If this is the first time you've gotten feedback on this particular work, you should not be surprised if it isn't very favourable.

The journey an idea makes from your mind, to words on paper, to the mind of the reader is a long and perilous one. Like Chinese whispers, something may get lost at every juncture: what you wrote may not actually be what you intended to write, and what the reader gets from it may differ from both what you actually wrote and what you intended to write (see Figure 8.1). But it is very difficult for you, as an author, to judge what readers are likely to end up taking away from your work. Others are more likely to see this than you are. You cannot sufficiently distance yourself from your work to view it as an outsider would because you are not an outsider. You already know what you were trying to accomplish. How can you tell how convincing an argument is when you are already convinced?

Blind spots occur at both the document level and the sentence level. At the document level, your job as a writer is to explain things step-by-step so that the reader can follow your logic. Because the steps seem so obvious to you – both because you have taken them many times before and because you already know the conclusion – you might, consciously or unconsciously, make a leap in logic, skipping a step that is critical for the reader but extraneous to you. This is also referred to as the 'curse of knowledge' or 'knowledge curse': the more you know something, the harder it is to imagine not knowing it, and thus the harder it is to explain to someone else. You notice leaps in logic in someone else's work and say to yourself, 'Whoa, hang on. How did he suddenly get here?' But you are unlikely to notice them in your own paper. Or you might be aware of this possibility and overcompensate for it by explaining in far too much detail. As much as you have tried to take your audience into account, you need a representative of that audience to tell you how well you have succeeded.

Figure 8.1 The communication gap between you and the reader

It is not always easy to know how your reader will interpret your text. Getting feedback early and often can help you better understand how your reader might be thinking.

At the sentence level, your familiarity with your own writing will make you see words that aren't there and overlook words that shouldn't be there (such as the game-changing word 'not'). Because you know what you intended to say, your eyes will not see repeated words, missing words, misspellings, easily confused words (such as 'it's' and 'its') and other errors. You will read your work through a thousand times and not see that instead of 'public policy' in your running head you have 'pubic policy'. But the moment it comes out in print, it will be glaringly obvious.

Tip

There are other ways to help you discover your own typos and oddities at the sentence level. They all involve changing the look of the document so your brain has a harder time seeing what *should* be there instead of what is:

- View it in a significantly different font/type size.
- Change the margins or put the text into columns.

- Print it out and read it in hard copy.
- Read it upside down or backwards.
- Put a ruler under each line of text to force yourself to read one word at a time.
- Read it out loud.

The only way most of us can review our own work with a sufficiently critical eye is to wait for an extended period – say, several months. Time does create distance. Have you ever picked up a paper you've written that has been lying dormant in a desk drawer for a year or two? When you put it aside, you thought it was 'almost finished'. Now you wonder, 'What was I thinking?!' Or perhaps you've forced yourself to reopen a document you'd long since given up on, only to discover that it wasn't half bad. Either way, because you may no longer remember exactly what you were trying to do in that paper, you have become a kind of outsider (albeit one with a distinct advantage). Most of us do not have time to put our first drafts in a drawer for a year or two. If we want to identify the problems that we can't see for ourselves, we are going to have to ask for help.

When and how to ask for feedback

Eventually, you will get feedback – whether you want it or not – when you submit your work to a journal or publisher with procedures for peer review. But you need not wait until then. When is the best time to seek feedback? It varies from writer to writer, and sometimes from paper to paper. But there comes a point in your writing when you have nothing more to give. You might be aware that there are some problems lurking, but you no longer care. You are shut down and locked tight. You have hit the wall. The only things you are willing to do are perform a spell-check, upload and hit 'submit'. You need to ask for feedback *before* you reach this point.

You can ask for feedback at any time in the development of your work – as long as you know what kind of feedback you need and are able to clearly communicate this to the person you are asking for help. If you are at a very early stage in your writing, when you are mostly concerned about whether your assumptions are reasonable and your logic is defensible, it is infuriating to get your paper back and find only red circles around your semi-colons with notes to use commas instead. You want to roll up your paper tightly, hit the reader upside the head with it, and yell, 'Did you even READ this?' Similarly, when you feel finished with a paper in every sense of the word, and are only interested in having someone read through to find typos or other small errors, you are not likely to welcome a comment along the lines of: 'But can this really be considered an independent variable in this case?'

If you give your work to someone shortly after you've gone through a creative phase, you are likely to feel that about half of what you've written is sheer genius and the other half is complete dreck, but you're completely incapable of knowing which is which. At this point, there are probably only five main types of comments that are useful for you:

- *Good*: Since you can no longer tell what's good and what's not, you want someone to point it out for you. You may be surprised.
- *Reformulate or restructure*: The content is good, but the way it is expressed is unclear in some way.
- *Expand*: Need more detail.
- *Tighten*: Content is good, but there is too much of it.
- *Cut*: Not useful information.

If you are in a later phase, you will be more interested in such specifics as grammar, style and the completeness of your reference list. The more clearly you are able to tell your reviewer exactly what you need, the more likely you are to get what you need in return.

This also applies if you are paying a professional editor or copy-editor to help you. There are many different kinds of editors: some work with you through the early stages and help you shape your argument, ultimately becoming as blind as you are to sentence-level errors; others focus only on the finer points of grammar and style, viewing the document under such a powerful microscope that they often aren't able to recall afterwards what it was even about. Substantive editors are best if you need help at the document level (structure and paragraphs, sometimes even ideas for content). But if you need help at the sentence level – that is, with grammar and style – you are better off with a copy-editor. Don't expect to find someone who can do both sentence-level and document-level editing at the same time (unless they are given sufficient time and an unlimited number of passes through the manuscript). An editor's perspective is rather like that of a camera's lens: if you focus on the foreground, the background will be blurred, and vice versa. Professional editors and copy-editors (good ones, that is) know that they should ask you what you want before they start, but it is you who will pay the price – both literally and figuratively – if you fail to make it clear.

It is also worth considering the extent to which the person giving you feedback should already be familiar with your argument. People who aren't already familiar with it have to try to understand your ideas based solely on what is actually written down. They do not have the benefit of having spoken to you about it at length before they read your work, so they will be able to give you good feedback about how convincing your written argument is. People who are familiar with your argument have an important role to play, too. They can measure what *is* written down against what they *expected* to find there. Both types of feedback are useful; it is up to you to decide what is most useful to you at the particular stage of writing you are in.

Many of us never get to the point of deciding whom we should ask for feedback. We simply don't dare ask anyone. Not only is it embarrassing to show people work that isn't finished, but we are acutely aware of how pressed for time our colleagues are. Unfortunately, this reluctance often ends up costing us all a lot more time in the long run. Say you submit to a journal a paper that no one else has really looked at. It is then sent around to about three reviewers, all of whom may point out the same structural flaws – or even worse, they were so confused by what you were trying to do that they give you completely different, and perhaps contradictory, comments. Your paper is then rejected or (if you are lucky) you are asked to revise and resubmit it. Had you first sent your paper to a single colleague, some of these flaws might have been caught. So, instead of daring to ask *one* colleague to spend a few hours of her time on your draft, you have used up the time of *three* reviewers and spent six months waiting for an answer.

Some people have overcome the problem of being too shy to ask for help from colleagues by establishing a colloquium whose members meet informally to review each other's work (see Chapter 2 and the text box 'Writing groups as a source of feedback' at the end of this chapter for ideas about writing groups). If one member has a paper he wants feedback on, he can distribute it to the group a few days before the meeting. At the meeting, the author can present his work, respond to comments and answer questions. (Note that, because the author is also presenting the work orally, those who have not had time to read the paper beforehand can still offer valuable feedback. See Chapter 9 on presentations.) Others have established writing groups or networks where members feel free to approach other members for feedback. And still others may choose one particular colleague with whom they feel comfortable. However, these groups or networks work only when members feel that they get as much out of it as they put in. If you are continually banging on the door of a colleague to get feedback on your work, but are suddenly too busy to read her work when she turns to you, you will soon find that door closed to you.

Digesting feedback

Until you get used to it, feedback can be hard to take. Even though we know there should be a difference between 'me' and 'my paper', feedback can very quickly feel personal: when you submit a manuscript, you feel like you are submitting yourself for evaluation, so when you get comments back from reviewers, it feels like they have scrutinized not just your paper, but you as a scholar (see Figure 8.2). Moreover, we have been so trained to see red marks on our papers as a final verdict that it is difficult for us to believe that the person giving us feedback might actually be on our side. Ideally, a reviewer acts as a buffer between our awkward first drafts and the permanence of publication. Sure, it's embarrassing when someone tells you that you have spinach between your teeth, but it is even worse when you get home and realize no one has told you anything and you've been sporting greens between your teeth since lunchtime. It is precisely the job of the reviewer to point out those things that we may not like to hear but that will save us from worse distress in the long run.

Figure 8.2   The communication gap between you and the reviewer.

Remember that reviewers do not always express themselves clearly either. You might need some feedback from colleagues to help interpret the feedback you get from reviewers.

For this reason, it is always a good idea to take seriously all the comments that you get on your work. You might discover that your audience is far more hostile than you anticipated and that you have stumbled into a pocket of controversy that you didn't expect. You might discover that you have some annoying writing tics that you do not even notice but that can be off-putting to your readers (for example, overuse of 'for example'). You might also discover that a small comment that you wrote almost as an aside in your conclusion may be the most exciting part of your paper.

But this does not mean that you should follow all advice slavishly and uncritically. The comments that you get will vary considerably depending on who has looked through your work and under what circumstances. Not all comments are equally useful. Reviewers do not always know what they are doing, and sometimes they have their own personal agendas, not to mention their own personal eccentricities. They may not be judging your work on its own premises, but rather in the light of how they would have done it. Comments that consist mostly of requests to cite works from the reviewer in question (who at this point has ceased to be anonymous, even though he might not have formally introduced himself) are a strong hint that the reviewer might not have your best interests at heart.

Colleagues, too, may be more interested in promoting their own work than in really trying to understand yours. Even if that is not the case, they may simply have too much on their minds to give your work their full attention. This is one reason why journals usually pick three or more reviewers in the external review process: it becomes more quickly evident if one of the reviewers is not giving it his best effort.

But even if your reviewer might not have been on target, you should pay special attention to any comments that indicate that he or she has not fully understood what you have written. This is the mirror at its most powerful. If one person misunderstands, then chances are good that other people will also misunderstand. You can, of course, tell yourself that the reader is an idiot if he doesn't get what you write, but what if your audience is made up primarily of such 'idiots'? So, when someone has misunderstood something, the first thing you need to ask yourself is whether that person can be considered representative of your audience. If you have asked your mother to read your paper on algorithmic game theory, you might not need to take into account all of her questions (unless, of course, she happens to be an expert in algorithmic game theory). But if your reader is a colleague familiar with your field, then you need to take her questions very seriously indeed.

Likewise, if an editor or a reviewer has made changes to your text that reveal that he or she missed the point, think twice before you simply override the changes and 'stet' the original wording. If the original wording was confusing enough to result in a bad edit, then the problem may not lie with the editor, but with the original wording. Start over. Try to find a completely different way of making the point, so that you avoid the kind of misunderstanding your original wording resulted in. And you may have to take a step or two back to do this: sometimes the source of the misunderstanding was something that you wrote in a previous section.

If the comments you have received are part of a formal review process, and the verdict is 'revise and resubmit', then once you decide how to address the comments you have received, you will have to describe these decisions in detail in a separate document (usually called something like a 'revision memo') when you resubmit your manuscript. For each of the comments from the reviewers, there are three main responses:

- The point is well taken and you have made the changes. Describe where you have made the changes.
- The point is well taken, but you have decided not to make the changes. Here, you need to describe why you did not make the changes requested by the reviewer. A typical answer here will be something like: 'Reviewer B requested that we expand our theoretical discussion. While we agree that a more in-depth treatment of the theoretical framework would have added to the value of this paper, word limits constrain our opportunity to develop this section as deeply as we would like. Instead, we have added references to other works where we discuss this framework in more detail.' This shows that you have

understood the reason for the comment, taken it seriously, but provided a good reason for not following the recommendation.

- You disagree with the comment entirely. If a reviewer makes a comment that shows that he or she has misunderstood your aim or your wording, then you need to point this out diplomatically. If you have taken steps to avoid similar misunderstanding on the part of other readers, then point this out. For example: 'Reviewer A objected to our exclusion of Phillis Wheatley and Jupiter Hammon in our discussion of eighteenth-century black poets. However, the aim of this article is to discuss only writers living in *Europe* during this period. Because this may not have been entirely clear, we have added a few more sentences to the introduction. See p. 2, paragraph 1.'

The revision memo can be one of the most important documents you write, and can convince the editor to take a chance on you. Unlike the article itself, the revision memo does not have word limits, which means this is the one time you can explain your point of view as fully as you like. This is especially useful if the audience is hostile in some way – the final article may not have space for you to make your case, but the revision memo will allow you to explain your reasoning in detail. The main thing to remember with feedback is that, unlike when you were at school, *you* get to decide what to do with it. It is not a command. It is a gift for you to do with what you please.

GIVING FEEDBACK

Wielding the red pencil is not necessarily any easier than reading its marks on your work. Because you have been asked to give feedback, you (hopefully) possess substantial knowledge of a subject area. Expertise in a subject area, however, doesn't guarantee that a person can provide useful guidance to another hopeful writer. That depends at least as much on understanding the writer and the writing process as it does on understanding the content.

Situations in which we give feedback vary in their formality, the extent to which the participants know each other, the power relationship between the participants, whether the feedback is given orally or on paper and what stage the draft is at. Acting as a peer reviewer for a journal is an example of formal peer review, where participants are anonymous, the reviewer is in a slight position of power, feedback is given in written form and the work should be complete. Acting as a supervisor for a student is also a formal relationship, although the encounters may be somewhat informal and often face to face, but here the participants know each other, there is a clear power imbalance and the supervisor works mostly with early drafts. Reading through a colleague's work is clearly more informal, the participants know each other and are presumably on relatively equal footing, and feedback may be given either in spoken or in written form, and at any stage in the writing process.

Step 1: Get an idea of what the author needs

The beauty of a mirror as a feedback tool is that it reflects you as you are – your strengths and your weaknesses. As a reviewer, you should do the same. But you cannot begin to give the author a picture of her strengths and weaknesses until you understand not only what she is trying to accomplish, but also how you can be of help.

Thus, the first thing you need figure out is what is expected from you, both in your general relationship with the author and in the specific feedback session. Sometimes, this means doing some groundwork before you even meet with the author or pick up the manuscript. If you are acting as a supervisor, for example, find out exactly what you are meant to be doing and make sure you and your student share the same expectations. For example, are you expected to provide an actual research question, or is it the student's job to formulate one? Are you expected to provide the student with references? Or is it the student's job to track them down? How many drafts are you expected to comment on? Some of this is likely to be written down somewhere (perhaps even in a formal contract), but many of these expectations may well be a product of departmental tradition, and thus asking your colleagues is the only way to find out. Finding out about these expectations will not only protect supervisors from students who expect their supervisors to do a lot of the work for them (such as finding a good research question and all the relevant literature), but will also protect students from supervisors who may either force their students to carry out research that will be of little benefit to anyone other than the supervisor, or refuse to provide comments on anything other than a finished draft. If you are acting as a formal peer reviewer, ask the journal whether they have guidelines for reviewers, and if they do, pay attention to them. And if you are reading a paper for a colleague, listen carefully to what they want from you before you start reading. If they don't tell you, ask! Two things to ask about specifically are: 'What is this I am looking at?' and 'How far along are you?' There is a big difference between a half-finished book chapter and a ready-to-submit journal article, and you need to know what it is you have in front of you before you can begin to give useful feedback. If the author wants your feedback on a manuscript they are revising to resubmit to a journal, then ask for the reviewer comments as well, just to get an idea of what the author needed to take into account.

The second thing to figure out is what the author ultimately wants to accomplish. One of the hardest things we ever do as scholars is to let go of our vision of how research should be enough to accept that others might have a different vision. You should not be asking, 'What kind of paper would I have written?' or 'What kind of method would I have chosen?' or 'What kind of research question would I have asked?' but rather 'What is the author trying to say?' and 'Does the research question reflect the aims of the author?' and 'Is the method appropriate for the research question?' You cannot criticize an apple for not being a bicycle: if the author has decided on a case-study approach, you cannot judge her work on the basis of it not being a large-n study. If you are acting as a formal peer reviewer, you thus need to look for the core argument: find something that looks like the research question, and something that looks like the answer to that question. (See the text box 'Active reading'.) The rest of your feedback can then be based on the extent to which the author did justice *to their own core argument*. Questions you can ask yourself include the following:

- What is the author's stated research question?
- How well does the author answer the question?
- What is the identified knowledge gap?
- Is the relationship between empirical data and theory clear?
- How clearly is the method or analytical framework explained?
- Are terms defined or operationalized as necessary?

Make sure all your feedback responds to your understanding of the author's aims – and does not merely reflect your own preferences.

Active reading

Working as an anonymous reader makes it much more difficult to 'listen' to the author. What is important here is to remember that before you can offer any advice or criticism, you need to have a clear understanding of the author's objectives. This means you have to read actively.

Active reading is similar to active listening in that you focus on finding out what actually *is* there, and not just taking the author's word for what is *supposed* to be there or assuming what is *likely* to be there. And in both cases, the fruitfulness of the session is determined by the type of clarifying questions you ask.

Indeed, asking questions is what separates active reading from passive reading. Reading a manuscript passively means just starting at the beginning and slogging through to the end. Reading actively means asking questions along the way.

The two most crucial questions to guide your reading are: 'What is the knowledge gap?' and 'What is the core argument?' You need to understand *what* the author is really trying to say and *why* it is important because the entire paper is built around the answer to these questions. You may have to look hard: the more implicit the knowledge gap or core argument, the more difficult it is to identify.

Looking for the answers to these questions is likely to lead to other questions:

- 'What is the point of this background section?'
- 'What exactly is the role of theory in this study?'
- 'How will he be able to back up that claim?'

The more questions you ask of the text and the more you search in the text for your answers, the more actively you are reading and the better equipped you will be to provide the author with useful feedback.

Reading actively does not necessarily take longer than reading passively. It can even reduce the amount of time you need to grasp the essentials. Indeed, learning to quickly locate a core argument will allow you to skim through any manuscript more effectively. It may even help you make a solid dent in your 'to read' pile.

If you are giving oral feedback as a supervisor or peer, you also have an opportunity to learn a lot by listening to what the author tells you (see the section on the 'Good conversation' further on in this chapter). It is always a good idea to begin each feedback session by letting the writer talk. One advantage of letting the writer talk first is that it allows him to get all his defensiveness and excuses out of the way so he can better hear what you are telling him. We are always acutely aware of the weaknesses in our own early drafts; when the person whose paper you have reviewed walks through your door, he is probably feeling apprehensive and vulnerable. Launching into 'constructive criticism' right away will only make this worse. But if you give him a chance to purge himself – 'I haven't really worked on the wording yet', 'The introduction still isn't quite right', 'I'm having trouble describing my method' – he will be more receptive to your comments. Allowing him to point out flaws in his work before you do will make him feel more capable as a writer. This is especially true if you can acknowledge his own evaluation as a preface to yours: 'As you say yourself, your research question isn't quite there yet. I, too, thought it was too broad. Let's talk about how you can tighten your focus.'

Note that there is a big difference between having the other person define problem areas in the paper and letting him inundate you with explanations for why this is so. 'I'm not sure whether I should use the theory to analyze the case, or the other way around' is a helpful point of departure; 'My dog ate my first draft' is a distraction. If the person you are trying to help is pummeling you with excuses, gently but firmly redirect the focus: 'Yes, I understand that finding good childcare is difficult. But let's focus on how to make the best of it. In the limited time that you have, what do you think you should be working on the most?'

Another advantage to letting the writer talk first is that allowing the writer to identify her problem areas for herself gives you a clearer idea of how *you* can be most helpful. Even if the writer thinks that her biggest problem is her references and you think her biggest problem is a lack of correspondence between her research question and thesis statement, if all she wants to talk about is references, you are better off addressing references first – and perhaps branching out to other subjects afterwards.

Listening actively to the author can also help you address the problems that arise when authors are unable to successfully explain in a written format what they mean. (See the text box 'Active listening'.) If the author can explain to you face to face what he is trying to accomplish, you will be in a better position to judge whether or not he has accomplished it in his manuscript. Do not underestimate the importance of asking questions: 'When I hear you talking it sounds like you are most interested in looking at the effect of news broadcasts on voter behaviour, but your research question makes it sound like you are interested in television in general. What is your main interest here?' While you might not hesitate to ask a student of yours what she is really trying to say, you might feel more uncomfortable asking a colleague – either because you do not want to make your colleague feel bad, or because you are afraid of revealing your own ignorance about something you feel you should know more about. If there was ever a place to sell new clothes to the emperor, it's in academia. Nowhere is the fear of looking ignorant more pronounced – or more crippling. But if you deny the other person a chance to explain, you rob them of an opportunity to achieve greater clarity for themselves – because there is no better way to understand something than to explain it to someone else. So it is better to ask too many questions than too few.

Active listening

Listening actively is harder than it sounds. It involves far more than just keeping your mouth shut while someone else is talking (although that's a good start). It essentially means paying close attention to what someone says, repeating it back to her and asking clarifying questions:

Sue: Let's order out for pizza tonight.

Bob: So, you feel like eating pizza tonight. Do you really want to order out?

This may seem pointless, but it forces you to focus entirely on the speaker. In ordinary conversation, we usually hear only about half of what someone tells us because we are mentally preparing what we will say next – that is, we're often focused on what we are thinking instead of what the speaker is saying. We hear even less if the speaker is trying to discuss a problem and we feel obligated to 'fix' it: The more we worry about having to come up with a solution, the less we are able to listen to the problem itself.

Repeating what you've heard also requires you to pay attention to what was *actually* said, not what you think might have been implied. We all have filters that make us hear what we *expect* to hear, which is not necessarily what was said. Returning to Bob and Sue, most of us have had conversations that sound something like this:

Sue: Let's order out for pizza tonight.

Bob: You think I'm a terrible cook.

Poor Sue. Bob's response is clearly grounded in his insecurities about his culinary abilities, not in what Sue actually said. Perhaps Sue just didn't want to mess up the kitchen. Maybe she felt sorry for Bob because he had been cooking his little heart out all week. Either way, it's probably going to be a tense supper.

For giving feedback in a scholarly setting, the implications are clear: when you are listening to someone explain what her paper is about or what challenges she is facing, focus on letting her talk and listen to what she is actually saying. To test whether you have heard correctly, ask clarifying questions like these:

- 'So what you are saying is that the main aim of your paper is to ...?'
- 'Am I right in understanding that when I read your work you want me to focus on ...?'

When receiving feedback, make sure you really understand what your reviewer has said. Avoid jumping to conclusions like, 'So, you are saying that I'm a hopeless scholar and I should consider a career in fast food,' and instead ask questions like, 'When you say I should consider looking into what Martinez wrote, do you mean that I should completely discount Sanchez?'

And, finally, sometimes just listening is enough. Consider the following scenario: a colleague bangs on your door, desperate to seek your advice on something. She starts explaining the problem to you, and every time you're about to say something helpful, she cuts you off and keeps talking. You eventually give up and just stare at her. You are actually thinking about where to eat lunch, but you nod every now and then just to make her think you are paying attention. Finally, she gets up and says something like, 'Thanks so much. You've really helped! I know what to do now.' You may feel that you have done nothing, but sometimes putting a particular problem into words makes the solution apparent. And since most people find talking to inanimate objects overly eccentric, they need a live human being who will allow them to think out loud.

It's not always easy to get authors to talk: sometimes, they have so much to say that they do not know where to start. You can help them get started by asking 'trigger questions', which are simply general questions that you can ask, without needing to read the manuscript first, to trigger conversation. Some good trigger questions include:

- What is the most interesting thing you have found so far?
- What are you finding most difficult to write about?
- What is it you want people to remember when they are finished reading this?
- What interested you in this topic to begin with?

No matter how the author answers these questions, you will get some insight into what they are trying to do, and what might be blocking them. The question,

'What is the most interesting thing you have found so far?' in particular is helpful: sometimes academics are so worried about being objective that they do not allow themselves to dwell on their own feelings about their work. If you ask them what they find interesting, they can express enthusiasm without having to feel like they have to be academic. You can then check the draft afterwards to see if you can find any vestiges of this exciting find: often it is disguised so thoroughly that you would have had no clue that the author found that part interesting if they hadn't told you. Asking authors what they have trouble writing about forces them to put into words what they are struggling with, and making this effort often gives them an idea of how to solve the problem. The last two questions – what they want their readers to remember and what interested them in the first place – ask the author to take a step back and think about *why* they are doing what they are doing.

Step 2: Respond

Once you know what the author wants from you and have done your best to understand the aim of the paper, you can start giving more active feedback. Before you say anything at all, remember that your job is to help the author, not to make yourself look good. Your ultimate measure of success is the degree to which the author walks away knowing what to do next, not the degree to which you have made your expertise apparent. With this in mind, there are three main areas to which you can address your comments: the content; the core argument or structure; and the general writing (including grammar, style and sentence flow).

If you have been chosen because you are an expert in the field, all comments you have on content are relevant (unless, of course, they are about how *you* would have approached the research). Comments on content can include pointing out omissions of important references or theory, questioning an interpretation of sources or data, or otherwise drawing attention to the scholarly or scientific strengths and weaknesses of the work.

Comments about the core argument or structure are also useful – even if you are not an expert in the field. Here, instead of drawing on your expertise on the content, you base your comments on your understanding of the writer's aims: 'Given that your research question narrows your scope of inquiry to the postwar period, I'm not sure I understand the function of your section on prewar economics.' Your goal here should be to point out places where it's not clear what the author is trying to say.

Sometimes, it's hard to understand what the author is doing because the author himself is unsure. In such cases, reading actively and trying to answer the basic questions about knowledge gap, core argument and structure will help you pinpoint the most important problem areas. Ironically, it is often more difficult to pinpoint problems in well-written papers than in mediocre or outright terrible ones. A good writer will keep you riding the wave of her prose, making it harder for you to stop and ask the critical questions. With poor writers, you have no choice but to stop and try to figure out what's going on.

Commenting on general writing style is where reviewers should exercise the most caution. First, at an early stage of writing, comments about grammar and punctuation are seldom welcome – or even useful. Second, you may simply not be qualified. Presumably, you have been asked to review a piece of work because of your scholarly expertise in the field, not because of your expertise in grammar or house style. The deep end of the grammar and style pool is no place for a novice. Even experts will disagree about whether to use 'which' or 'that', or whether splitting an infinitive is excusable. Moreover, grammar, usage and style all vary according to geographical region (e.g., US vs UK English) and, more important, according to journal preferences. You may have learned to always write out 'per cent', but the journal for which you are acting as a reviewer may use '%'; if the author has diligently read the instructions to authors and replaced every 'per cent' with '%', he will not take kindly to a snide comment from you about writing out 'per cent'. What makes this especially important is that once an author dismisses one comment as irrelevant or erroneous, he will tend to view the rest of the reviewer's comments with greater scepticism. So, if you have told an author to spell out 'per cent' when he knows he did it right the first time, he may be inclined to sneer at your valid point that the figures in his tables do not add up. This does not mean that you have to completely overlook the author's use of language. Comments like the following can be useful – and welcome: 'This sentence is awkward and unclear', 'Who is the agent here?', 'The referent in this sentence is ambiguous' and so on. Even at the sentence and word level, your comments should go toward improving the clarity of the writing, not toward airing your own linguistic bugbears. It is well within your prerogative to suggest that an article might benefit from professional copy-editing, but leave comments on specific grammatical choices and house style issues to the journal editors.

Tip

If you are not a native speaker of English (even if you are a native speaker of English, for that matter), and a copy-editor or reviewer has 'corrected' your language, but you do not understand why (or suspect that something is wrong), ask an editorial expert (or Google the usage). Reviewers can introduce language errors because they misunderstand particular grammar or usage rules ('I learned in primary school never to start a sentence with "And", so it must be true.'). Copy-editors can misunderstand what you are trying to say, which can leave you with grammatically perfect sentences that bear no resemblance to what you intended to write. Since this is ultimately *your* manuscript, make sure you can stand behind all the changes that are made.

The main thing to remember here is that, regardless of what you are commenting on, if you want to move beyond making queries or pointing out problems and into the realm of giving advice, the author will be most receptive to your advice if she feels you have understood her aims. If the author does not feel understood, then everything you say – even the useful advice – is likely to be disregarded.

Step 3: Plan the next step

The final and most overlooked step of every review session is to reach agreement about where to go next. A long face-to-face session of receiving feedback can be very overwhelming for the author, particularly a student receiving feedback from a professor. It is very likely that when the student leaves the office, he will no longer remember everything that was discussed. It is even possible (probable) that at some point he stopped listening to what you were saying because he got hung up on something you said earlier. So, before the student gets up to leave, have him repeat back to you the main points of the discussion. Agree on what steps need to be taken and in which order – and have the student write them down. This also helps them start thinking about what they will *do*, not just about all the things that might be wrong with their work.

The same applies to written comments: the comments are likely to vary widely in their importance, but the sheer number of them may make it difficult for the author to sort out which are the most important. For this reason, most journals request that reviewers not only make specific comments about particular elements in the text, but also write a brief summary indicating the reviewer's overall impression and assessment of the most pressing problems.

Even if you are meeting informally with a colleague, try to end the session by asking, 'So, what is your next step?' At the very least, the author will have to focus attention forward, so that he leaves the session thinking productively about what to do next instead of obsessing about how his current draft isn't good enough. The mirror works best as a tool for feedback when it shows you not only where you are now, but gives you a glimpse of where you want to be.

THE GOOD CONVERSATION: PEER FEEDBACK AT ITS BEST

Informal peer-to-peer feedback between colleagues is something that I do not think we do enough of. Either we think that it will take too much time, or we find it too embarrassing, or both. Certainly reading a single-spaced 30-page draft and marking every possible typo is something none of us really have time for – unless you are a copy-editor getting paid by the hour. But the good face-to-face conversation is something that we should all manage to squeeze in. The object here is not to provide detailed written comments, but rather to engage in a conversation that will leave the author feeling like he can't wait to get back to writing. If the author has been writing only to his computer the entire time, engaging with a live human being is likely to be a revelation.

Face-to-face feedback allows you to go beyond just the sentences on the page and into the ideas behind them. Trigger questions can get the conversation going.

The aim of the good conversation is not to provide 'advice', but rather to provide a format for allowing the author to think systematically through a draft and share his thoughts with another person. This is just as powerful, and useful, for students as it is for full professors. The trick is to understand what makes a conversation 'good'. One of the best conversations I ever had with a supervisor was one where he asked me a question, one that seemed innocuous at the time, and I gave a superficial answer. But on the train on my way home, the implications of the question started to sink in. By the time I got home, I knew I had to rewrite my entire chapter. If he had *told* me to rewrite that chapter, I would have been defensive, and concentrated on proving him wrong. But he merely asked a question – and waited for me to figure it out myself. Now that I am on the other end, I realize that it is not always easy to know what the good questions are. But over the years, I have put together a set of broad questions that comprise a good starting point.

Below, I give an overview of how to initiate a good conversation – one that encourages the author to keep thinking even when the conversation is over. Because the questions I suggest are at a fairly high degree of abstraction (that is, they do not focus on individual sentences), you can use them even if the author is at a very early stage of writing and has almost nothing on paper, or if for some reason you were unable to read the draft very carefully (or at all).

Before reading the draft, ask the author trigger questions

- Where are you at now with this work, and what do you need the most help with?
- Why did you pick this topic or question in the first place?
- What do you most want people to remember after reading your work?
- What is the most interesting thing you've found out so far?
- What is the most challenging aspect of writing this paper right now?

As described earlier in this chapter, this step ensures that you get a good idea of what the author wants and needs from you. And because not everyone knows what they want or need, asking trigger questions can indirectly get them to talk about what you can help them with. For example, if you ask them: 'Why did you pick this topic in the first place?' they might answer, 'Because it seemed like a good idea at the time. But now it seems like this topic has been researched to death. I have nothing new to add.' This will tell you that part of your job might be to help the author see their own claims more clearly in relation to the existing literature so they can pinpoint their contribution to the discourse.

While reading the draft, ask yourself guiding questions

- Who is the apparent target audience?
- What is the knowledge gap?
- What questions are they asking?
- What claims are they making? (What are the thesis statements?)
- How do they provide support for their claims?
- What theoretical lenses do they use to view their material?
- What do you, the reader, find most interesting about the draft?
- What do you, the reader, expect to be most problematic for the author?
- Do the title and headings fairly represent the content?
- Can you read the tables and figures out loud?

These questions ensure that you read actively. Looking for the core argument and trying to define the audience and knowledge gap based on what you have in front of you helps you find not only what *is* there, but also what is not. For example, the author may have written an interesting introduction, but when you start looking for the knowledge gap you might not be able to find it. In other words, you cannot see why this topic is relevant, or what is new in this particular study. This will give you something to discuss with the author.

Meet with the author for conversation

Peer feedback works best if you can meet face to face. Not all queries translate well to written comments. 'Explain!' for example, might just make the author think 'Explain *what*?!' or 'What do you mean? I just spent three paragraphs explaining this!' By asking the author face to face to explain something, you get a chance to help the author understand what you do not understand. The author's response to your query might then affect some of your other comments – either answering other questions you had, or raising new ones. Either way, the conversation helps the author see how a reader understands her work, and gives her a better idea of how she can make it clearer. (See the text box 'Writing groups as a source of feedback' for ideas about how you can make feedback a group endeavour.)

The questions suggested in the previous step provide a good point of departure for a discussion with an author. If nothing stands out as demanding immediate attention (or if there is very little on paper), you might just want to go through all the questions systematically – until something unexpected turns up. Here it is important to take nothing for granted. Don't just say, 'I understand who your audience is, and your research question is clear.' Say, 'It looks like you are writing for quantitative political scientists and that your research question asks whether armed conflict is likely to decline in the future.' Telling the author what you think they are doing is a powerful way to hold up the mirror. This allows them to say:

> Wait, no. Even though I am a quantitative researcher, this particular paper is meant to be for an audience that has a lot of qualitative researchers as well. And that isn't really my question any more. The main thing I am trying to do is talk about the different types of non-violent protests that are likely to become more common. Didn't I say that?

This unexpected response from the author allows you to pursue this further: 'No, but now that you say it, the whole second half of the paper makes much more sense now. Let's talk about how we can make it clearer.'

Writing groups as a source of feedback

Writing groups can be found in any number of flavours (see Chapter 2 for more ideas). Some are formed specifically to be a source of regular feedback. If you are most interested in feedback at a sentence or paragraph level, you can meet in a 'writing circle' of about four and take turns reading one to two pages from your manuscripts; this gives everyone a chance to get feedback, and also motivates you to have something to show your group each session. Groups like this should meet often – about once a week. Sessions should be relatively short, maybe about an hour. (This also means that time should be spent on the readers giving their feedback and the writer saying as little as possible.)

If you are more interested in getting feedback on argument and overall structure, you will need a different format. One way to do it is to get about six to eight people to commit to meeting about once a month for about 90 minutes. You might want to begin with a short round around the table where each person spends no more than a few minutes talking about the progress she has made on her writing goals since the last meeting; this should probably take no more than 30 minutes total. The remainder of the meeting can be spent focusing on one of the participants in particular. Ideally, the writer in the spotlight will have circulated a copy of a draft paper about a week before the meeting and everyone will have read it. In reality, however, many (if not most) will not have made the time to read it – or at least not in detail. For this reason, you might want to assign one or two people the role of 'discussant', so that at least a couple of the people read the paper in full. More important, however, is that the author prepares a 5-10-minute presentation of the paper, focusing for example on the knowledge gap, the core argument and the writing challenges she is currently facing. The short presentation will make it possible for those who haven't read the paper to follow along, and will give those who *have* read the paper some extra information: sometimes the main message is far clearer in a 5-minute presentation than it is in a 20-page draft paper. The act of preparing the presentation will also be useful for the author (see Chapter 9). One of the participants can facilitate the discussion, using the questions described earlier in this chapter as a guide. The goal of the discussion is to create 'the good conversation' in a group format.

Remember

Peer review helps ensure that contributions to the scholarly dialogue are sound. To participate in this dialogue, you will be expected to review the work of other scholars and to have other scholars review your work – to both give and receive feedback.

Giving feedback requires you to listen and read actively so you can give the author the most accurate insight into how his or her message comes across.

Receiving feedback allows you to see how your work appears to others. It doesn't tell you what to do: it is up to you to revise as you see fit.

The good conversation can help you talk about your work constructively and show you where your writing needs to go.

FURTHER READING

- Belcher, Wendy Laura (2009) *Writing Your Journal Article in 12 Weeks: A Guide to Academic Publishing Success*, Thousand Oaks, CA: Sage. The chapter on 'Responding to journal decisions' provides excellent advice for responding to reviewers, planning your revision strategy and writing revision memos.
- Elbow, Peter (1998) *Writing with Power: Techniques for Mastering the Writing Process*, 2nd edn, New York: Oxford University Press. The chapters in section V are all focused on feedback. Although he describes these chapters as helpful for you to get control over *getting* feedback, they are also very helpful for *giving* feedback.
- Germano, William (2008) *Getting It Published: A Guide for Scholars and Anyone Else Serious about Serious Books*, 2nd edn, Chicago, IL: University of Chicago Press. Unlike most of the other sources that I've listed here, Germano looks at getting feedback in the context of book writing, not article writing.
- Murray, Rowena (2013) *Writing for Academic Journals*, 3rd edn, Maidenhead: Open University Press. Chapter 9 addresses how to respond to reviewer feedback, and very helpfully talks about how to handle hostile and contradictory reviews.
- Wellington, Jerry (2010) *Making Supervision Work for You: A Student's Guide*, London: Sage. Although promoted as a guide for students, this book is very helpful for supervisors in thinking about what kind of feedback students need. Much of this is also relevant to giving feedback to peers.

NINE

Saying it out loud
Presenting your paper

Many journal articles and book chapters begin their lives as a presentation at a scholarly conference. Presentations also extend the life of published works; scholars are often invited to present a paper they have already published – sometimes to very different audiences. There is just no getting around it: giving presentations is as much as a part of research as writing is. Indeed, giving a presentation can be seen as part of the writing process: it forces you to put your ideas into words, and you get an immediate response from your audience. But we seldom dwell on the benefits of giving presentations because most of us associate them with either boredom (if you are the listener) or terror (if you are the speaker) – or both.

When we put children to bed at night, we often read them a story. We pick up a book and read word for word what's written on the page. Our voices washing over them have a hypnotic effect; their eyelids get heavier and heavier, they struggle to stay awake, but the monotonous sound of our voice is relentless and finally they give in and sleep overtakes them. This is a tried-and-true method. Perhaps doing the same thing from a podium is not the most effective way to present your material to an audience who you hope will still be awake when you finish.

But one reason scholars persist in reading from a prepared manuscript is that most of us hate the very idea of speaking to a live audience. Quipped comedian Jerry Seinfeld, 'According to most studies, people's number one fear is public speaking. Number two is death. … That means to the average person, if you have to go to a funeral, you're better off in the casket than doing the eulogy.' Because making a presentation is so terrifying, we spend as little time preparing as we possibly can. Thus, we resort to picking up our published article, breaking into a cold and clammy sweat, and reading it verbatim to an audience that looks as if it has had its collective brain sucked right out of its head. Both we and the audience are counting the minutes until the torture is over.

Another reason is that we have internalized the notion that scholarly lectures are supposed to be boring and that neck injuries from nodding off during a presentation are an occupational hazard. True, multimedia shows with bouncing balls, spinning text, a choir singing in the background and elaborate pyrotechnics are out of place at a scholarly conference. But there is an important difference between *entertaining* and *engaging*. To entertain means you cause time to pass in a pleasant way. You distract your audience for a while, perhaps giving them a laugh or two, but when you leave you (or at least your message) may be quickly forgotten. To engage means that you give people something to think about. When they leave, they take something with them.

When you present your work to a live audience, you have an opportunity to engage your listeners so that they take your research home with them, think about it and perhaps build on it. What's more, switching from a written to a spoken medium may help you hone your argument, and perhaps explore the ramifications of your work in a different way. Just as holes in your thinking become more obvious when you try to write them down, holes – and other problems – in your writing become more obvious when you try to say it out loud.

Presenting your work orally is an important way to participate in the scholarly dialogue. Drawing on some lessons of rhetoric (see the textbox 'Contributions from classical rhetoric'), this chapter describes not only how you can give more effective presentations, but also how you as an author can get the most out of them – whether you have been asked to present your work at a conference, or you are invited to be a guest lecturer at another university, or you simply wish to get feedback from your colleagues.

Contributions from classical rhetoric

Rhetoric is a discipline that focuses on the science of persuading through the use of language, and is thus a natural place to turn to when looking at what makes an effective presentation. This chapter is structured around an admittedly liberal interpretation of the following elements from classical rhetoric:

Intellectio: Doing the groundwork. In its strictest interpretation, this step is limited to choosing your topic. I argue that preparation involves far more, particularly defining your audience.

Inventio: Finding your argument and evidence. This step is generally considered a continuation of the first step, where you narrow down your topic to a specific argument. For scholars, it focuses on identifying and refining your core argument.

Dispositio or *collocatio*: Structuring your presentation. In classical rhetoric, the structure involves providing a factual background and then refuting contrary arguments. I argue that in a scholarly context, structure must do more than this.

Elocutio: Choosing your words. In this chapter, as in classical rhetoric, the focus is on the words you use rather than what you say with them. However, classical rhetoric explores this area in far more depth than I have done here.

Memoria: Remembering what you want to say. Having originated a couple of millennia before the invention of teleprompters and PowerPoint, classical rhetoric naturally focuses on tricks to help the speaker memorize the presentation. I use this step to focus on the types of visual aids most scholarly presenters use to jog their memory and help them tell the story.

Pronuntiatio and *actio*: Using your voice and body language effectively. As in classical rhetoric, this chapter uses this step to focus on the use of voice and gesture in delivering the presentation. I have limited my discussion to the areas most relevant for scholars, especially scholars speaking in a non-native language.

Analysis: Analyzing your performance. Although often left out, this step is important if you want to not only become a better public speaker, but also get constructive feedback on your work.

DOING THE GROUNDWORK

You have just published a groundbreaking paper on black holes and you get a phone call asking you to speak at a conference. You agree, and set about making transparencies of your complex line graphs and equations. When you arrive at your destination, you realize that you are not facing a group of fellow astrophysicists, but rather a group of game designers and science fiction authors. By the time you realize your mistake, it is too late. You were already nervous; now you are petrified. (See the text box 'Managing nervousness'.) If only you hadn't skipped rule number one for giving presentations: Know what you are getting yourself into.

Managing nervousness

Nervousness need not spell doom for your presentation. The trick is to learn how to make it work for you, and not against you. Realize that it does not mean that you are

(Continued)

(Continued)

incompetent, but rather that you care about what you are doing and are not indifferent to your performance. The resulting adrenaline boost you get can help you focus and stay connected with your audience. Likewise, a complete lack of butterflies may make it hard to concentrate on what you are talking about. Some of the best presenters are always nervous before they speak, but they know how to act confident even when they don't feel that way (see 'Using your voice and body language effectively' below). And because they do not fear the nervousness itself, and are able to make use of that adrenaline boost, they come across as committed and sincere rather than terrified.

You can try picking up tips from guides on presentations skills, or by talking to other presenters to learn what they do to get their nerves under control. Some people listen to music, perhaps even a 'theme song' they use every time, before they present to help get themselves in the right frame of mind. Others might wear a particular piece of clothing that makes them feel more confident. Figure out what works for you. But by far the best way to get your nerves under control is to be prepared: arrive early, have a plan B if things don't go as planned, and focus on the main parts of your story. Remember, people are listening to you because they want to hear what you have to say, not because they want to judge your speaking skills.

Knowing what you are getting yourself into means first finding out exactly to whom you will be speaking. Even if you are asked to present a published paper, you may be addressing an audience different from the one for which you wrote the paper. Perhaps they are friendlier; perhaps they are more hostile. Perhaps they are less interested in the academic aspects of your work and more interested in the practical implications. It's almost impossible to overdo the groundwork. The more you find out about your audience and what they expect from you, the more able you will be to give it to them. This applies to any presentation, from scholarly conferences, to teaching, to brown-bag lunches with colleagues, to dinners at the Rotary Club. It may be time-consuming, but the success of your presentation is directly related to the work you put in beforehand. You can probably reach more people by doing one presentation properly than stumbling through five poorly prepared.

Just as important as finding out what your audience wants from you is figuring out what you want from them. Perhaps you want to present a fully developed argument and try to convince your audience of its validity, or perhaps you want to present an idea that is not fully developed to try to get useful feedback from the audience. Maybe you just want them to learn something. Knowing exactly what you want to achieve will determine how you shape your presentation. If you want to convince, you emphasize the validity of your evidence and argument; if you want feedback, you may want to emphasize the problematic aspects and uncertainties; if you are teaching, you should think about not just the message, but how people learn. If you work in applied research you also need to think about how you want to communicate to a non-academic audience and decide whether you want to inspire action or reflection. Do you want them to jump up, bang their fists on the table, and shout, 'By gum, he's right! To arms, men!' Or do you want them to nod sagely and say, 'Point taken. I think I'll take this into account in my work.'

In addition to learning about your audience, groundwork may include looking into any or all of the following.

Location, location, location. The venue, the way the room is set up, and the available equipment matter for how you interact with your audience. This is why many scholars prefer smaller workshop-oriented conferences.

What kind of room will you be in? Is it a big room? A small one? Will it be filled to capacity? Can you move the chairs and tables around to your liking? Where will you stand? The more accurately you can picture the room beforehand – how many people will be in it, where they are sitting and where you will be – the more likely you will be able to enter the room with confidence. If you are especially nervous, try to visit the room a day or two before your presentation, preferably when no one else is there. Walk around it, stand where you plan to stand, and generally give yourself a chance to feel like you own the room. This way, when the big day comes, you'll be less likely to feel that you're walking into hostile territory.

What kind of working equipment is available to you? The projector you saw attached to the ceiling may not be in working order. Find out what you can borrow, and what you yourself need to bring. If you are doing a computer slide show, do you need to bring your own laptop? Or can you bring just your file? Can you bring a memory stick? Do you have access to the Internet? Can you play a sound file? Find out what other equipment is available: overhead projector? flip chart? chalkboard? whiteboard? Do the pens work? Is there chalk? How about an eraser? Do you need an extension cord? There are few things more disconcerting than technical glitches. Even a seasoned presenter will be thrown off if she finds herself standing there with a laptop that has a cord too short to reach the nearest outlet, or a memory stick and no place to insert it.

When will you be speaking? Will you be speaking early in the day? If so, be prepared to deal with stragglers and to compete with coffee cups. Will you be speaking just after lunch? If so, be prepared to deal with the notoriously sleep-inducing post-lunch sugar rush. Will you be speaking at the end of the day? If so, be prepared to deal with people who may have reached their saturation points and be looking forward to dinner.

Who else will be speaking? If you can, find out who will be speaking before you or after you – and try to find out what they are talking about. Experienced speakers learn how to use other speakers to frame their arguments – even if they are presenting opposing views. Keep in mind that some people sign up for a conference just to hear one person speak – and that one person may not be you. And if there is a wide variety of speakers, the audience is likely to be varied as well. You may have to work extra hard to capture the interest of such audiences. (See the sections on structuring your presentation in this chapter and in Chapter 4 on hostile and mixed audiences.)

All this advance preparation may seem an unnecessary nuisance – until the first time you walk through the door and discover things are not as you expected : 'I was expecting a much smaller group! I only have enough handouts for half these people!' Likewise, it may not seem important who will be speaking before or after you, until you learn that the person who spoke right before you made a very good argument for precisely the opposite of what you want to say – or said the very *same* thing you want to say. If you are prepared, you can weave responses into your presentation. If you are not prepared, your self-confidence may take a beating. There are no shortcuts to quality: do your homework. And the more prepared you are, the more confident you will feel.

FINDING YOUR ARGUMENT(S) AND EVIDENCE

Once you know who your audience is and what they want from you, you can begin to find your argument. If you think you did this once and for all when you wrote your paper, think again. Remember, your audience may be more interested in the policy implications of your work than in the scientific implications. Or vice versa. One thing you can be certain of: you have more in your paper than you will be able to get across in your presentation. This is because writing can support a level of detail that speaking simply cannot. And if you try to present the same level of detail in your lecture as you did in your paper, you run the risk of overwhelming your audience, perhaps to the point where they get nothing at all out of what you say.

If you want to engage your audience, you are going to have to make some tough choices about what to include and what to leave out. Since you have done the groundwork and now understand who your audience is likely to be, and you have thought long and hard about what you want to get out of the presentation for yourself, you can narrow down the field. Go through your paper with a fresh sense of purpose and figure out which aspect of it you want to focus on. Perhaps you want to focus on your case study. Perhaps the method will be particularly interesting to your listeners. Maybe you want to draw attention to your conclusions – or one conclusion in particular. Perhaps it is a more specific formulation of your research question that is interesting. The most important thing to remember here is that the core argument of your paper may not be the best core argument for your presentation.

If you have narrowed down the focus of your argument, you will also have to be selective about the evidence you use to support the argument you are making in your presentation. Again, go through your paper with a fresh set of eyes. Which of your findings are relevant to the argument you are trying to make in the context of *this* presentation? If you have summarized your evidence in tables or figures, choose carefully which ones to use. As a rule, tables and figures make effective visual aids, as long as you are able to explain them sufficiently and the point they make fits into your overall argument.

And when you are reviewing your evidence, remember that in a presentation, less is sometimes more. One principle of rhetoric is that three pieces of evidence are not only sufficient to make your point, but are also easier for both the speaker and the audience to remember. If you have seventeen good reasons why non-governmental organizations can be more effective than international organizations, you will not convince your audience any more thoroughly than if you had presented only three. Instead of becoming more convinced with each piece of evidence you throw at them, they will become overwhelmed, and after a while impatient and thus sceptical – especially since some of the reasons are bound to be rather thin. Then they will go away not only thinking that some of your reasons were thin, but possibly not remembering the evidence that was solid. Pick a few of your best reasons. You may want to suggest you have more, but keep your focus on the best ones.

In addition to the core argument for the presentation, you need to think about *how* you will persuade your audience that your points are valid. Rhetoric identifies three argumentative approaches to persuading your audience: *ethos*, *pathos* and *logos*.

Ethos is persuasion on the basis of your credibility. When you appeal to ethos, you are saying, 'Believe me because *I* say so.' Your use of language, your appearance and your mannerisms all help you establish authority. What constitutes 'authority' will vary from context to context. Most of the time your academic authority will be the most important, which you can demonstrate through any previous research you have done, your understanding of the current research, your position in your field and your demonstrated familiarity with your research subjects. But authority can also be derived from your practitioner experience: 'As a practising clinical psychologist working with substance abusers for the past 20 years ...' One way to draw on ethos is to explicitly state your institutional affiliation, title and experience. Another way, however, is to work it more indirectly into your presentation through the use of images (Figure 9.1).

Pathos is persuasion through the emotions of the audience. When you appeal to pathos, you are saying, 'Believe me because your gut tells you to.' You connect with the beliefs and values of your audience. In academic writing and presentation, this is perhaps the most risky approach. On the one hand, people tend to understand things first through their emotions while their intellect needs a

Figure 9.1 Ethos is persuasion on the basis of your credibility

Here, the researcher is photographed in a minefield in Sri Lanka wearing mine-clearing protective equipment. By adding this fieldwork slide to her presentation while she is talking about her methods, the researcher makes an appeal to ethos: 'Believe me because I was there!'

Source: Photo by Wenche Hauge

little time to catch up. So, showing a picture that plucks a string in the viewer means that you've captured their interest long enough to substantiate your point (Figure 9.2). When you first see pictures that are full of pathos, your critical mind is momentarily shut down. You are simply thinking, 'Holy cow! That's awful!' or 'Isn't that wonderful?' But because you are an academic, you will quickly move to critical thinking: 'What is actually going on here?' A skilled presenter will answer your questions before they are fully formed in your mind. This is how pathos can help you create engagement in your audience.

On the other hand, pathos can backfire when you do not follow up the images with relevant scholarship. This can leave the audience thinking, 'This isn't research! This is sensationalism!' In an academic setting, people trust reason more than they trust emotion, so use pathos with caution – perhaps limiting it to your introduction where it is likely to do the most good. Those of us working in fields inherently filled with pathos – war, poverty, crime, healthcare, child abuse, addiction and so on – have to work hard to strike the right balance and not overdo it. For those of us who work in fields that have less pathos – discourse analysis of government documents, urban settlement patterns, attitudes to public transportation, median incomes, for example – we might have to work hard to find any pathos at all. Pathos is not 'academic' in nature, but an argument or an image that generates an emotional response allows the

Figure 9.2   Pathos is persuasion through the emotions of the audience

Launching straight into statistics about child soldiers might simply cause your audience to tune out because statistics are harder to see than individual people. This picture of child members of the Fatah-affiliated youth organization 'al-Ashbal' taken in a Palestinian refugee camp in Lebanon in 1982, however, puts faces on those statistics.

Source: Photo by Are Hovdenak

audience to 'get it' at a visceral level before they 'get it' intellectually. And used with caution, this instrument of persuasion can be powerful even in an academic context.

Logos is persuasion through logic. When you appeal to logos, you are saying, 'Believe me because the evidence is indisputable.' In an academic setting, this is the gold standard. You believe me not because of who I am or how I make you feel, but because my argument is so good that you simply have no choice. The structure of the academic article is built on an appeal to logos: you identify a gap in the knowledge, define a relevant research question, and answer that question on the basis of evidence you have gathered from your well-described method (see Chapter 6). In an oral presentation, (relevant) images can help you make your point better than words alone (Figure 9.3).

Compare the two slides in Figure 9.3. Which one gives you a better mental image of what is happening? With the first slide, the presenter can tell you the exact numbers if necessary, but most importantly allows you to look at the different shapes of the curves. The second slide just gives you the numbers but without letting you see the shapes of the curves and making it difficult to get a visual of how they fit together.

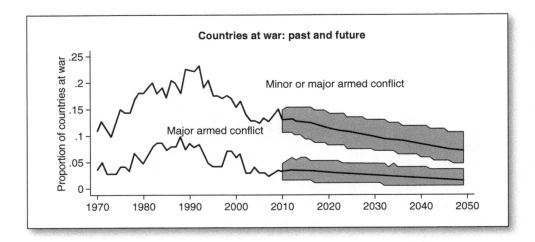

Countries at war: past and future

- Time period date collection: 1970–2009
- Forecasted period: 2010–2050
- Proportion of countries in conflicts:

  – Minor or major armed conflicts

  - From 0.1 in 1970 to 0.24 in 1994
  - Decrease to 0.13 from 1995 to 2010
  - FORECAST: Further decrease to 0.7 in 2050

  – Major armed conflict

  - From 0.04 in 1970 to 0.01 in 1988
  - Decrease to 0.03 in 2010
  - FORECAST: Further decrease to 0.015 in 2050

Figure 9.3 Logos is persuasion through logic

Just because an argument is based on solid research-based findings and logic does not mean it cannot be presented more intuitively for the reader through images.

Source: Håvard Hegre, 'Forecasting', available at: http://havardhegre.net/forecasting/, last accessed June 2014; and Håvard Hegre, Joakim Karlsen, Håvard Mokleiv Nygård, Håvard Strand and Henrik Urdal, 'Predicting armed conflict, 2011-2050', *International Studies Quarterly*, 57 (2) (2013): 250-70 (DOI: 10.1111/isqu.12007)

STRUCTURING YOUR PRESENTATION

As suggested above, your presentation should be structured so that it rests on logos – although use of ethos and pathos, particularly in the first minute or two help establish your authority and pique the interest of the audience. So, in addition to having to adapt your core argument to a spoken medium, you will also have to adapt your structure. For one thing, you will probably need to get to the research question a lot faster. Most journal articles present a couple of pages (about 700 words) of background before they culminate in the research question. If you wait that long in a presentation, you may have to shout to make yourself heard over all the snoring. When you are speaking, your introduction needs to be simple and concrete. If you do not manage to communicate to the audience within the first few minutes what your entire presentation is going to be about, and make them feel that what you are talking about is important, then chances are they will be lost the entire time. Likewise, once you have your audience with you, the rest will almost run by itself.

After you have introduced your research question you can dwell a bit more on the background or context. Just as in writing, the temptation here is to include too much. Restrain yourself – with force, if necessary. The only aim of the background segment is to answer the question: 'Why should you listen to this?' You do not need to go into detail about *all* the relevant work other scholars have done that might have a bearing on your own conclusions. Your job is to focus on the knowledge gap, not to demonstrate your broad grasp of the material.

Next, you present your thesis statement and supporting evidence. In a spoken presentation, it is virtually mandatory that you present your thesis statement before you present your evidence. The audience cannot rewind and listen again to what you said, so you need to make sure they get it the first time. Presenting your thesis statement before your evidence prepares your audience for the evidence that is coming. They know what it is supposed to be proving, so they are in a better position to be able to understand its significance.

Finally, you reach your conclusion. Again, remember that the conclusion of your presentation is not necessarily the conclusion of your paper. Go back to your motivation: What is your aim in giving the presentation? If your aim is to get good feedback, then your conclusion should put the focus on the areas you would like to discuss when you get questions afterward. If your aim is to convey a fully thought-out idea, then recall your main argument and focus on what it all means.

But the main thing to remember here is that you need to tell a coherent story. When we go through our material picking out what we want to cover, we tend to focus on the highlights: the key findings, the main uncertainties and so on. Here, the danger lies in focusing too much on detail at the expense of the overall story. How many times have you seen a slide titled 'Background' with seven bulleted points that did not seem to have anything to do with each other? See Figure 9.4: most of us know this as the story of Cinderella. Our misguided scholar, however, used the slide to provide unnecessary background detail (including words he would probably find difficult to pronounce) and definitions of basic concepts copied directly from *Wikipedia* without source referencing (ever notice how the definitions of simple words like 'glass' can transform a familiar substance into something unrecognizable?), and a singularly unhelpful and irrelevant figure of some sort of family tree. What's missing here is the actual *story*. What *happens* and why it happens. Nervous researchers often fear that they will forget the 'important' details, so they put all those details in the slides. And of course when they get up there and their minds do go blank, they inevitably spend the entire presentation talking about these details and completely forget the actual story, which might have made these details relevant. Details only make sense when they add something to a basic story: the basic story has to be there first. And the basic story should be the one thing you can talk about without any extra assistance. Should the projector explode and your notes burst into flames, you should still be able to take a deep breath and just tell your story. In the oral tradition of storytelling, the storyteller did not have bullet points to follow. Or even a manuscript. He was able to remember the story and the listeners were able to follow it because the story had a narrative flow: a beginning, a middle and an end. Each flowed from the other. When you are considering your structure, take a step back and try to see how your main points flow from one to the other.

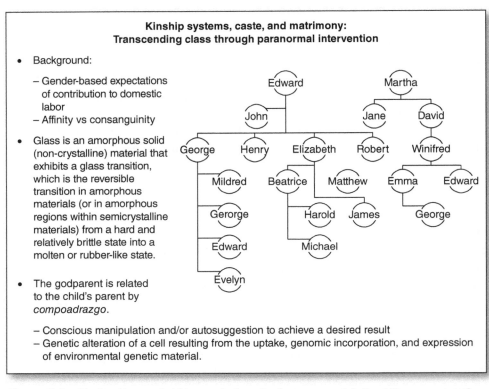

Figure 9.4 Cinderella as retold by a scholar who focuses on details at the expense of the story

One way to do this is to take into account the audience's evolving state of mind throughout the course of the presentation. Here, we can draw on lessons from the learning cycle (see Figure 9.5).[1] We first experience things in terms of how they relate to us (moving from concrete experience to reflective observation). Then we can listen to what other people have to say about them and achieve a more general understanding (moving from reflective observation to abstract conceptualization), which we can apply in our own work or to our situation (moving from abstract conceptualization through active experimentation to a new level of concrete experience).

---

[1]Based on David A. Kolb, 'Learning and Problem Solving', in *Organizational Psychology: A Book of Readings,* ed. David A. Kolb, Irwin M. Rubin and James M. McIntyre (Englewood Cliffs, NJ:. Prentice-Hall, 1974).

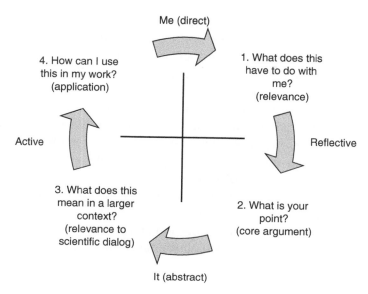

Figure 9.5 The experiential learning cycle

In a scholarly presentation, we have to respond to four types of questions from our audience, each of which corresponds to a stage in this learning cycle. First, your audience is asking, 'Why are you telling me this?' Before they can listen to anything you have to say, they need to know that your presentation is relevant to them in particular. For example, when our astrophysicist was facing an audience of game designers, he would have stood a better chance of getting them to follow his entire presentation if he had begun with: 'As gamers, what do you really need to know about black holes to make your products as realistic as possible?' By appealing to them directly, you establish a connection that will prepare them for your main message. Clearly, this is a special challenge if you have a very mixed audience. At the next stage, the dominant question from the audience is: 'What is your point?' Once they are convinced that what you say is relevant to them, they will be willing and able to hear your argument and conceptualize it. This is where you present your main message.

The final two stages require the audience to step beyond the context of your main message and think about how it can be applied to the scholarly dialogue in general and to their own work in particular. At the third stage, the question dominating your audience is: 'How is this relevant in a wider context?' They are still thinking at a conceptual level, but are actively trying to apply your argument, either to a real-world context or to the broader scholarly discourse. And, finally, at the fourth stage, they are ready to ask: 'If this is so, what does it mean for me? How can I use this in my own work?' Here, they are ready to integrate what they have learned and move forward with it. This is where they decide to what extent your presentation is valuable for their own work.

To take advantage of this learning cycle, a speaker will first establish a connection with the audience before lecturing on content, and then allow the audience to actively make connections to the larger picture, and finally encourage them to integrate what they've learned into their own work. Most scholarly presentations take place only at stage two, lecture – which is why they can be so boring. The audience does not get a chance to feel any connection to the material, and once the material is presented, they are not given an opportunity to do anything with it. Ideally, your preparation should allow you to know your audience well enough to establish a connection before you present your material. And, fortunately, most speaking contexts will allow you to take questions from the audience, which will stimulate active processing. In most academic contexts, you probably will not be able to arrange for your audience to break up into smaller groups so that they can discuss the wider implications of your work and how it may be integrated into their own work. But you can certainly make sure you do not extend your presentation into the time allotted to answering questions and structure your presentation so that you start by establishing a connection and end by bringing it back around to the relevance to the audience, perhaps by suggesting some of the implications of your work for future research.

CHOOSING YOUR WORDS

Say 'operationalization' three times fast. For that matter, say it once slowly. Some words that are friendly on paper can suddenly become your enemies if you try to say them out loud. This is especially true if you are giving a presentation in a language that is not your mother tongue. Even if you can use such words comfortably on paper, you might want to avoid them in a talk. Sometimes, just knowing that you will have to say the dreaded word is enough to increase your anxiety to such levels that you are doomed to mispronounce it no matter what.

Tip

If a difficult word is unavoidable – say it's the name of the village where you conducted your case study – make sure you write it out on some kind of visual aid: a slide, a transparency, the chalkboard or what have you. When you get to the word, you can turn slightly and point to it. You draw attention toward where you are pointing and away from your mumbling.

Even if you are able to pronounce multisyllabic words with equanimity, you might want to think twice about using them anyway. Written language can afford to be a notch or two more formal than spoken language. (A reader can always take time out to look up troublesome words. This is much harder in a conference room, not only because it's rude, but also because by the time you've looked up the difficult word, the speaker has moved on.) And what can seem both eloquent and distinguished on paper can sound pompous and cumbersome when spoken aloud. Not to mention boring. Written language supports both longer words and longer sentences more comfortably than spoken language. You can almost always tell if someone is reading a manuscript out loud – even if they are reading fluently. The word choice will sound unnatural, and they will often almost run out of air by the time they get to the end of the sentence. Spoken language, on the other hand, is choppier. The short sentences, sentence fragments and repetition that would seem amateurish in a piece of writing are far more effective in an oral presentation.

The difference between written and spoken language affects the ways in which you can most effectively present your evidence. The numbers and statistics that work very well in a written paper might be harder to grasp when spoken aloud (without the benefit of an accompanying visual aid). Similarly, figurative language that would seem out of place in a written paper often works very well in a spoken setting. An anecdote that isn't scientific enough to make it into print may be the perfect way to introduce your subject. Many scientists who would never dream of quoting Shakespeare in their manuscript on clinical psychology might find a line or two from *Hamlet* the perfect way to sum up a point. And a metaphor that seemed far too literary to include in a scholarly article may work perfectly well in a roomful of PhD students.

A word of caution: if you decide to venture into the world of figurative speech, choose your metaphors, similes, aphorisms and allegories with care. They work because they draw on people's common understanding of a familiar object or relationship – but using them requires that such a comparison be justifiable. The term 'the greenhouse effect' works not only because most people know what a greenhouse is, but also because it expresses a very complex climatic phenomenon in simple and relatively accurate terms: people picture a greenhouse and they get a very good idea of how heat stays trapped in our atmosphere. But if you pick an unfamiliar reference ('The relationship is like that of Eurybia to her sons') or an image that can't be grasped immediately ('The political system of Sweden is like a bicycle'), you simply confuse people, unless you are prepared to spend a considerable amount of time explaining yourself. This is also true if you bombard your audience with several different types of figurative description for the same phenomenon ('It's like a tree-house or a horse or even a bowl of fruit'). But perhaps the main reason to be careful about figurative language is that a poor choice can draw the focus in the wrong direction. Say you are describing an artist who never had more than a second-rate talent, so he channelled his frustration into politics. You think of comparing him to Hitler. However, a thwarted artistic background is not the first thing we think of when we think of Adolf Hitler, so comparing your artist to Hitler may cause your audience to read far more into the comparison than you intend.

The relative informality of the spoken language is evident even in highly formal settings. In almost any context, the speech that makes the greatest impact is the one given in language that people can understand immediately – language that does not require rewinding or rereading. Dare to speak more directly, with less qualification, when you present your material orally. This is not to say that you cannot use your complex figures and tables. People absorb information in various ways, and one of them is visual. Explaining a complex figure in simple language lets your audience use both the visual and audio senses and can be more powerful than either of them on their own.

When you are thinking about word choice you might also want to consider how you can make ethos and pathos work for you. While your structure should be firmly grounded in logos, you can build your authority (ethos) through your word choice. Using technical terminology can position you as an 'expert' ('believe me because I know what I'm talking about'); using the vernacular can position you as a 'real person' ('believe me because I am one of you'). From your own experience, you have probably noticed that presenters in an academic context tend to overdo the 'I'm an expert, just listen to my big words!' approach. Remember, it is one thing to use technical terminology correctly and position yourself in the field through your choice of concepts; it is another thing to use a long word at every opportunity. (It is helpful to think of jargon like cayenne pepper: a little goes a long way, and too much makes the dish inedible.) Likewise, you can also appeal to pathos through language by drawing from poignant quotes from informants, anecdotes that bring statistics to life and generally emotionally charged words (for example, 'liberty' and 'equality' have more charge than 'democratic systems of governance'). It is the balance of ethos, pathos and logos that is important. If you are new to academia, you might want to err on the side of over-formality to demonstrate authority. If you are a well-established expert, you might want to err on the side of informality to demonstrate accessibility. In any case, it should be a conscious, deliberate choice.

REMEMBERING WHAT YOU WANT TO SAY

Once you have decided how you are going to present your ideas to your audience, you can start thinking about how you are going to remember what you want to say. The old Greeks and Romans who developed the study of rhetoric did not have PowerPoint. Nor did they have 3-by-5 note cards. What they did have was a clear sense of purpose when they spoke. A clear sense of purpose is your most important memory aid: knowing exactly what you are supposed to be doing, having a clear sense of your storyline, will help you regain your focus should your words fail you.

Once you feel confident about saying your central message out loud, close your eyes and imagine yourself giving your talk from beginning to end. Picture where you will stand, where you will look, how your voice will sound and what you will say. When the time comes to actually give your talk, the visualizing you did beforehand will not only make it easier to remember what you were going to say, but also make the situation feel more familiar and therefore less threatening.

For most of us, though, a clear sense of purpose and a clear vision of what we want to do isn't enough. We almost always have with us something that will help us remember what we want to say. Fortunately, we have a wide variety of options at our disposal. Unfortunately, the ones that seem the most helpful might actually work against us.

Reading a prepared manuscript

Many of us feel our safest crutch is a fully prepared manuscript. The more terrified we are, the more we feel we need to see the words right in front of us. We fear that if the words aren't written down, we will never get them out of our mouths. But as noted above, sentences written and words chosen for the printed page are more often more difficult to say out loud. The more we struggle to get our mouths around our well-crafted but long sentences and the more we see our audience getting restless and bored, the more nervous we become – making the manuscript harder to read and the audience even more restless. As the audience starts to squirm, we start talking faster, as if we think we can physically hold them in their seats if we can only bury them in enough words. And the faster we talk, the less the audience understands, and the cycle continues.

If you simply must have a fully prepared manuscript, then at least spend the necessary time rewriting the manuscript so that it can be read out loud. Shorten the sentences, use simpler words and make sure you know how to pronounce everything. You can even include informal phrases like 'let's say', and note where you should pause. You will also need to make sure it is easy for you to see the words on paper: double-space the entire manuscript and choose a font size that you can see comfortably. Read the manuscript through from beginning to end several times to weed out any problem areas and to time yourself. Contrary to what you might think, reading from a prepared manuscript requires more rehearsal than speaking extemporaneously. The more familiar you are with your manuscript, the more natural the words will sound, and the more often you will be able to look up and establish eye contact with your audience.

The more you can wean yourself away from a fully prepared manuscript, the greater the contact you will likely be able to establish with your audience. Jot down key words and phrases on those old standard 3-by-5 note cards, just to jog your memory. The less you write down, the more you will have to say extemporaneously. This will automatically encourage you to use less formal and stilted language, which in turn will make it easier for your audience to understand and remember what you say.

But it is also possible to choose visual aids that not only help you remember what you want to say, but also actively help you get your message across to your audience. Computerized slide presentations, chalkboards/whiteboards and flip charts are all valid options.

Computerized slide presentations

Computerized slide presentations, such as those prepared using Microsoft's PowerPoint, Prezi or other similar programs, are the most modern and probably most common visual aid used today. Slide presentations allow you to write down bulleted lists of points or key words and phrases, as well as figures and tables, ahead of time. The advantage of this is clear: not only do the slides help you remember what you want to say, but they also help your audience refocus if they drop out momentarily (especially if you use animations to introduce one point at a time). The disadvantages are perhaps not as clear: you may wind up competing with it for the audience's attention – and losing. *You* are the most important visual aid you have (see the next section), and the more you draw attention away from you, the less you communicate directly with your audience. The most common problem with slide presentations is that the slides contain far too much information. Most people cannot read one thing while listening to something else. They will tend to read what's on the screen and ignore you, or maybe listen to you and ignore what's on the screen – or most likely, try to do a bit of both and end up failing on both counts.

For your slide presentation to be effective, make sure only a small amount of text appears on the screen at a time. Your bulleted points should appear one at a time (and, please, just make them appear: no bouncing, spinning, singing or dancing). If you simply must have a large number of words on the screen at once – say you are showing an important paragraph of legal text – then read the text *with* your audience: use a pointer and read the text out loud so your audience can follow along. This way, you make sure you direct your audience's focus where you want it. If you ask them to read it to themselves, as many presenters do, you risk over- or underestimating the length of time it takes to read, and most likely you will carry on talking, making reading difficult.

If you spend too much time looking at the screen, you draw attention away from what you are saying and the audience is robbed of their most important source of information: you.

The second major mistake people make when giving slide presentations is that they turn their backs to the audience to see what is on the screen, and then they end up talking to the screen. This makes it harder for your audience to hear, and it causes them to miss out on the valuable information they can get from your facial expressions. Make sure you have a monitor in front of you that is showing what is on the screen behind you. Then you won't have to turn around to check what's up on the screen, and you'll be less tempted to talk to the screen instead of your audience.

Flip charts, chalkboards and whiteboards

Far more old-school, and comparably undervalued, are flip charts, chalkboards and whiteboards. The genius of these is that you can draw as you talk – letting your ideas develop visually as they flow. Most of us remember at least one wild-haired professor waving his arms around with chalk in hand, drawing arrows in all directions, spittle flying. Chances are you never fell asleep during his classes. It's hard *not* to be engaged when the speaker is so clearly engaged, and the less you are a slave to your visual aids, the more you can let your engagement steer you. The more you want to interact directly with your audience, the more you need a visual aid that does not require prior preparation, or will not flummox you with technical glitches. If you are planning to answer direct questions from your audience, the last thing you want to have to say is: 'Wait a second, hold that thought. Let's see, if I press ESC, I get out of the slide show, but how do I start a new slide? No, I don't want the bullet points. How do I draw a line on this thing?'

USING YOUR VOICE
AND BODY LANGUAGE EFFECTIVELY

Whatever system you use to help you remember what you want to say – and to help your audience both understand and remember your message – make sure you do not play a supporting role to your visual aids. Your body and your voice are your most important aids. And in a contest between your body language and the words coming out of your mouth, your body language will always win. Remember when you were a kid getting yelled at by your father for, say, putting cans of Coke in the tumble dryer to see what would happen? You knew that if he even for *one second* cracked a smile, you had nothing to fear. No matter how emphatically he said, 'Now, Bobby, I'm really angry with you', the smile overruled everything. The same will happen when you are up on the podium. No matter how often you say that your results are exciting and you have confidence in their validity, if you stand there cringing like a minion, nobody will get excited and plenty of people may wonder how much confidence you really do have (Figure 9.6).

Which one of the people in Figure 9.6 would you rather listen to? If you look like you are interested in what you are talking about, your audience will be interested, too. Likewise, if you look like you are indifferent, you are sending a strong signal to your audience about how they should feel as well. This is a serious challenge if you are terrified of public speaking. The less confident you seem, the less confidence your audience will have in what you are saying. The good news is that the more public speaking you do, the more confident you are likely to become.

Figure 9.6 The importance of body language

It is not just action that speaks louder than words: inaction and facial expressions send a strong message to the audience about your confidence and level of engagement.

Until then, however, you may have to learn to fake it until you make it. Here are some things you can do to seem more confident and in control:

Practice 'power poses': Avoid crossing your arms, sitting hunched over with your legs crossed or any posture that makes you smaller. Practice standing with your shoulders relaxed, with your arms wide open, loose at your sides or your hands on your hips. (See Amy Cuddy's TED talk, 'Your body language shapes who you are', available at: www.ted.com/talks/amy_cuddy_your_body_language_shapes_who_you_are.) Do this for a few minutes before you speak, and when you are speaking, you do not need to strike a Superman pose, but remembering to stand up straight with your shoulders back and your arms uncrossed can send a signal not only to the audience but also to yourself that you have this under control.

Avoid apologizing: If you are late, simply say, 'Thank you for your patience.' If you have forgotten to bring the handouts you prepared the night before, just say, 'If you would like additional written material, contact me afterward.' And whatever you do, do not begin a speech by apologizing for what a bad public speaker you are. You may feel like you are scoring points by bonding with the audience on a human level, but what you are actually doing is calling attention to a shortcoming the audience probably would not have noticed until you brought it up. See for yourself: next time you have people over for dinner, halfway through the meal apologize for the uncomfortableness of the chairs and watch them suddenly squirm in a newfound awareness of how they are sitting. And the worst thing you can say is: 'I'm sorry I didn't have time to prepare.' You might think you are telling them, 'No, really, I'm better than this. Don't let my bumbling performance fool you', but what you are actually saying is, 'I couldn't be bothered to prepare properly. You are not a high enough priority.'

Dress to mirror your audience: One of the best ways to inspire confidence is for your body language to say, 'I'm one of you.' If your audience is in jeans, you can wear jeans. If they are in business attire, you should be, too. It is safer to err by being a bit too formal than a bit too informal. One other note regarding clothing: the best clothing to wear is the kind that is not remembered afterward. If your audience pays attention to what you are wearing, they are clearly not paying attention to what you are saying. This means that all loud, jangling jewellery of any kind should be left at home.

Keep nervous tics to a minimum: Do you feel you have to do something with your hands at all times? Hold on to a pen, a piece of chalk, a pointer or something. This might keep you from scratching various body parts or fiddling with your hair or clothing – any of which are infinitely more distracting. And while moving back and forth a bit can help keep both you and your audience more awake, try to avoid rocking or swaying, which can have a less-than-desirable hypnotic effect.

Maintain eye contact: The more you look at your audience, the more confident you will appear. Even if they seem like a blur to you, just lifting your face to look in the general direction of where people are sitting helps tremendously. Sometimes, you will find some people who look particularly interested in what you are saying; if you focus on them, you can boost your confidence, in addition to achieving better contact with the audience in general. But please avoid staring at just one person in particular; in addition to making that person feel extremely uncomfortable, you make everyone else feel left out.

Speak loudly and slowly: Nothing inspires confidence more than a clear, resonating voice. And for most of us, the more excited or nervous we get, the faster we talk. Slow down! This is especially true if you are speaking in a non-native language.

Use silence: Do not be afraid of pauses. Most people find silence uncomfortable and rush to fill it. But if you show that it does not scare you, then your audience will cave first – and instead of tuning you out, they will focus their attention on waiting for you to say something. So, instead of saying 'umm' or 'uh' or whatever filler you favour, practice just letting silence descend. This not only lets your audience think, it also shows them that you are in charge.

And if you are speaking at a conference in a foreign language, or if you in any other way feel intimidated by the other speakers or audience, try to interact with them as much as you can beforehand. Ask questions, circulate, mingle. This will give you both an opportunity to warm up in speaking the language of the conference and a chance to learn something about your audience.

ANALYZING YOUR PERFORMANCE

The final step in giving a good presentation is to analyze how it went. First, ask yourself what went well, and what went less well. If you take just a few minutes to think about what worked and what didn't, you can apply this to your next presentation. Next, you can ask someone from the audience how it went. It is always a good idea to ally yourself with a partner at every speaking occasion. Get someone from the audience to pay particular attention to how your presentation went *as a presentation*. And like any feedback situation (see Chapter 8), the more background you can give your partner on what you need help on, the better the feedback you will get. Are you most worried about distracting mannerisms? Your pronunciation of some words? Your visual aids?

When it comes to scholarly presentations, however, the most important aspect to analyze is usually the content. The feedback you can get from a presentation, where people can ask you questions directly about your work, can be far more valuable than almost any other kind of feedback. If you use the opportunity to integrate this feedback, then presenting your work becomes more than just an unavoidable part of being a scholar – it becomes an invaluable tool.

Remember

Giving presentations does more than help you reach a wider audience with your message. It is also an important part of the writing process. Presenting your material out loud and answering questions from your audience both help you further hone your ideas.

FURTHER READING

- Aristotle, *Rhetoric*. Sometimes it is useful to go back to the beginning. In this case, Aristotle is the undisputed father of modern rhetoric. Aristotle's pamphlet on rhetoric is available in any number of forms: I have a Kindle version by Acheron Press. What is amazing about Aristotle's writing is how much of it is still relevant today, after more than 2,000 years.
- Curry, Mary Jane and Lillis, Theresa (2013) *A Scholar's Guide to Getting Published in English: Critical Choices and Practical Strategies*, Bristol: Multilingual Matters. Curry and Lillis discuss the reasons why you might want to attend a conference and give a presentation.
- Duarte, Nancy (2010) *Resonate: Present Visual Stories that Transform Audiences*, Hoboken, NJ: John Wiley and Sons. A follow-up to her previous book *Slide:ology*, which focuses on the visual presentation of slides, this book focuses more on the art of connecting with an audience. Although scholars are not the main audience, we have a lot to learn from some of the ideas that she offers. She also has a website that is worth taking a look at: www.duarte.com, last accessed June 2014.

- Reynolds, Garr (2012) *Presentation Zen*, Berkeley, CA: New Riders. In *Presentation Zen* and its follow-up book *The Naked Presenter*, Garr draws from lessons he learned about simplicity by living in Japan. Like Duarte, Garr does not explicitly target academics here, but he has a lot to offer. He also has a blog worth visiting: www.presentationzen.com, last accessed June 2014.
- Thody, Angela M. (2006) *Writing and Presenting Research*, London: Sage. This is one of the few books on scholarly writing I have seen that explicitly talks about presentations. See chapter 13 'Becoming a presenter'.
- Tierney, Elizabeth P. (1996) *How to Make Effective Presentations*, London: Sage. Most books on presentation skills focus on presentations in the context of business, which as we all know is not the same thing as a scholarly conference. As part of the Sage 'Survival Skills for Scholars' series, this book focuses on the important issues of giving presentations in the context of academia.

TEN

Delivering the goods
Following author guidelines and submitting your manuscript

It's the thought that counts, right? When you were little and presented your mother with breakfast in bed on Mother's Day, she didn't mind that the toast was burnt and the coffee was tepid black water. She looked past all that to the effort and love you'd put in, reached over and ruffled your hair, and all was well. Surely journal editors, too, should be able to look past your messy reference list, your lack of editing, your handwritten notes in the margin. They should be able to recognize your brilliance and embrace your work, warts and all. But the truth is that burnt toast is only charming when it comes from your own kid – and even then only once a year. Get served burnt toast every day and even a Mother Teresa might hurl it across the room and shout, 'How hard can it be to make a freakin' piece of toast?!?' Journal editors feel pretty much the same way. I'm sure not a day goes by that they don't want to hurl a manuscript across the room and yell, 'How hard can it be to make a freakin' reference list?!?'

Most journals and publishers provide guidelines for authors who are preparing to submit manuscripts for publication. Making an effort to track down, read and follow those author guidelines shows that you are serious about submitting your work to that particular journal or publisher. It also shows you have an eye for detail, which implies that you are equally exacting with your research. (And, yes, the converse is also implied: if you are sloppy about these details, the managing editor may wonder about the quality of your research.)

Finding the most up-to-date set of author guidelines for your target journal is your first challenge. A few years ago, most journals published their guidelines in the journal itself. Today, virtually all journals make their author guidelines available on the Internet. Some even have them in both places, vividly demonstrating how more is not necessarily merrier – especially when the two versions disagree. The print version may say, 'Do not use footnotes,' while the web version says, 'Footnotes should be reserved for clarification of content. Simple references must be placed in endnotes.' Because web pages can be instantly updated and there are no real space limitations, it is logical to assume that the web version is the most current and complete. But like any assumption, this one can get you into trouble. When in doubt, consider calling or emailing the managing editor for clarification. You can also try looking at the most recent version of the journal, or talking to a colleague who has successfully submitted work to it. (See the text box 'Journals: The human element'.)

Journals: The human element

As I pointed out in Chapter 4, it is easy to forget that journals are run by people. Moreover, these are people who are not doing this full time. Journals are less like perfectly mechanized and thoroughly professional systems, and more like part-time businesses run on a volunteer basis by people who have too much to do to begin with. Journal editors, and those sitting on the editorial boards, are almost always publishing academics themselves, which means they also conduct research, write, teach and do all the other things other academics do – on top of editing a journal. They have good days and bad days; they occasionally lose stuff and forget stuff. Most important, they differ from one another with respect to how they work (especially with respect to how organized they are and how much they prioritize their work on the journal) and what they like or don't like. I once asked four journal editors how they felt about a researcher calling them with an article idea to ask if the journal would be interested. One was vehemently negative: 'Talk to me when you have a full draft. In fact, don't talk to me then, either. Just submit it.' Another was surprisingly positive: 'One of the things I like best about this job is working with authors and ideas.' The other two were somewhere in between. This range of responses is evident for almost everything. For example, some editors merely shrug philosophically when authors send in manuscripts that are already 1,000 words over the limit and just say, 'We'll take care of it in the revisions.' Others send back submissions that are even a syllable over the limit, mentally reserving a special place in hell for that author. Although in this chapter I describe how *most* journal editors feel about things, keep in mind that I cannot possibly do justice to the natural variation. So, it is not only important to read the author guidelines carefully, but also to perhaps read between the lines – and always remember that humans are fallible.

Once you have a set of guidelines in hand that you feel you can trust, go through it systematically. The more experience you have with publishing your work in journals, the clearer it will be that different journals have very major differences in their in-house preferences. Some journals have author guidelines that are so detailed they could be published as a book. Others are as general as 'Double-space everything and send it in.' Few make for exciting reading, but some contain unexpected gems, like this one from the author guidelines for *African Affairs*: 'Sadly, too many submissions contain simple ideas expressed complexly.'

Understanding the preferences of your target journal is your next challenge. You might think that holding a set of typed instructions in your hand would make things easier. But you would be wrong. Most author guidelines are written to make sense to copy-editors, not authors. Copy-editors know, for example, that 'MW12' means the twelfth edition of *Merriam-Webster's Collegiate Dictionary*, a recognized authority on American English; most authors don't. This is unfortunate, and goes a long way toward explaining why authors give up, send the manuscript in as is and simply hope for the best. This chapter looks at some of the most important and confusing areas covered in instructions to authors, and suggests areas that deserve your particular attention. The focus is on academic journals, but much of it applies to books as well.

WORD LIMITS

There is not much to say about word limits except that they apply to everyone – yes, even to you. They should be considered absolute and inviolable. A word limit of 8,000 words does not mean 9,000 words, or even 8,100. Thinking 'surely they will make an exception for my fine work' is likely to result in, at best, a polite but firm revise-and-resubmit letter that concludes with 'and please make the necessary cuts so that the article does not exceed 8,000 words'. There are two reasons for strict word limits. One is that print journals usually have a fixed and finite number of pages at their disposal. The other is that journal editors know from experience that journal articles will expand to fit the space allotted to them. Almost everyone struggles to make their work fit the word limit – no matter what that word limit is. If editors allow authors to exceed the limit – or, heaven forbid, impose no word limit at all – they will be able to publish only a very few, very bloated journal articles instead of a larger number of concise and streamlined articles.

Word limits offer two potential traps for the unwary author. The first is that the word limit often depends on the *type* of article you are submitting. Journals often have several different classes of articles: research articles, review articles, commentaries, letters, features and so on. Each type has its own word limit. So, read the guidelines carefully, and make sure you adhere to the word limit that corresponds to the type of article you are writing.

The second trap is notes and references. Most journals specify that the total word count *includes* notes and references. If you find you are over the limit, it does not help to cut paragraphs from the main text and turn them into footnotes. Sorry!

FORMATTING

When it comes to formatting, many author guidelines say something simple like 'Use double-spacing throughout, including footnotes', and leave it at that. Some ambitious authors, proud of their desktop-publishing skills, try to go a step further: they try to make their articles look like the journal's finished product by adding text boxes, columns and other 'finishing touches'. Don't be tempted! This makes it more difficult to process your manuscript. What you send in is essentially treated as raw text, which is then digested and spit out by a proper typesetting program. Many types of typesetting software find certain things indigestible, such as automatic bullets or automatic numbering (e.g., in footnotes and endnotes). This means that when they get your manuscript, editors have to manually strip out all the bullets, numbered footnotes, and other specialized formatting codes and replace them with codes that the software can read. This is why some of the instructions may seem quirky, like asking you to use endnotes, even though the final article will be printed using footnotes. Endnotes are simply easier to manage during this process. The instructions in the author guidelines are written with the journal's specific typesetting software in mind. They are there for a reason.

Many journals offer a template that you can download and use to format your article. Although using these kinds of templates should be intuitive, it can often be a teeth-grinding experience. If you manage to make it work, then you know you have your article formatted according to the preferences of the journal. If you do not have a template, then you need to learn how to follow instructions.

Formatting instructions normally include a specification for styling headings, tables, captions and other design elements. Sometimes, the conversion from word processing software to typesetting (or page layout) software makes everything go wonky. If you have been very consistent about your use of styles, this is fairly easy for the typesetter to repair using a basic search-and-replace function. But if you have used several different styles for the same level of heading, or used the same style for more than one level, this may create a big mess. This often happens when more than one author is working on an article. Each author has her own set of available styles, and each uses what she thinks is best based on how it looks on the printout. But how it looks on the printout is far less important than how it is defined at the formatting level. Similar-looking headings may be defined very differently, with one called 'Heading 2' and the next called 'Heading 2 + double spacing' and a third called 'Heading 8' and the fourth just 'Normal', to which someone has added bold. If everything has gone wonky in the conversion process, all of these may wind up looking different. This means extra work for the editors and layout artists, who then have to find out which headings are supposed to be at which levels. It is far easier to handle a document with no formatting styles than to process one with inconsistent styles.

Different journals and publishers are also equipped to handle different kinds of word processing software. Virtually all can handle Microsoft Word or any other software that can produce an .rtf (Rich Text Format) file. Many others can handle various versions of LaTeX. But if you are using a word processing program that is somewhat unusual, then you should check to see whether the journal or publisher can handle it. By the way, manuscripts should never be submitted in PDF format, although PDF may be used in the first round when the article is sent to peer reviewers. Think of a PDF file as a photograph of the document: you can see what the document looks like, but editing is difficult at best.

File types are also a concern when it comes to artwork (photographs, tables and figures). Journals always specify what file types they can accept, such as .gif, .png or .jpg. Do not take it for granted that the relatively common file type you are using will be acceptable to the journal.

HOUSE STYLE

In the world of clothing and fashion, 'style' has to do with how the clothing *looks*. The basic function of clothing is to keep you warm when it's cold, to keep you dry when it's wet, or to keep you from sticking to your leather chair. Colour, shape and various frills and trim seldom keep us warm, dry or unstuck, but they do help make a statement to the world about who we are. In the world of publishing, style is likewise more about fashion than function. In the context of format (see previous section), 'style' refers to how a particular heading or block of text should look: bold, italic, 12-point Times Roman, double-spaced and so on. But in the world of copy-editing, 'style' covers everything that isn't merely a question of grammar. 'House style' refers to the specific preferences of a given journal or publisher in at least some of the following areas:

- *Abbreviations (including acronyms and initialisms)*: Are they allowed? Should they be given before or after the full name? Should they be listed in a separate appendix? What about Latin abbreviations such as e.g., i.e., cf., etc. and so on?
- *Capitalization*: Is title case or sentence case preferred for headings?[1] What about various titles (President or president)? Short names for proper nouns (the Protocol or the protocol)?
- *Foreign terms*: How should you treat untranslatable terms? Should place names be anglicized (Venice or Venezia)? What do you do with names of foreign organizations or titles?

---

[1]Title case (Like This, Where All Main Words Are Capitalized: Also Known As 'Upstyle') is somewhat more common in the United States and for main titles whereas, sentence case (Like this, where only the first word and proper nouns are capitalized: Also known as 'downstyle') is more common in the United Kingdom and for subheadings.

- *Lists*: Should lists be bulleted or marked off with letters or numbers? Should you capitalize the first word in each item? How should they be punctuated?
- *Units of measurement*: Do you use metric or imperial? Do you write out or abbreviate?
- *Currency*: How do you style, for example, one hundred US dollars? USD100, 100 USD, US$100, or 100 US dollars?
- *Dates and time*: Numbered or written dates, and in which order? For example, 04.02.64, 2/4/64, 1964–02–04, Feb. 4, 1964, or 4 February 1964? A 12-hour or 24-hour clock, as in 1 p.m. or 1300?
- *Quotes*: Should you use double or single quote marks? When is a quote long enough to set off in a block? When should you use ellipses?
- *Punctuation*: Should you use a serial comma (Oxford comma)? Should you use em dashes (—) or en dashes (–)?
- *Spelling*: Which type of English spelling is specified? American, British, Australian, Canadian or other? Is a particular dictionary specified, such as MW12 or the *Oxford English Dictionary*? What is the policy about open or closed compound words?
- *Gender neutrality*: Is gender-neutral language required? If so, are preferences stated about pronoun use for unspecified persons, such as 'he/she', 'he or she', alternating 'he' and 'she' in examples, or 'they' as a singular? What about titles, such as using 'chair' or 'chairperson' instead of 'chairman'?
- *Numbers and symbols*: When should you write out numbers? Under ten, twenty or one hundred? Should you write 'percent', 'per cent' or '%'?

Yes, it is overwhelming and confusing. Perhaps the most confusing aspect of it all is that there is no one 'right' answer. This is the most important thing to understand about house style: it not about right or wrong; it is about preference. And in matters of taste, there are no absolutes, only many strong opinions. (If you want to see a real blood sport, try locking up a bunch of copy-editors in a room and have them slug it out over the proper use of the serial comma or 'which' vs 'that'.)

Often a journal will claim that it uses a particular style guide, such as the *Chicago Manual of Style* or the *APA Publication Manual*. But usually they also have their own in-house preferences that differ from and overrule some of the specifications in these manuals (especially with respect to references; see the section on getting help later in this chapter). So, you are far better off learning to read and follow instructions rather than learning a particular style by heart.

If following the instructions on style proves daunting, or if instructions are absent, you can avoid the worst of the pitfalls by simply following the overriding principle of consistency. With respect to style, your motto should be: 'Better to be consistently wrong than occasionally right.' If you are not sure about whether to write '*Stortinget*', 'the Storting', 'the Norwegian Parliament', 'the Norwegian parliament' or 'the parliament in Norway', the worst possible choice you can make is to use all of them in the hope that at least one of them is correct. You not only instill confusion in the reader – who will wonder whether 'the Storting' is a different thing than 'the Norwegian parliament' – but you will also create a genuine nightmare for the copy-editor who has to find every variation that you've used and make it consistent. When in doubt, pick one and stay with it. If you are wrong, at least the copy-editor only has to do one round of search-and-replace!

REFERENCES: GIVING CREDIT WHERE IT IS DUE

The area that is most likely to trip up authors in the homestretch is references. When you think your article is finished and you are about to press 'submit', stop. Take another whole day and work on your references. I am neither kidding nor exaggerating. If you could see my face right now, you would see a grim line where my mouth usually is. Even if you have used bibliographic management software such as EndNote or Zotero, you still have a long road ahead of you.

When (and who) to reference

The goal of referencing is to enhance the transparency of your argument, and thus your credibility as an author. When a reader thinks to herself, 'Where did he get *that*?' she should be able to find the answer. Facts, data or ideas that originate anywhere other than in your own head should be traceable. Plagiarism is a serious offense in scholarly work, and it is worth spending some time making sure you understand when referencing is required (for an overview of what constitutes plagiarism see, for example: www.plagiarism.org). Here, as in every other aspect of the law, ignorance is no excuse.

Obviously, when you copy *word for word* what someone else has written, the copied material must be set off either in quotation marks or, for longer passages, as a block quote. After the quote, you must cite the source in accordance with the citation format required by the journal or publisher. Less obviously, you must also give credit for ideas borrowed from someone else, even when you have put them into your own words. If you have paraphrased, then quote marks are no longer called for, but you still need to cite the source. Lest this sound like every single word you write will have to be cited, let me point out that you do not have to cite generally accepted truths. You can state that 'the capital of California is Sacramento' without citing a source.

Whether or not you should add a page number to your citation is not as straightforward as you might think. The general rule most of us have learned is that you give the page number when you have cited verbatim and omit the page number when you paraphrase. But keep in mind that the ultimate goal of referencing and citation is to give your readers enough information that they can check for themselves. Say you write something like: 'According to the UN Millennium Development Goals Report 2013, the main obstacle to childhood education is household poverty, which makes children three times less likely to complete school.' This is not plagiarism because you have stated your source. And you have paraphrased the original text, which is as follows:

> Household poverty is the single most important factor keeping children out of school. This is one of the findings of an analysis of data collected through household surveys in 63 developing countries between 2005 and 2011. Children and adolescents from the poorest households are at least three times as likely to be out of school as their richest counterparts. (p. 15)

But if you do not add the page number to your paraphrasing, you make it very hard for a reader who wants to know where the figure 'three times less likely' came from or to find out more about poverty as an obstacle to education – especially if the report or book you refer to is in the hundreds of pages. You may also unwittingly start a game of 'academic whispers', which is like Chinese whispers except instead of children sitting around in a circle and whispering what they thought they heard from the person on their left into the ear of the person on their right, we have academics paraphrasing what they thought they read from someone who paraphrased from someone else. This can result in claims like 'the UN claims that rich children are three times more intelligent than poor children'.

The spectre of 'academic whispers' should not only encourage you to add page numbers when you paraphrase specific facts (rather than summarize an entire work, or a large part of a work), but also encourage you to find your way back to the original reference. Say you are reading a book by Smith. In this book, Smith quotes Jones. You think that the quote eloquently sums up what you want to say, so you use it, too. If you write 'Jones, as quoted in Smith', you give Smith the citation credit. On the one hand, we operate in a world where our merit is measured by the number of times that we are cited. If Jones spent five years meticulously researching and writing his article, sweating and pulling his hair out over the perfect formulation, it seems unfair for Smith to get credit for just taking the time to read Jones's work and type up a sentence from it. On the other hand, much of the work we do as scholars involves trying to make sense of what others have said before us. If Jones has a reputation for being unreadable, and Smith has done the work of making Jones accessible to others and finding the one quote in Jones's 12-volume work that actually makes sense, then Smith deserves the credit. Likewise, if Jones is a thirteenth-century French author who wrote only on sheepskin and whose works are available for viewing only by monks who find the secret entrance to the cave under an unspecified cathedral in Paris and thereafter take a vow of silence, you can cite Smith with a clean conscience and admire his dedication. But if the only reason you give the citation credit to Smith is because you are too lazy to go to the library to find Jones, you are not excused. Do your best to cite original sources – at the very least to make sure that Smith quoted Jones accurately!

How to reference

There are three main documentation systems, each of which has about a gazillion variations. If you use a reference managing software (such as EndNote or

Zotero), switching from one documentation style to another can be done quickly and relatively painlessly (although there might be some things you have to fix manually afterwards, such as filling in entire first names if you have imported references with only first initials). If you do not use a reference managing software and manage all your references manually, you can approach the question of style in two ways: either figure out which system your target journal wants *before* you start writing so you can do it correctly as you go, or do it the way you've always done it and then spend a horrific week at the end restructuring all your references, still getting it wrong, giving up and paying a copy-editor to do it for you. It's really up to you.

Author-date (Harvard, APA)

The author–date system, most common in the social sciences, is so called because in the text you cite your source by the author and the date, like so:

Adams argues that 'with age inevitably comes wisdom' (2001, p. 3). Recent studies, however, have shown a moderate inverse correlation between age and IQ (Brown 2006; Dixon 2004; Carter and Dixon 2003).

You then have a reference list at the end that contains all the references in full in alphabetical order, like so:

Adams, Annette (2001) *The Meaning of Life*, Oslo: Know-It-All Publications.

Brown, Bobby (2006) 'Being 42 isn't enough: How Annette Adams misses the mark', Review of the book *The Meaning of Life*, *Journal of Intellectual Snobbery*, 12 (2): 37–51.

Carter, Celine and Dixon, Diggory (2003) 'Does intellect have an expiration date? IQ and age', *Social Science of the Ages*, 3 (5): 119–24.

Dixon, Diggory (2004) *An Impossibly Impenetrable Report*, August 2004, Town, State: United States Department of Arcane Statistics, available at http://USDAS/impenetrable/reportcemetary/.org (accessed 12 January 2006).

What's important to remember here is that your reference list should contain *only* works actually cited in your manuscript, and that all the works cited in your manuscript must be listed in full in the reference list.

Numbered (Vancouver)

The numbered system earned its name because, not surprisingly, the in-text references are marked by numbers. The numbers can appear in either round (1) or square [2] brackets, or as superscripts[3]. The numbers direct the readers to an entry in the full reference list, which is located at the end of the article. This system is most useful when there are a lot of citations, when several works may be cited for a given statement, and when it is common for each work to have a large number of authors, as in the natural sciences and medicine. For example, the in-text references may look like this:

> Many recent studies have provided convincing evidence that the presence of dust-eating nocturnal feather mites can be used to estimate the age of the slant-eyed emu [1, 2]. However, Skodvin et al. argue that densely populated urban settlements with pronounced use of artificial lighting disturb the feeding patterns of the feather mites, thus reducing their life spans and thereby their use as an indicator [3].

The references at the end of the article are not listed alphabetically, but rather in the order in which they first appear in the article. Because the aim of this style is to save space when there are so many references and so many names, most use a first initial instead of a full first name for each of the authors. To save even more space, some journals leave out titles of journal articles, using only the author names, journal name (or abbreviation), page numbers and year. Book titles, however, are given in full. Thus, the reference list will look something like this:

1. Gillott, J., K. Palau, A. Bakti, F. Saadane. *Insect Bio.* 34, 112 (2004).
2. Banks, M., J. Pursley, S. Soergel, P. Ballingall, J. Shinkle, J.R. Ewing. *Bio. Insecticus* 23, 456 (2005).
3. Skodvin, T., T. Hauglid, D. Hestnes, A. Bjorshol, H. Hole, J. Tonnesen, K. Greiner, K. Oyen, K. Aanensen, L. Lindstad, M. Helle, T. Helle. *Of mites and men: Feather mites and human settlements.* (Pseudo-Science Publishing, Berkeley, CA, 2006).

Footnote (Chicago, Turabian)

Footnote references are perhaps most common in the humanities. Here, there is seldom a separate literature list at the end, but rather all important information is included in the footnote. For the first mention, the full reference is included, while subsequent mentions include only the author name, short title if necessary and page number. For example, the text might state:

> Discourse analysis of modern texts shows that an improbably long shelf-life, or *self-life*, is a goal to which the modern female aspires, thus undermining the assumptions of post-modern, intra-feminist, urban self-defeatism.[1]

The footnote would then read: Laura Walker, 'I'm pink, therefore I'm Spam', *Journal of Consumer Philosophy*, 12 (2005), p. 23. On second reference to the same article, the footnote would say something like this: Walker, 'I'm pink', p. 38. And you are allowed to use 'ibid.' if a footnote cites the same source as the footnote immediately above.

Problem references

There always seem to be one or two references that do not fit into any of the familiar categories. What do you do about websites with no authors? Papers that were handed out at a conference but not published elsewhere? What about archive material? Personal communications? If the instructions to authors do not describe how to treat these anomalies, your best bet is to pick up some recent issues of your target journal and skim through them to see how other authors have dealt with the same thing. If you cannot find any examples that are comparable to yours, then call or email the editor of the journal.

One particular class of problem references worth discussing here is foreign references, that is, bibliographic material written in languages other than English (if English is the language of publication). Journals have different rules for whether and when you are expected to translate the titles of such material. The *Journal of Scandinavian History*, for example, might assume that its readers have a working knowledge of Scandinavian languages and thus not require translation. So, if the author guidelines do not specifically say whether or not you need to translate the titles of non-English works, then check out some back issues of your target journal to see what other authors have done.

If you do need to translate the title, in your reference list the original title *must* come first and the translated title must follow in square brackets, not the other way around. Listing the English title first implies that an English document with that title exists somewhere. If no such document exists, it will prove very frustrating for a reader who is trying to dig deeper into your subject matter. But before you start translating everything in sight, see if the work has already been published in translation. Government papers (such as parliamentary White Papers) and many classic works of world literature, for example, are often translated into English. Some styles specify that if a published translation does exist, then you put the title in the same format as the foreign title (e.g., italics or quote marks): for example, *Et dukkehjem* [*A Doll's House*]. Moreover, if you have quoted the document in your work, using a published translation means you can lift quotes from the translation without having to translate them yourself. If you do this, the translation should also be listed in your references. If no English-language version of the document exists and you have translated the title for the benefit of the reader, then you can leave the translated title unformatted: for example, *Ibsens hemmelig liv* [Ibsen's secret life].

If you translate quotes yourself, then put the translation in quote marks. If you are using the author–date system, write something like '(Olsen 2002, Author's translation)'. If you are using a numbered system, then you will have to make a separate note that says 'Author's translation', and use that note number every time it is applicable. For the footnote system, simply add 'Author's translation' to the footnote. If you have many translated quotes, consider putting a footnote at the earliest possible point in your manuscript – no matter what documentation system you use – that says, 'Unless otherwise specified, all translations from the [fill in the language here] are the author's.' This applies even if you have hired a professional translator to do the translating. If a published translation does not exist, then you are responsible for the translation in your manuscript even if you did not do it yourself.

Variations

All of the three main documentation systems described above have innumerable style variations. Each journal or publisher has its own house preferences for how references should look. Pay particular attention to the following categories:

- *Capitalization in titles*: Some journals always use title case; others always use sentence case. But many use a combination: for example, sentence case for the titles of journal articles and book chapters; title case for the titles of books, reports and journal names.
- *Author names*: Journals using the number system usually require just the first initial, while journals using the footnote style usually require the full first name. Journals using the author–date system vary widely. Note: if your style requires full first names and you have only the first initials, you (or your copy-editor) may have a lot of research ahead.
- *Inversion*: After the first author, do you list subsequent authors first name first or last name first? First authors are always listed last name first, but journals vary as to whether they want the names of subsequent authors inverted as well.
- *Order*: What comes after what? Most journals require that the bibliographic entry start with the last name of the author. After that, variation is the name of the game. Sometimes it's a date, sometimes the title. Sometimes the publisher comes before the city, sometimes after.
- *Separators*: And how do you separate the parts of the bibliographic entry? Journals vary widely (and often incomprehensibly) in their conventions for setting the elements of a bibliographic entry off from one another. For example, some set off dates in parentheses; others use a period, comma or semicolon.
  - *Italics and bold*: When do you use them? It is common to set book titles and journal names in italics, but by no means universal. Some journals set the volume number of the journal in bold.
  - *Use of quotation marks*: Some journals like to enclose the titles of journal articles or book chapters in quotation marks. Others do not.

Remember that reference style always follows the target journal, not the source document. If your target journal wants book titles in lower case, put them in lower case regardless of how they look on the book.

DOES IT REALLY MATTER?

Why, you may be asking yourself at this point, do journals have to be so different from one another? Why can't there be just one way of doing things so we don't have to go through this torture every single time we want to submit something? The reference and other style preferences of the different journals are not merely the whims of the managing editor – although personal preferences certainly play a role. They are very often the result of the publishing culture of the disciplines represented in the journal, the country the journal is published in and perhaps the idiosyncrasies associated with the journal's subject matter. Whatever the reasons, you are better off spending your time trying to follow the particular preferences of your target journal instead of trying to understand why they are what they are.

The real question, though, is how much does this really matter? For an initial submission to a journal or publisher, the answer is usually: 'Less than the author guidelines imply, but more than you think.' Guidelines for style (including the styling of references) are sometimes incomprehensible to authors. And your motivation for attempting to follow them is inarguably dampened when you factor in the likelihood of having to send your work to a second journal with a completely different set of preferences. It is no secret that authors often submit to more prestigious journals first, and if their work gets rejected (some of the top journals reject about 90 per cent of the articles submitted to them), they work their way down their list of preferred journals. Attempting to conform to the house style of each journal can prove time-consuming, so many authors ignore the house style. It's understandable, but is it smart?

The answer is that it depends on the journal, and whether this is the first time that you have submitted the article to that journal. Some journals, especially the most prestigious, will reject the article on sight if the submission guidelines are not followed to the letter. Most journals, however, will allow some deviation from the guidelines – at least in the initial submission. There is no question that you need to follow the guidelines with respect to word count, formatting and documentation systems. (Your article may not even get sent to review if it exceeds the word count or is not formatted acceptably.) But with respect to style (and the styling of references), there is admittedly some leeway. The main things the reviewers will be looking for are whether your core argument is relevant and makes sense, your method is valid and your work is sound. When it comes to references, they are not likely to notice whether you have used title case or sentence case, but they may notice if important information is missing, if author names are misspelled, or if a study referred to in the text does not appear in the reference list. So, at the very minimum, you must perform a basic quality check (which becomes significantly easier if you have used reference management software):

- Make sure that all in-text references correspond correctly to a full entry in the reference list. Imagine a reader trying to match up an in-text reference that says 'Parker 2002' with a reference list that shows only 'Parker 2001' and 'Parker and Wattenberg 2002'. Only *you* know whether you meant to write '2001' but your finger slipped, or whether you forgot to write 'and Wattenberg', whether the reference list is wrong and should have been 2002, or whether 'Parker 2002' is a completely new reference that you have forgotten to put in. Likewise, if you are using a numbered style, only *you* know whether the number of your citation corresponds with the bibliographic entry of the same number on your list.

- Make sure your reference list contains only works *cited* in your paper.[2] Sometimes you might cut a paragraph that has a reference in it, without cutting the reference from your list. If the reference is important, then you might want to refer to it elsewhere. If not, you must cut it from your list. Only you can make this decision.
- Check the spelling of all the names. A reader does not know whether 'Browne' is a misspelling of 'Brown' or another person. And what if you have a lot of names like 'Silbriborkalodeliftov' or 'Abbadilliborrinahai'? Since you presumably have access to the correct spelling, you are far better off doing the double-checking yourself.

If you are asked to revise and resubmit your work, devoting yourself to slavishly following the style guidelines should be on your list of priorities. At this stage, you know that the journal is interested in what you have to say; now is your chance to use every means at your disposal to show that your work belongs in that journal.

GETTING HELP

Doing everything in your power to follow the guidelines might mean seeking outside help. This can be a smart move. Not only are many of the explicit instructions to authors difficult to understand, but there are also many other implicit conventions. For example, one thing authors don't always realize is that it doesn't matter how the bibliographic information looks in the original article, book or report. What matters is how it is supposed to look in *your* reference list. The journal article you want to cite may be styled using title case in the original – 'A Very Insightful Article' – but if the journal you are submitting to wants the titles of journal articles in sentence case, then you must write 'A very insightful article' in your reference list. This is not very intuitive, which is why God made copy-editors.

When you are very close to submitting for the first time, or are preparing to resubmit, a copy-editor can be invaluable when it comes to style and references. They will know what to look for and how to find it – even if the guidelines offer no real guidance. But be careful about expecting a copy-editor to check all your references for accuracy. For others to successfully complete a quality check, they have to read your mind. A likely scenario is that you will have to pay the copy-editor for the time it takes to try to figure things out, give up, and type up a list of queries – which you will have to deal with anyway. So count on doing that part yourself.

Many journals and presses have in-house copy-editors who will edit your article for style. An in-house copy-editor has the distinct advantage of knowing

---

[2]Books will often allow bibliographies, which contain relevent works not cited in the manuscript. But journals seldom allow bibliographies and stick to reference lists that contain only the works cited.

the journal's house style by heart. (And any effort you put into trying to understand the instructions to authors will pay off when you can understand *why* a copy-editor made the changes he did. Much time is wasted when copy-editors edit according to the house style, authors 'stet' the original version because they like it better, and then editors have to restore all the changes because they are required by the journal or press.) However, a copy-editor who works for a journal or press is very seldom able to establish a close working relationship with any particular author; generally this kind of copy-editor does not even have direct

While perfectionism can work against you in the early writing stages, it definitely works for you in the final stages. Preparing to submit means a lot of tedious hours getting everything just so.

contact with the author, only with the journal or press. Moreover, it is becoming more and more common for journals (and even for some book publishers) to require that the author take responsibility for copy-editing, either by doing it themselves or hiring a copy-editor. Do not underestimate the value of finding and cultivating your own professional copy-editor. Copy-editors know and understand style, both for references and everything else. They also know grammar, and they can help you with any awkward formulations. And, more important, if they work with you long enough, they will begin to understand your work. A copy-editor who is familiar with both your field and your work can be an invaluable ally.

If you are a non-native speaker of English (and, honestly, even if you are a native speaker of English), you might also want to consider getting help with language issues, not just style. As discussed in Chapter 8, many different kinds of copy-editors are available, and some of them specialize in sentence-level clarity. That is, they are less concerned with issues of style, and more concerned with issues of grammar, sentence flow and voice. They can help polish the writing of non-native and native speakers alike. This is a point I do not think I can stress enough: your main job as a scholar is to focus on your research and your core argument. If your language is clumsy, either because you are a non-native speaker or because you simply are not comfortable writing, there is no shame in asking for help in expressing your ideas more clearly. A more relevant question, however, is *when* you get language help. Obviously, if you have unlimited resources and unlimited access to a good language consultant, you should get your work language-edited at least once (if not two or three times) before initial submission and then again after you make any revisions. Unfortunately, the reality for most of us is that good language editors are expensive and hard to find, and every round of editing takes time, so you might only be able to afford one round of editing. There is no absolute rule for when you should invest in the editing, but the more your argument depends on clarity of language (that is, the less it relies on statistics and other hard data), and the more the reader's comprehension of your message is impaired by language problems, the more important it will be to get a round of editing prior to the initial submission. If your language is relatively clear, or your argument rests on your tables and figures, then you might want to wait until you have received comments from the reviewers before you undertake a language edit. It is a judgement call.

SENDING IT IN

Now you are ready to submit your manuscript. Even here, journals differ considerably in what they want. Today, most want manuscripts submitted electronically either as email attachments or uploaded directly. But some still prefer hard copy and will ask you to send, say, four copies (some specify that they want the pages held together with strong paper clips; others want staples).

Author guidelines: Specifications for your target journal

Here is a checklist of questions to keep in mind when you read through the author guidelines:

- What are the word limits for the article itself and for the abstract?
- Is a particular style guide or dictionary specified?
- Are tables and figures submitted as separate files or integrated in text?
- Are there fees for colour figures?
- What is the policy on footnotes or endnotes?
- What reference documentation system is used?
- What are the requirements for file types for text and graphics?
- Hard copy or electronic submission? If hard copy, how many copies should you send in?
- What size paper (European standard A4 or US standard 8.5" x 11")? Margins?
- What should the title page include?
- Are key words required? Is there a predefined list to choose from?
- What steps should the author take to anonymize the manuscript?

Electronic submission is, of course, the simplest. Often the journal will provide an online form for you to fill out; this takes the place of a cover letter. If no form is provided, or if you are submitting by mail, then you do need to compose a cover letter. It should include the following:

- *The name of the journal to which you are submitting*: Some publishers house several different journals under a single roof and thus share a single postal address. To make sure your article gets to the right place, be sure you specify the exact name of the journal you want to submit to.
- *The type of article you are submitting*: Since most journals have more than one classification of article, you need to state whether your article is a research article, review, commentary, letter or something else.
- *Whether or not this is a resubmission*: Although the journal should have a record if you have submitted the same article earlier, it is a good idea to state something along the lines of 'This is a revised version of an article I originally submitted last year. My response to the reviewers' comments is enclosed.' *Note*: This only applies for resubmissions to the *same* journal. If you are submitting an article that has previously been rejected by another journal, treat it as a first-time submission.
- *The contact person*: If the article has many different authors, be sure you specify who should be contacted regarding the status of the article. And make sure the contact information for this person is up to date, especially if it differs from the address or institutional affiliation given in the article.
- *Legal release*: State that you are submitting your article for publication. If you do not, the journal technically is not allowed to send it out for review.
- *Details of accompanying matter*: Make sure you state what you have enclosed or attached to the manuscript: photos, figures, comments to reviewers and so on.
- *The total number of words*: State whether this includes footnotes and references.
- *Confirmation that the manuscript is new*: You must state that this article has not previously been published and is not currently under consideration elsewhere. Whether you have submitted it elsewhere and been rejected doesn't matter. The only issue at hand is whether or not it exists in a published form elsewhere or whether it is currently being considered by another journal. This is not always black and white. For example, many research institutes publish working papers on their websites. Working papers are early drafts of papers that are to be revised for journal publication; they haven't been reviewed. Some journals, particularly in the social sciences and humanities, do not consider this to be previous publication, and will have no problem accepting a paper that has an earlier draft available on the Internet. Other journals, particularly in the natural sciences, will not accept this. Similarly, some journals will accept previous publication in a different language, especially Asian languages that few native English-speakers understand, but others will not. It is your responsibility to find out what your target journal finds acceptable and to fully disclose the status of your work in the cover letter.

AND NOW, THE WAIT ...

You've done all you can do. You've defined your audience and figured out how to reach it. You've honed your core argument to make sure you've asked a good question and managed to answer it; you've structured your argument so it makes sense to someone other than yourself; you've revised your tables and figures to augment your argument; and you've double-checked your references and sent in

Sometimes submitting an article feels like you've sent off a part of yourself. You can make the wait easier by making sure you always have articles in different stages: some just started, some in revision, others awaiting review.

your manuscript in accordance with the guidelines. Now all you can do is wait. And wait. And … wait.

But while you're waiting, things are happening to your manuscript. The journal editor first has to track down experts in the field who are willing to take on the job of reviewing it (see the text box on the peer review process in Chapter 1). Sometimes you will be asked to provide the names of experts who could act as reviewers (or people who you would prefer *not* be contacted as reviewers), but usually the journal takes care of this. Once the reviewers receive your manuscript, they have to find time to read it, think about it and write their responses. Reviewers aren't paid for their work, and their schedules are already tight. What this means is that it may be anywhere from three to six months before you get your answer. Don't contact the editor every week to ask if the reviewers are done yet. But contacting the journal to ask when you might expect an answer (if they haven't told you already) is a reasonable request. And if several weeks pass without a confirmation that your manuscript has been received, or if no answer is forthcoming after several months, a follow-up call or email is not only reasonable, it's recommended.

Eventually you *will* get an answer. When you do, it will be one of three main possibilities: accepted, rejected or revise and resubmit. If you don't get an 'accepted' answer on the first try, do not lose heart. An unconditional acceptance is very rare indeed. An answer of 'accepted with minor revisions' is cause for celebration; this means that your article will be accepted if you make the revisions specified by the editor.

Your paper may well be rejected. But this does not mean it's time to head for the paper shredder. As argued in Chapter 1 of this book, if your work is relevant and the scholarship is sound, there is a home for it somewhere. A rejection does entail taking a hard look at your work, considering the comments from the reviewers, and deciding whether you want to completely rewrite your work, or revise your thinking about your target audience – or both.

One of the best answers you can get, and one of the most common, is 'revise and resubmit'. This means that your reviewers believe you have a very valid point to make, but that you can make it better. And they will provide specific points for how they believe you can improve. Armed with your reviewer comments and your knowledge about how to respond to them (see Chapter 8), you have the opportunity to refine your argument further and ensure that your contribution to the scholarly dialogue is as effective as possible.

So don't be discouraged if it doesn't work for you on the first try, or if it seems to take a very long time. If you have something valid to say, you will eventually get the chance to say it for an attentive audience. If you can make sense, you will be heard. And, hopefully, someone will respond, which will make all your hard work and the long wait worthwhile. You might get a call or an email from someone who would like to collaborate with you; you might be asked to present your work to a wider audience; and you might find your work cited in the works of others. No matter what kind of response you get, it is likely to give you something to think about and perhaps something new to say. After all, the beauty of the ongoing scholarly dialogue is that there is no such thing as having the last word.

Remember

Don't trip just before the finish line. In the homestretch, details matter.

For the first submission, don't forget to check word limits and formatting requirements. Make sure your reference list is complete.

For the final submission, also double-check style (including for references), and get help from a copy-editor if you need it.

FURTHER READING

- American Psychological Association (APA) (2010) *Publication Manual of the American Psychological Association*, 6th edn, APA style is the most commonly used style in the social sciences. Although different journals will all have their own local variations, it is worth having this manual as a general reference.
- Belcher, Wendy Laura (2009) *Writing Your Journal Article in 12 Weeks: A Guide to Academic Publishing Success*, Thousand Oaks, CA: Sage. Belcher's chapter on 'Sending your article!' has very useful advice about writing cover letters and some of the other important finishing details.
- Lillis, Theresa and Curry, Mary Jane (2010) *Academic Writing in a Global Context: The Politics and Practices of Publishing in English*, New York: Routledge. Although the book addresses the issue of publishing in English far more broadly than just the issue of editing (and it thus provides relevant further reading for more than just this chapter), their concept of 'literacy brokers' is particularly relevant here.
- Rekdal, Ole Bjørn (2014) 'Academic urban legends', *Social Studies of Science*, 44 (4): 638-54. Rekdal writes engagingly (and entertainingly) about the dangers of sloppy referencing practices. Using real case examples (such as a decimal point error that has us all believing that spinach is a good source of iron), he turns referencing from a tedious chore to a meaningful activity. He has two other articles also published in 2014 that deserve a look as well: 'Monuments to academic carelessness: The self-fulfilling prophecy of Katherine Frost Bruner', *Science, Technology & Human Values*, 39 (5): 744-58, and 'Academic citation practice: A sinking sheep?', *Portal: Libraries and the Academy,* 14 (4): 567-85.
- University of Chicago Press (2010) *The Chicago Manual of Style* (CMS), 16th edn, Chicago, IL: Chicago University Press. Although CMS might be more common in the humanities than in the social sciences, it is still an extremely useful (and highly detailed) style manual that is worth getting to know.

Postscript

It goes like this:

A big 'Woo!' followed by an even bigger 'Hoo!' (Alternatively, 'Yee' and 'Hah!' or just 'YESSSS!') Hands up in the air, a victory lap around the room, a little shimmy, high-fives all around, and the hugging of any people in the immediate vicinity – even if they are relative strangers.

The Acceptance Dance.

All the years of behind-the-scenes efforts to help others get their work published did nothing to prepare me for the sheer joy of having my work accepted by a publisher. Who wouldn't feel unbridled elation? Is there any other way to feel? (Except maybe 'It's about freakin' time!') You've spent years thinking about something, writing draft after draft, waiting for someone to pay attention, and *finally* someone says, 'Yes, I think you have something to say, and we're going to give you a chance to say it.'

How can you *not* do the acceptance dance (at least in your own head)?

I suppose the only feeling in the world that could possibly compare is the profound satisfaction of holding the finished product, the published work, in your hand. All the work, all the hours, all the agonizing have finally borne fruit. People are listening to you. You're being heard. There's nothing else quite like it.

Just wait. You'll see.

Glossary

Academic discourse   Also referred to as 'the scholarly dialogue' or 'the scientific dialogue', academic discourse is the conversation that is taking place in academic journals or books about a given topic.

Applied research   In contrast to basic research, applied research is meant to directly contribute to solving an identified social problem or technological challenge.

Basic research   Also called 'pure' or 'fundamental' research, basic research is undertaken with no clear practical goal in mind, but rather a desire to increase knowledge about a particular phenomenon.

Claim   A claim is any assertion you make that needs some supporting evidence, such as reference to other studies or your own data. (See also entry on 'Thesis statement'.)

Core argument   Your core argument consists of the question you are asking (research question) and the answer you are providing (thesis statement). The concept of core argument comprises both the question and the answer because everything in your manuscript should function either to convince your reader that your question is a good one, or to help you answer the question.

Essay   As used here, 'essay' refers to a paper that argues a point using primarily logic or reasoning. Although data or other empirical evidence might be presented as examples, the argument itself rests primarily on the author's analytical reasoning. (See entry on 'Theoretical research'.)

Ethos   Persuading the reader by appealing to your authority or credibility. (See 'Pathos' and 'Logos'.)

Faux objectivity   Faux objectivity refers to actions taken by academic writers to make them appear objective, but which are not actually related to objectivity.

One example of this is using the passive voice to disguise a personal involvement with your own research: 'interviews were conducted'.

Free-writing   Free-writing means to write down your thoughts as they occur to you, without censoring, without focusing on grammar or structure, for a certain length of time, or for a certain number of pages.

Friendly audience   A friendly audience comprises readers that essentially agree with not just with what you are saying, but how you are saying it, and how you went about your research in the first place.

General public   Also referred to as a lay audience, the general public is a non-specialist audience outside of academia.

Hostile audience   A hostile audience comprises readers that are fundamentally sceptical about at least one aspect of your work: your conclusion, your methodology, your theoretical perspective and so on. Interdisciplinary audiences can usually be considered hostile because they are likely to comprise audiences that have differing epistemological or ontological assumptions.

Hypothesis   A statement that asserts a proposed relationship between two or more variables and can be tested.

Hypothesis-generating research   Research (usually qualitative) that aims to result in one or more hypotheses that can be tested in subsequent research. Here, the hypothesis is part of the thesis statement.

Hypothesis-testing research   Research (usually quantitative) that aims to test one or more hypotheses derived from a theoretical discussion. Here, the hypotheses function as research questions or sub-research questions.

IMRAD   IMRAD is an acronym for the standard elements of structure in an academic article: introduction, methods, results and discussion.

Knowledge gap   Knowledge gaps are aspects of the academic discourse that are still disputed or unclear. A knowledge gap might represent something that is not known, something that is known but in dispute, or something that has been more or less taken for granted but the author provides a good reason to cast doubt.

Literature review   A literature review is a presentation of the academic discourse relevant to your research question and is designed to give the reader a sense of how much is known about a certain issue, and where knowledge gaps might be located. (See 'Theoretical framework'.)

Logos   Persuading the reader by appealing to logic or reason. (See 'Ethos' and 'Pathos'.)

Method   Methods are the particular tools you use to gather data, such as interview, survey, participant observation and so on.

Methodology   Methodology represents the larger philosophical principle that justifies why you choose your methods to begin with. Examples of methodology would be logical positivism and interpretive methodologies such as social constructionism.

Mixed audience   A mixed audience comprises members of fundamentally different groups, such as practitioners and academics, experts and non-experts, or groups from different disciplines.

Objectivity   In the context of this book, objectivity refers to the researcher's ability to change his or her original viewpoint should the evidence point in a different direction, and to point to external (non-personal) justifications for any given viewpoint.

Pathos   Persuading the reader by appealing to emotion. (See 'Logos' and 'Ethos'.)

Peer feedback   Peer feedback refers to comments on your written work or oral presentation given by a colleague. Unlike peer review, peer feedback is generally not anonymous.

Peer review   Peer review is the anonymous evaluation of your work by an expert in the field to judge whether it is worthy of publication by a given journal or press. Peer reviewers are selected by the journal or press to act as gatekeepers – to ensure that the article, book chapter or book meets the rigorous standards of the journal or press.

Plagiarism   Plagiarism refers to the unlawful copying of someone else's words, ideas or data and presenting it as your own and without sufficient reference to the original author.

Qualitative research   Qualitative research seeks in-depth explanation and thus investigates a smaller number of cases or informants in great detail, often using interview-based methods. Based on, for example, interpretive methodologies, phenomenology, or ethnography, it is a particularly suitable approach for answering questions about why people might engage in certain kinds of behaviour.

Quantitative research   Quantitative research seeks to explain phenomena in more general terms, and thus requires a much larger number of cases to be able to say something about what might be 'typical' or 'a trend'. Based on a methodology of, for example, logical positivism or realism, methods can include survey and statistical analysis.

Research productivity   Research productivity refers to the amount of written scholarly output produced by a researcher in a given amount of time. Usually, only peer-reviewed, published material (such as journal articles, books or book chapters) is counted.

Research question   Here, the research question refers to the question you intend to answer in your article, book, or book chapter – the rhetorical starting point of your overall argument. It may differ from the original research question of your research project.

Results   Also referred to as 'findings', results are the data you harvest as a result of the methods you employed. Results might be in the form of statistics, themes that emerged from what your informants said, or evidence from documents you have examined.

Rhetoric   Rhetoric refers to the study of argument and persuasion.

Target audience   Your target audience is the main group of people you are aiming to reach through your writing or presentation.

Theoretical framework   Sometimes called an analytical or conceptual framework, the theoretical framework presents the concepts and ideas that drive the research. These concepts and ideas should be used actively in the research, informing the question, the methodological approach and the analysis.

Theoretical research   Also referred to in this book as 'non-empirical research', theoretical research is research based on ideas, concepts, logic and argument. The extent to which you have collected data is less relevant than the extent to which you have examined closely the ideas and concepts you wish to discuss.

Thesis statement   The thesis statement is the 'answer' half of your core argument. It represents the rhetorical destination of your overall argument. It can be expressed in the form 'X is Y because Z', where 'X' represents the topic you are discussing; 'Y' refers to the claim you are making about this topic; and 'Z' refers to the basis on which you can make that claim (i.e., the reasons or evidence you will present to your reader as support for the claim you make).

Transparency   Transparency refers to the extent to which you show your reader what you have actually done and why you made the choices that you made.

User group   User groups can include policy-makers, decision-makers, business and industry, teachers, nurses, social workers or any other professional group that is outside academia and is interested in research for their professional practice.

Index